A HISTORY OF SIN

$\mathscr{A}$ HISTORY OF SIN

ITS

EVOLUTION

TO TODAY

AND BEYOND

JOHN PORTMANN

ROWMAN & LITTLEFIELD PUBLISHERS, INC.
Lanham • Boulder • New York • Toronto • Plymouth, UK

ROWMAN & LITTLEFIELD PUBLISHERS, INC.

Published in the United States of America
by Rowman & Littlefield Publishers, Inc.
A wholly owned subsidary of The Rowman & Littlefield Publishing Group,
Inc.
4501 Forbes Boulevard, Suite 200, Lanham, Maryland 20706
www.rowmanlittlefield.com

Estover Road
Plymouth PL6 7PY
United Kingdom

British Library Cataloguing in Publication Information Available

Library of Congress Cataloging-in-Publication Data

Portmann, John.
  A history of sin / John Portmann.
    p. cm.
  Includes bibliographical references.
  ISBN-13: 978-0-7425-5813-7 (cloth : alk. paper)
  ISBN-10: 0-7425-5813-4 (cloth : alk. paper)
  1. Sin—Christianity—History of doctrines. 2. Catholic Church—Doctrines—
History. I. Title.
BT715.P66 2007
241'.3—dc22

                                             2007000382

Printed in the United States of America

♾™ The paper used in this publication meets the minimum requirements of
American National Standard for Information Sciences—Permanence of Paper
for Printed Library Materials, ANSI/NISO Z39.48-1992.

In loving memory of Father Gerald Cohen,
whose intelligence leavened Yale
and inspired many

Our transgressions and our sins are upon us, and we waste away because of them; how then, can we live?

—Ezekiel 33:10

The Christian focus is overwhelmingly on sin sin sin sin sin sin sin. What a nasty little preoccupation to have dominating your life.

—Richard Dawkins, *The God Delusion*

CONTENTS

CONTENTS

ACKNOWLEDGMENTS

Virginia Germino and Bill Germano furnished useful comments on an early version of the manuscript. I am grateful to them both.

Hara Estroff Marano posed useful questions about the argument of the book as the project unfolded. More important, she showered me with good humor on a daily basis.

John Loudon reached out for this project, expressed consistently useful enthusiasm, and deftly shepherded the project to publication.

Daniel Ortiz supported the writing of this book in important ways. Again and again, I thank him.

Thank you, St. Jude.

INTRODUCTION:
SIN TODAY

God has made a comeback, and with him, inevitably, sin. For you can't have one without the other. God looks a little different in each century, and sin does, too. Through one, we can effectively get to know the other. An update on sin will reveal what really matters to God today and highlight the somewhat quirky sensitivities his people have taken on.

God himself conditioned us to think of sin as his foil. Of course, God gave us rules to obey. Any time we broke those rules, we sinned. But beyond that, he compelled us to think in terms of a work ethic. In order to get something, we have to give something. What we gave up, more often than not, was pleasure. Sin often feels really good. Just as we appreciate more the things we pay for, so do we love God more because we've worked to please him. Psychologically, the relationship works beautifully.

Even if you were to claim that God amounts to nothing more than the projection of man's highest hopes onto the sky, still you would see how useful a study of God would be. Whether you believe in God or not, he holds the key to understanding much of humanity. As a combination of the divine and the defective, man has spent many centuries trying to overcome his dark side—to little or no avail, usually.

Since September 11, 2001, religious enthusiasts and skeptics alike have warmed to the divine in a way we have not seen for decades. God waits for us still, as does sin. What does God look like now? He has changed, or at least he has revealed more to us in such a way as to make us think he has changed. He first gave Noah one basic rule (to drain animals of their blood before consuming them), then Abraham another (to circumcise himself and all men in his tribe), and Moses a host of others, totaling 613. Then Jesus and, more decisively, St. Paul overturned many of those rules. Circumcision became optional, as did marrying your brother's widow and following various dietary rules.

This cycle of severity and paucity, of emphasizing the letter or the spirit of the law, continues today. Prior to the epochal Second Vatican Council (1962–1965), for example, it was sinful for Roman Catholic women to enter a church without a veil, just as it was sinful for all Catholics to eat meat on any Friday of the year. No longer. Think of usury or shopping on the Sabbath as well (or even slavery—the Vatican approved of this institution well into the nineteenth century, and the Talmud accepts it as a natural component of the economic and social systems). It seems what God expects of us changes over time: it is easier to accept this than the idea that God himself changes over time. For if God is perfect, he doesn't change. Any change would only make him worse.

What makes us worse is sin. While it may be clear now what sin used to be, it is far from obvious what it is now. Gay marriage, the ordination of women as rabbis or priests, maybe even abortion, could one day go the way of usury. Exodus (22:25), Leviticus (25:35–37), and Deuteronomy (23:19–25) forbade the Israelites to lend at interest. Despite the prohibition, the Book of Ezekiel (22:12) indicates that usury was common in Jerusalem. For their part, Greco-Roman philosophers, particularly Plato and Aristotle, protested against lending at interest. We do well here to remember Aristotle's analysis, given the long shadow it cast over the scholastic tradition. According to Aristotle, the moneylender deserves more blame than anyone else, because he pretends to grow fruit from something unnatural: coins. Coins do nothing other than measure things (*Politics* I:10), and so moneylenders don't make a proper contribution to society.

Jesus counseled to "lend, hoping for nothing again; and your reward shall be great" (Luke 6:35). Although Jesus did not condemn lending at interest, both the Greek and Latin church elders inveighed against it. According to early Christian theologians (e.g., Clement of Alexandria, St. Gregory of Nazianzus, St. Basil, St. Gregory of Nyssa, St. John Chrysostom, St. Ambrose, St. Augustine, and St. Jerome), the usurer reaps where he has not sown. Lending at interest offended early Christian sensibilities because it amounted to taking other people's belongings. The rich must freely lend to the poor. Today, rich nations debate whether to forgive the staggering debt of poor nations, yet no one deplores the institution of the International Bank. It is impossible to imagine the American economy without Wall Street, and it is understandable (if not forgivable) why some Americans insist on turning away desperately poor foreigners who risk their lives in order to sneak across U.S. borders. America will lose some of its affluence if the rich should have to shoulder the burden of accommodating penniless strangers. The poor from Mexico and Central America are accused of stealing the belongings of hardworking Americans, who may not wish to lend without recompense.

The increasing atomization or tribalization of America forges alliances along not only economic but also ethnic, religious, and political lines. With the help of the Christian Yellow Pages, Americans have already begun to choose friends, schools, and neighborhoods with an eye to aligning themselves with others who agree on what is a sin. Today Americans support ethnic and racial diversity, but we still wince at moral diversity. It is one thing to proclaim the value of different races, but another thing to value the views of people who disagree with us on abortion, gay marriage, or national health care. We want to associate with people who believe what we do.

Meanwhile, sin forges ahead of civilization. Sin has a very long history and an even longer future. This realization raises some hope, for it is often sinfulness that spurs us on to the extraordinary achievements of civilization. We see in contemporary art and drama that sin—especially blasphemy—propels a culture to new and exotic harbors and illuminates the leading edge of a culture. Moral outrage fuels cultural progress, which explains in part the usefulness of sin.

SIN MAKES ANOTHER COMEBACK

Western Christianity differs from most other religions in the rollercoaster path it continues along. After two millennia, Christians continue to slip and slide between permissiveness and repressiveness. The Enlightenment, to take an obvious example, relaxed puritanical morals in the eighteenth century. Then along came the Victorian age, which tightened the screws on personal conduct (except behind closed doors) in the nineteenth century. Decades later, the 1960s ushered in the sexual revolution and a new age of permissiveness, an unorchestrated attempt to shake off an oppressive Christianity that had terrorized the faithful with its doctrine of an angry and vengeful God. Americans didn't like thinking of God as a cruel authority figure and perhaps learned to be less judgmental themselves. The 1980s then partially reversed this trend, but not so conspicuously as on September 11, 2001, when a new wave of religious fundamentalism was unleashed that promises to hang on for decades, if not longer. Sin—that unpopular boor pushed out of our minds to whatever extent a generation can manage it—is making a powerful comeback.

It seems there can be no religious fervor without persecution of sin. The blame for social ills rests with rampant sinfulness, according to Christians of various stripes. Just being Jewish or Christian strikes some Islamic fundamentalists as sinful; the more fervor fundamentalists can foment, the more they will consider pandering to Judaism and Christianity a sin worthy of terrorist acts. The more sin we see around us, the richer our experience of God might become. Yet religious believers today certainly do not take a remarkably permissive and sinful world as a blessing in disguise. The sixteenth-century Inquisition is back, except Christians are the bad guys this time.

Sin surprises us by the basic assumption surrounding it: everyone knows what it is, so it needs no introduction. Yet sin is a beast remarkably more supple and complicated than we sometimes suppose. What the ancient Greeks called *hamartia* corresponds nicely with what subsequent generations referred to as "sin." Hamartia offers the familiar example of missing the bull's-eye: you aim the arrow at the center of a target, but your arrow lands somewhere beyond its goal. Moral wrongdoing presupposes righteousness, as well as knowledge of the bull's-eye. Ancient Jews, following Abraham and Moses, placed God at the center of the bull's-eye, not as a target to be hit but as the beneficent father to be pleased and obeyed. For Jews, sin was largely communal: the Jewish community believed that united they would stand and divided they would fall. A single errant member could bring down or pollute the rest of the group. Christians came to conceive of sin as something more personal: the idea wasn't so much to save your community as to save yourself. Every man for himself; every tub on its own bottom.

ORIGINAL SIN STARTS TO FLAG

Christians set themselves off from both Jews and ancient Greeks in the pivotal notion of Original Sin. The influential fifth-century Christian theologian Augustine nailed down the tenet, ever since canonical in Roman Catholicism, that the Fall of Adam and Eve forever spoiled humanity. The concupiscence of lust that leads to sexual intercourse between a man and a woman passes along Original Sin to each new generation; each child is born stained. Unless the stain is washed away in baptism, a person's soul cannot attain heaven. The idea that babies are born stained finds no perfect counterpart in Greek paganism, Judaism, or Islam.

Augustine formulated his doctrines in a time of great theological peril. Make one false move as a theologian, and you could find yourself labeled a heretic, excommunicated. One of the most famous theological debates in Christian history plotted Augustine against Pelagius, a thinker who believed that nothing we humans might do could possibly "earn" us salvation. For being wrong, the church cast out Pelagius as a heretic, a particularly dangerous kind of sinner. Intellectuals have long threatened Christian leaders, most notably Roman Catholics. Learning, like acquiring material wealth, makes you suspicious in the eyes of some religious zealots.

One intellectual, a poet, bequeathed us an enduring account of what happens to heretics specifically and sinners generally, once death takes them. Dante's *Inferno* has done more to shape the Western imagination than any other work, at least in terms of helping us envision where transgressors end up. Dante, like Augustine before him, parsed sins into component parts and ranked them in order of seriousness. Early Protestant reformers such as Luther and Calvin objected strenuously to this practice, insisting that a sin is a sin is a sin. By distinguishing between a venial (merely bad) and a mortal (extremely bad) sin (as Roman Catholics continue to do), you send the tacit message to ordinary believers that venial sins aren't really anything to worry about. Wrong, said the first Protestants. Wrong as well, said some Jesuit theologians in the 1960s and 1970s, for there really wasn't anything a person could do to alienate God forever. Although Roman Catholics continue to believe that all sins can be forgiven (provided a proper confession is made), mortal sin remains a cornerstone of Catholic theology. Teenagers and adults still defend themselves by insisting, "There are worse things I could do" (just as Stockard Channing did, to great effect, in a song by that name in the popular film *Grease*, from 1978).

Dante and Augustine both considered sins of the flesh easier to forgive than sins of the spirit, such as blasphemy. Lying is worse than fornication, according to Augustine. Augustine also makes other friendly concessions in an otherwise harsh admonition not to sin. He allows "sins that alleviate," for example, telling a dying man who worries about his son that the son still lives, even though you know he doesn't. Augustine also asserts that a raped woman is not responsible for any sin; the fact of illicit intercourse does not besmirch the soul of the raped woman, who should not even consider harming herself out of guilt.

With Original Sin comes the presumption of guilt. Original Sin thwarts the underlying presumption of Western legal codes: that people are innocent until proven guilty. Original sin suffered a mortal blow of sorts in 2005, when Roman Catholic theologians officially discontinued the centuries-old belief in limbo, the place where unbaptized babies and virtuous heathens went. And as scientists tell us more and more about the first humans, it seems somewhat less likely that there was a rudimentary pair of humans who populated the Earth. It could be that lots of Adams and Eves came into being at roughly the same time. If so, then the Original Sin idea would fade away from Christianity, much as limbo has done (neither Jews nor Muslims believe in Original Sin).

THE DEMISE OF SIN

Sin did not fare well in the heady 1980s and 1990s, as fewer and fewer Westerners seemed to think about it. Sin became an endangered species, as theologians of various stripes joined believers in redefining sin and salvation. In *A New Christianity for a New World*, the controversial Anglican bishop of Newark regretted the idea that "human beings are born in sin and that, unless baptized or somehow saved, they will be forever banished from God's presence." To Bishop Spong and plenty of other Christians and Jews, religion just seemed too harsh, sin too constricting. For a variety of reasons, Christians had come to imagine sin not only as something relatively minor but also as something very personal—entirely between oneself and God. Largely forgotten was the biblical wisdom that sin hurts the life of the whole community and that God will punish it severely.

Because of a deepening sense of justice, Christians are slowly becoming aware that personal sins have social consequences and that the two are reciprocal. Personal sins lead to sinful social structures, and sinful social structures encourage personal sins. For example, individual greed gives rise to greedy social structures (think of tax laws that favor large corporations or of the breathtaking salaries of CEOs), and the latter encourage new people in their greed.

Since September 11, 2001, the West has become more religious—not just Muslims, but Jews and Christians as well. Organized religion is making a terrific comeback, for better or for worse, so we can expect the world to get tough on sin in the next few decades. Even as brows begin to furl anew, though, old sins challenge the old ways to accommodate science and new sensibilities. Take masturbation, for example. Like artificial birth control and the loss of virginity before marriage, masturbation is supposedly capable of keeping Roman Catholics out of heaven. Since so few people believe in them anymore, these over-the-hill sins risk ruining the reputation of other, genuinely dangerous sins.

Temptation itself became a good thing in the twentieth century, or at least more explicitly a good thing. Good temptations wandered the gym floor, where middle-aged men and women pedaled, pushed, and panted in order to beat themselves into good physical shape. After the workout, as before, they would pour themselves into tight-fitting clothes that attracted the erotic interest of others. When other people make you feel you're still desirable, you see yourself as a good temptation. The temptation to live in a mansion or drive a fancy car or own a great work of art compelled people to work harder, just as the desire for a better life drove the poor to raise themselves above the poverty line. Ambition became a social good.

Pride in general swelled in importance in the late twentieth century. As the world became more and more competitive, it seemed time to bless pride as a sine qua non of personal and professional success. Early in the twentieth century, an influential Christian thinker had reaffirmed an ancient bias against pride and strengthened pride's position as the worst of the seven deadly sins. In *Mere Christianity*, C. S. Lewis calls humility one of Jesus's most praiseworthy characteristics; furthermore, pride—the opposite of humility—is the "complete anti-God state of mind." No doubt pride really is the source of many evils, relating to greed, selfishness, and the general idea of self-importance and egotism. Lewis maintains, "As long as you are proud, you cannot know God." Christians striving to avoid sin today will likely say to themselves that pride is simply something they can't do without, that previous generations failed to realize the necessity of having it. The effect of time on sin will come up again and again in a history of sin such as this one. Striving Christians today will feel powerfully drawn to the conclusion of Bishop Spong: "God is Being—the reality underlying everything that is. . . . You worship this divine reality by having the courage to be all that you can be—your deepest, fullest self." Our deepest self (read: a gloriously successful self) is what we moderns dream to become.

Sin evolves over time. Science and medical research can weaken the case for considering a particular act or attitude sinful. Masturbation in the Catholic Church serves as an excellent case in point here: as long as a religious group outlaws masturbation, it denies itself the advantages of in vitro fertilization (IVF), nor can it vigorously enforce the border against other forms of fornication. Any group that condemns masturbation will naturally recoil in horror at stem cell research, despite the wondrously life-saving promises such research holds out. If usurers and masturbators make us yawn today, so may objections to stem cell research tomorrow. One of the principal arguments of this book is that sin fatigue has already set in.

The effects of sin also deserve attention. A contemporary reverence for what are now called "human rights" unites a dazzling diversity of people in opposition to suffering. Consideration of suffering raises interesting questions about racism and the American social policy of affirmative action. Sinning in order to reverse the case of previous sin (the sins of our fathers) requires some effort to understand and renews our understanding of both the importance and danger of sin. Philosophers have spoken of intergenerational justice in terms of the environment (especially pollution, global warming, butchered forests, etc.) and national debt, but no one seems to have noticed that it bears importantly on affirmative action as well. Young white people in America pay for the sins of their fathers in a variety of ways, and older white Americans who have already graduated from college and established careers do not foot the bill equitably for affirmative action. Young white Americans today feel sin most palpably in and through racism: blacks and whites alike resemble characters trapped in a Greek tragedy, trying hard to find a way out of an inherited mess.

The idea that self-understanding, social awareness, and general sensitivity will enable us to forgive anyone or anything comforts me, as I am convinced that few if any of us realize how much suffering we cause to others, how many sins we commit without even knowing it. The most puzzling question to emerge once one accepts this forgiving attitude toward all human sin is whether God shares it. If God fully understood us faulty, neurotic humans, how could he ever refuse to forgive us anything? Why would there be such a place as hell? The answers to these questions remain a mystery in various corners of Judaism and Christianity. The questions reveal not so much a loss of faith but a growing appreciation of moral complexity. The questions point to a sin fatigue that compels believers to look beyond simplistic, black-and-white accounts of wrongdoing. This is progress.

MODERN "SINS"

Even as traditional sins make a comeback, distinctly modern sins have begun to appear. These sins question the difference between sin, which generally refers to offenses against an almighty lawgiver, and garden-variety vice. Modern sins seem capable of uniting a variety of people of different religious and ethnic backgrounds. These sins include harming the environment, engaging in racism, denying the Holocaust, being depressed and not seeking pharmacological relief, not reaching your potential, and being overweight.

Modern sins have increasingly switched the focus from individuals to institutions. Distrust of institutions swept through American culture in the 1960s and 1970s, and Westerners have grown accustomed to holding up large organizations to scrutiny. Corporations, at least in the United States, may be the most fertile breeding ground for sin today. But religious institutions play a role as well. Beginning with a story by Nobel Prize winner Isaac Bashevis Singer, for example, Barbra Streisand directed the film *Yentl* (1983), in which a woman pretends to be a man in order to study the Talmud. Having always wanted to study the Talmud, Streisand's character compels viewers to wonder who the greater sinner is: the woman who lies in order to get closer to God, or the Orthodox Judaism that forbids women from studying the Talmud? Similarly, in Louise Erdrich's novel of 2000 *The Last Report on the Miracles at Little No Horse*, a nun pretends to be a man in order to help convert Native Americans in the Dakotas. Readers are left to ponder whether the sin of a Roman Catholic nun who lies in order to save souls exceeds the culpability of a church that denies ordination to women.

As women, gay people, and people of color acquired civil rights in the late twentieth century, distrust grew around groups suspected of thwarting these disenfranchised subsets of society. On college campuses, for example, fraternities suffered public relations setbacks, as voices from many quarters accused fraternities of widespread contempt for women, gays, and blacks.

Other films and news items have augmented this trend to associate sin more with groups than individuals. The 2003 film *Magdalene Sisters* depicted the cruelty of Irish Catholic nuns charged with reforming young women who had had premarital sex or simply worn their skirts a little too high. A year earlier, Michael Moore's *Bowling for Columbine* presented the National Rifle Association (NRA) as the real culprit behind the gruesome massacre in a Colorado high school. And the sex scandals that rocked the Roman Catholic Church in 2002 and 2003 further fueled the idea that institutions, not individuals, commit the truly egregious sins—moreover, *that institutions somehow compel individuals to sin*. The power of groups to abuse individuals takes many forms, of which one of the most vivid must be the systematic doping of East German women swimmers in the 1970s and 1980s. These women believed the coaches who had told them that "vitamin supplements" (which were really anabolic steroids) would simply give them an energy boost. Instead, the drugs resulted in multiple birth defects in the children subsequently born to these women. A new distrust of authority separates us from forebears who might have sensed that power corrupts but who never quite articulated or grasped the idea that those setting the rules may be more guilty than those occasionally breaking them.

Corporate America likely generates more sin than any other group or association today. The American conglomerate Wal-Mart came to stand for much of what's wrong with big business. Wal-Mart employed over 1.6 million people in 2006, making it the largest employer in the history of the world. Through rigid cost control and denying health care benefits to over half its employees, Wal-Mart kept prices low, but perhaps at terrible human cost. Enron workers arguably had it even worse, though, as their pensions evaporated overnight in 2002. Across a number of sectors, Americans continue to work longer hours in order to hold on to jobs and benefits. How much of a worker's well-being a company has a right to claim in order to earn a salary lies close to the heart of contemporary sensitivity to sin.

CONTRITION IS NO FUN

Worshipping God takes time, just as repenting for sin does. Time gets increasingly scarce in the modern world, and atonement fatigue creeps into the picture. Traditional Jews read aloud from the Torah at least three times a week, and good Muslims face Mecca five times a day to pray. What do ordinary believers have to show for themselves, other than some bumper stickers and lip service to "family values"? Part of the Western sin fatigue stems from the inconvenience of contrition. Saying we're sorry for something we really wanted to do gets in the way of our enjoying life. Further, one of the difficult questions sin poses is why people regret it so deeply—is it to show love for God or to protect ourselves from a more severe punishment?

We are supposed to regret our sins, to suffer pangs at having offended a mighty and loving God. We are supposed to promise ourselves not to fall back into the same trap. True contrition makes us detest ourselves for sinful behavior. However, contrition sometimes amounts to little more than fear of punishment from an omnipotent God (this theme runs throughout the Book of Job). Fear, like sin, may have fallen out of fashion as liberal voices in the American media lament that Evangelical Christians seem to specialize in arrogance and holier-than-thou attitudes: Evangelicals such as Pat Robertson and Jerry Falwell retort that they aren't afraid because they are confident in "their salvation."

As we ponder the motivation for our contrition and our good behavior, we can detect an important parallel. Our lives individually conform to broad patterns in both Hebrew and Christian scriptures. Creation is followed by sin, which is followed by violence and catastrophe, which is followed by redemption, which is a new creation of sorts. Sin goes on and on; sin falls away from popular consciousness and then returns; sin leads to our downfall and, ultimately, our strengthening. At the end of the path lies wisdom, often acquired after a parade of mistakes, when we find ourselves sadder but wiser. This book argues for optimism about human potential. Just as Jews walk to flowing water on Rosh Hashanah and symbolically cast their sins into the purifying waters, so, too, can contemporary believers choose to rid themselves of personality traits and compulsions they would prefer to live without.

For better or for worse, Jewish, Christian, and Muslim communities will likely hang on for at least another century or two. They will keep alive an ancient but evolving notion of sin, whose future appears robust indeed. Wherever there are humans, there will be sin. Precisely what that means invites fascinating debate, but it seems safe to assume that our idea of what we can be will always outrun what we really are. Only long after the dust from any particular age has settled will we see how helpful sin has been in enriching science, art, and culture.

Note to readers: Many of the examples and illustrations in this book come from Roman Catholicism. This is because the author writes as a religious believer, not simply a historian. Hopefully readers of all backgrounds will find something of use within this perspective.

I

THEORY

1

SIN FATIGUE

The Dilution and Demotion of Sin

By 2000, the word *sin* in America indicated more about the person saying it than about the act to which the person was referring. The few who used the word in public took themselves entirely too seriously, or perhaps not seriously enough. Sin was decidedly out, and that was that. Already more than a century ago, one of the greatest of scholars of religion noted in *The Varieties of Religious Experience*, "We have now whole congregations whose preachers, far from magnifying our consciousness of sin, seem devoted rather to making little of it. They ignore, or even deny, eternal punishment, and insist on the dignity rather than on the depravity of man."[1] What's old is new again. In the twenty-first century, sin is even more passé in America than it already had been a century earlier.

Even now, it is easy to forget that the word ever amounted to more than a metaphor for faux pas outside of small enclaves of Orthodox Jews, conservative Catholics, and Evangelical Protestants. A 2004 review article in the *New York Times*, altogether representative of the new century's moral vocabulary, ran under the headline "In a Show about Sexual Exploits, Blushing Is a Sin."[2] In a sense, blushing *is* a sin in contemporary America, as doctors have declared war on it. Today, thousands of Americans take beta-blockers to get over social anxiety disorder, which used to go by the name of blushing. It's hard to get health insurers to pay for your blushing treatment; *social anxiety disorder* sounds much more threatening. And putting up with a curable problem that makes others feel uncomfortable sounds, well, sinful. But this is to beg the question of what exactly we mean by "sinful." This chapter will sketch the downfall of a Western terror whose glory days stretched over some eleven or twelve centuries. Now defanged, sin fails to strike fear in the hearts of many religious believers: the West has venialized sin, stripped it of its awful glory. A religious subculture in the modern West now strains to find its bearings in a sexually charged landscape.

I argue that sin doesn't really make much sense divorced from the context of God, even though the word *sin* as it is frequently used today has no more to do with God than Sunday or Christmas do. Whether we can believe in sin but not in God (some atheists might claim this position) raises as many vexing questions as whether we can believe in God but not in sin (some conservative believers accuse liberal believers of this position, more or less). More than just semantics is involved, for either arrangement requires a somewhat dizzying cultural adjustment. I also argue that sin (or at least our thinking about it) has evolved significantly since the 1950s and continues to do so, such that Fidel Castro's confident *cri de coeur* from the early 1960s, "History will absolve me," could work today for a great many religious Jews and Christians wrestling with their conscience. Even people who consider themselves traditionally religious will passionately defend things once considered terribly sinful—say, masturbation, marijuana, a sexually experienced bride, suicide, miscegenation, pride, abortion, or same-sex marriage. The most interesting aspect of sin's evolution is a contemporary sensitivity to how well a religious law serves social needs, as distinct from how religious doctrines square with each other. It's as if modern believers hold God accountable for his rules, much as we might expect in an annual performance review down at the office.

I will try to make clear the intellectual force of the old adage "*Tout comprendre, c'est tout pardonner*" (To understand everything is to forgive everything). Boredom and fatigue also function as wondrous solvents— to fail to see the sinfulness in another's act is essentially to forgive it. Even more effective than forgiving others is reassuring them they did nothing wrong in the first place. Even this attitude—offensive as it may be to traditional believers—is forgivable, once you take a look at sin's slide from prominence in the public square (9/11 notwithstanding).

DEFINITIONS OF SIN

Court cases such as *Roe v. Wade* (which legalized abortion in the United States in 1973) and *Lawrence v. Texas* (which legalized sodomy in the

United States in 2003) stand as convenient watershed moments in the venialization of sin. The argument that sin has lost its sting naturally begins with an attempt to define sin. Ordinary people rely on such definitions no less than courts do. We'll see that a particular sin can bear a certain amount of sneering before it collapses under the burden of our opposition to it. Boredom plays a crucial role here as well. Sin fatigue is the weary condition of having to decide whether to hold on to or discard a transgression that just doesn't excite us anymore. Like a soap opera character who suddenly goes from bad to good, a sin can reveal its instability in a way that leads us to tire of it. We hold against a sin the effort required to readjust our attitude to it. With a wink and a nudge, we use the word *sin* in a way that undermines it. What did it mean?

Ancient Greeks thought of sin in terms of a modern-day target practice: someone who missed the bull's-eye had gone astray (hamartia), had sinned. Sometime later, Aristotle argued that every virtue lay between two corresponding vices, and that the goal of virtuous men was to hit the "golden mean." Ancient Greeks worried a lot about pride and understood the concept of "forbidden knowledge" as sinfully encroaching on the domain of the gods (think for example of Prometheus and fire).

Not surprisingly, early Christian theologians defined sin as an act that defies the law of God, one done knowingly and freely. Various definitions of sin came to absorb secular definitions of vice (familiar from ancient Greek philosophy); like vice, sin meant a refusal to master our physical and psychological impulses. In the Hebrew Bible, sin is the violation of a divine command: God commands us to resist temptation and to worship him. The trouble we save ourselves through swearing off greed, lust, pride, and so forth is also a way of saving time. Were we to give in to temptation, we would only end up miserable and contrite, on our knees before God, begging forgiveness. Of course sin can involve a third component—other people. When we sin against our neighbor, we also sin against God, because he wants us to be compassionate to one another. St. Basil the Great (d. 379) defined sin as an abuse of our God-given powers to do good. This strikes me as the best definition of sin available, capturing as it does our relationship to ourselves as well as to God and to other people, and, moreover, *power*. (If we take that definition to include negligence, many believers will quake in fear.) This entire book revolves around St. Basil's way of framing the idea.

CHAPTER 1

St. Augustine and St. Thomas Aquinas cast the net broadly, calling sin an offense against reason, truth, and right conscience. For them, sin demonstrates a failure in genuine love for God and neighbor. A perverse attachment to certain goods causes sin, which weakens human solidarity. It's hard to stand firm with your neighbor when you envy his car or compete with him for a promotion in the same office. Implicit in the notion of sin favored by Augustine and Aquinas is St. Basil's notion of free will or individual power.[3]

Pride would emerge some centuries later as the worst of the seven deadly sins. Not surprisingly, Augustine and Aquinas tie the very notion of sin to pride, or a revolt against God through the will to become "like gods" (Genesis 3:5). If we could determine for ourselves what is good and evil, we would be our own god. But ours is not to question the law; ours is simply to accept it. Sin is thus "love of oneself even to contempt of God" (Augustine, *The City of God* 14, 28). This proud self-exaltation can become our downfall. The obedience of Jesus ought to inspire Christians to follow, not lead.

We can make out an important contrast here, as pivotal figures in the Hebrew Bible called God's judgment into question, or at least asked him to explain himself. Think here of Job, Moses, and especially Abraham, who cross-examined God over the destruction of Sodom and Gomorrah. When Abraham asks God whether he would spare a wicked town for the sake of fifty good souls, God concedes he would. Like a skilled bargainer in the marketplace, Abraham then begins to drive down the price of salvation, as it were. "What about forty-five good souls? Forty?" and so on. Various prophets in the Hebrew scriptures inspire us not so much to disobey God as to try to understand him. Figures in the New Testament show less inclination to challenge divine authority (with such exceptions as doubting Thomas, or the story of Mary and Martha at the feet of Jesus). Nonetheless, such characters sometimes struggle to understand wrongdoing and its consequences (think of curiosity over the man born blind, who was given his sight by Jesus).

Various scholars have distinguished between evil and sin.[4] Following these scholars, I consider evil something that emanates from received social structures (more or less passively) and sin an act or attitude deliberately chosen by an individual. The psychological process of habituation can shape a person's character and conscience, which makes it difficult to hold evil and sin entirely apart from one another (think of good people who are born into racist, sexist, or homophobic communities).

Who decides what sin is? A deceptively simple question raises a difficult question. For if we answer confidently that God decides, we have to be prepared to grapple with another question: why God considers any particular act or attitude a sin. Take murder, for example. Is murder a sin because God says so, or does God tell us that murder is a sin because murder is immoral? If we try to insist that murder is bad because God says so, then we risk making God seem arbitrary, inscrutable, or both. What if God considered wearing blue and green together a sin? We might insist that obedience counsels us to do whatever God says, but we might also find ourselves wondering why wearing these two colors together is such a big deal. Shouldn't the concept of sin be rational, transparent?

An even bigger obstacle emerges if we try to argue that God calls murder a sin because murder is heinous. If murder is awful in and of itself, then it seems that God is following someone else's rules, and that just can't be right. Surely, God makes all the rules; no one lays down rules before God. But if we try to argue that God recognized murder as heinous the moment he got to it, we seem to imply that something comes before God—namely, murder's awfulness. Philosophers refer to this conundrum as "the Euthyphro problem," after the Platonic dialogue *Euthyphro*. Before turning to a brief summary of that dialogue, I'll mention that St. Thomas Aquinas devised an elegant solution to the problem I've just outlined. Aquinas separates God's will from his essence. All that is good in the world issues from and conforms to God's essence (or the list of things that God is). And so when God tells us what is good, he is simply willing to be what he is. And when God eschews a sin, he is merely avoiding the opposite of what he embodies. There is something of an infinite regress here, as we might next ask, "Where did God's essence come from?" The answer is a mystery.

Long before Aquinas devised this solution, Plato wrote a story about his mentor Socrates that illustrates the thorniness of this pivotal question: who gets to decide what is and isn't a sin? The *Euthyphro* frustrates any search for a pat answer. When Socrates meets a young man headed to court, where he plans to argue that his father should be put to death, Socrates wonders whether he has finally found someone who can explain sin and virtue for him, once and for all. Euthyphro, whose name in Greek means "straight thinker," leads Socrates around in circles; the young man fails miserably in his attempt to explain it all for Socrates, who exposes the foolishness. If you're going to have your own father put to death (for a death he did not directly cause), you'd better be pretty sure of your reasoning, Socrates says. The best reason Euthyphro can give for moral certainty is "the good is whatever the gods will." This circular answer falls short of Socrates' standard, though, as he points out that different gods issue different instructions at different times. The *Euthyphro* leaves us humbled, with not only a chilly reluctance to put our father to death, no matter what his mistakes may be, but also with a deeper appreciation for the difficulty of defending our moral views.

Our recently recovered humility, evident in our sensitivity to the imperfections of the American justice system and the frequency of moral leaders going astray, now bears some of the blame for sin's demise. The humility also leads to the psychological impulse to excuse the sin of someone else by filing it under the category of "venial" or "not important enough to protest publicly."

Now let's take a look at various kinds of sin.

ORIGINAL SIN

Of all the links that unite us with people who lived long ago and far away, regret must be one of them. We may occasionally find ourselves wondering how we could have made such a mess of our lives and how the world became such a rotten place.

The fall of Adam functions as a vivid depiction of the human condition today, not just as an explanation for how human sinfulness arose. According to some, Adam's sin led to the sins of future generations of people who mistreated one another (the sin also led to the necessity of working for a living and of pain during childbirth). Jews, Christians, and Muslims all recognize that God cares deeply about how humans treat one another; treating other people well is a way of honoring God in each of these three traditions. Why religious Westerners so frequently break their own rules cries out for some overarching explanation. Enter Original Sin. Although Jews and Muslims deny Original Sin (at least in the sense Christians think of it), Original Sin has so changed the way Christians think of the world that it is difficult to grasp the extent of the difference this story has made in the West.

Some Jews are surprised to learn that the doctrine of Original Sin actually fits with Judaism. The Jewish theologian David Novak has written, "Most Jews (at least most liberal Jews) are surprised if not shocked to learn that Judaism affirms [it] as does Christianity after it, albeit with some important differences."[5] The idea of visiting the sins of fathers upon their sons dovetails with Augustine's doctrine of Original Sin, a doctrine that can explain why human beings behave so badly toward one another. As the fourth century drew to a close, Augustine codified his extraordinarily influential account of why we see misery and suffering in a world created and governed by a benevolent and omnipotent deity.[6]

The classical doctrine of Original Sin comprises two distinct parts. The first concerns the two original humans, Adam and Eve, who disobeyed God and ate of the tree of knowledge (that infamous apple). The account of Adam and Eve found in the book of Genesis has given us the enduring pattern of a morality play.[7] The second part concerns the source of all human wrongdoing: whereas human nature had once been virtuous, as God had planned, it was now forever tainted. That tainting predisposes us to a wide variety of transgressions. Christians groping for a persuasive explanation for the persistent human inclination to sin may feel affirmed by twenty-first-century murmurings among scientists to the effect that there seems to be one common female ancestor for all human survivors of evolution. Maybe scientists will claim that there really was an Eve after all.

Ongoing disagreement over Original Sin continues to divide the three major branches of Christianity: Roman Catholic, Orthodox, and Protestant. Fundamentalist Protestants regard the Bible as scientifically accurate (which means that the Earth could not possibly be 4.5 billion years old, as scientists claim), whereas the Roman Catholic church holds that the Genesis creation narrative includes figurative language and therefore leaves room for competing scientific claims. (Still, according to the catechism of the church, the Fall of man did indeed take place at the beginning of human history.) Moving even further to the left, liberal Protestants such as Anglicans regard the story of the Fall largely as a metaphor, a myth that points to the symbolic "first man."

St. Paul writes in Romans 5:12–21 that through one man, sin came into the world. Paul believes that we are all affected by the sin of Adam, but Paul does not exactly explain how this is. Sin began and spread; we perpetuate the disastrous cycle and so are in need of redemption. Sin results in death, and since we all die, we all sin. To liberate ourselves from sin, we must die to sin with Christ, Paul explains (Romans 6:1–23).

Augustine presses on Paul's insights and "carries the ball further," as it were.

In one of the more interesting theological controversies in Christian history, Pelagius, a contemporary of Augustine, argued that the sin of Adam and Eve was merely personal—that is, that the sin of Adam and Eve was not transmitted to subsequent generations (which is, generally speaking, the Jewish and Muslim understanding as well). According to Augustine, concupiscence transmits Adam's sin to us—that is, the lust and sensual enjoyment that usually occur during sexual intercourse. This pleasure, this desiring, stains every new human being. Without faith and baptism, that new human being is destined for damnation. According to Augustine, circumcision functioned as a channel of grace. Circumcision functioned to override Original Sin (*On Marriage and Concupiscence* II.24). Circumcision represented the cleansing of Original Sin, just as baptism from the time of its institution began to serve a similar purpose. According to Augustine, baptism brings about a "circumcision of the heart," thus making physical circumcision unnecessary.

In subsequent centuries, Christian theologians understood Original Sin in terms of a lack of sanctifying grace, for which Adam's wrongdoing was responsible. More recent Catholic theologians, such as Karl Rahner (d. 1984), take a broader view of Original Sin, arguing that it should not be understood in terms of a sinful act committed by the first man. Rahner considers Original Sin a mystery, just as grace itself is. Changing accounts of what Original Sin amounts to might give educated people pause; these accounts might also bring on fatigue.

The loss of limbo might bring on Original Sin fatigue. For many centuries Catholic Christians believed that an unbaptized person would fail to make it to heaven, because of the seriousness of mortal sin, into which category Original Sin fell. Although Catholics no longer believe in limbo, the doctrine of Original Sin remains for Catholics "an essential truth of the faith."[8] In 1950, Pope Pius XII insisted in the encyclical *Humani Generis* that the Fall really happened. According to the catechism, "The Church, which has the mind of Christ, knows very well that we cannot tamper with the doctrine of original sin without undermining the mystery of Christ."[9] Jesus overcame the sin of Adam, as Catholics believe that the sacrament of baptism effectively washes away Original Sin. Although Paul made reference to Original Sin (1 Corinthians 15:21–23 and Romans 5:12–21), it was Augustine, as I've said, who formalized the doctrine of Original Sin, which turns on the Adam and

Eve narrative. Clearly, Jews knew something about baptism, as John the Baptist made it a practice to baptize people, but most Jews do not believe in Original Sin. Twentieth-century theologians such as Karl Barth and Emil Brunner disagreed with Pius XII; for them, as for other Protestant thinkers, the Fall was not a historic fact. That is, some Protestants hold on to Original Sin even though they don't believe the actual story of Adam and Eve ever happened.

Christians have also disagreed over whether everyone needs baptism. Pope Pius IX proclaimed the Virgin Mary the Immaculate Conception on December 8, 1854; this meant that Mary was conceived without Original Sin and had no need of baptism. In the eyes of traditional Catholics, who are spiritually bound to acknowledge this *ex cathedra* belief, Mary shares this rare designation with her son. Because she was incapable of sin, she led a morally perfect life. Protestants objected (and no doubt still object) to this view because it seemed to make Christ less special. Instead of having only one example of a perfect human being, we have two. And instead of Christ having come to the world to save absolutely everyone, it turns out that there was one person who did not need to be saved. Protestants pointed out that one searches the New Testament in vain for corroboration that Mary was born without any taint of Original Sin. The greatness of Christ's sacrifice on the Cross would have been compromised if the world already contained a redeemed human, some Protestants maintain. The very idea of the Immaculate Conception, which had been floating around for centuries before Pius IX issued his *ex cathedra* ruling, was anathema to Luther.

Like the Virgin Mary, science has something important to do with our grasp of Original Sin. The Jesuit geopaleontologist and religious mystic Pierre Teilhard de Chardin (1881–1955) focused on the direction, survival, and fulfillment of the human species on Earth. He envisioned a mental evolution that would eventually unite spiritually the entire human species. Teilhard shepherded into modern religious thought Darwin's insights into the organic beginnings of plant, animal, and human life.

In the early 1920s, Father Teilhard de Chardin was teaching science at the Institut Catholique in Paris and also talking to seminarians about his ideas on Original Sin. His unpublished essay "Note on Some Possible Historical Representations of Original Sin," intended for theologians, made its way to the Superior General of the Jesuits. Sometime later Teilhard was told to confine himself to science and sent off to work in China. He continued to write on theological topics, and his ideas continued to circulate. His remarks on Original Sin appear to have changed very little in the 1930s and 1940s, despite the opposition they aroused.

His first essay on geocentrism challenged received ideas. The traditional formulation of Original Sin was, he held, the chief stumbling block to reconciling science and religion. Monogenism, for example, that is, the origin of the human race from one couple, is impossible for science to accept. A whole new way of seeing the universe "is introducing an intrinsic imbalance into the very core of the dogma." It affronted Teilhard's sense of the immense size and age of the universe that a universal fall be attributed to the action of one human on one small planet. This geocentrism was unacceptable not only in regard to Adam and Eve but also in regard to the way the faithful see Christ. "Let me say frankly what I think: it is impossible to universalize the first Adam without destroying his individuality."[10] He concluded that strictly speaking, there was no first Adam. An original sin itself simply symbolized the inevitable chance of evil manifesting itself in human activity.

These themes continued to repeat themselves over the years. "The more we bring the past to life again by means of science, the less we can accommodate either Adam or the earthly paradise." Because Original Sin expresses the perennial and universal law of imperfection that operates in humankind, the Fall thus takes on cosmic proportions for Teilhard. He almost pinned responsibility for it on God. He insisted that Original Sin was "a static solution to the problem of evil." But moving from a static view to an evolving universe made evil less of an incomprehensible element in the structure of the world and more of a natural feature.

In July 1966, Pope Paul VI convened a conference of experts on Original Sin at the Gregorian University. Some commentators at the time concluded that he granted theologians freedom of research with one hand and took it back with the other by placing limits on that research. In any event, Catholic theologians concur that it is a mistake to infer that humans lack freedom simply because of Original Sin. We can and must overcome our immoral proclivities, Catholic theologians will insist. The struggle is unending and imperative.

As we've seen, the consequences of Original Sin are sickness, suffering, pain during childbirth, the necessity of working to make a living, and death. Like suffering, sin remains a mystery. We don't really understand why God includes either in the world. To the extent we have an answer, it's that we've brought these problems on ourselves. We must pay for the sins of our forebears. Given that all humans find themselves in the same boat, any coherent theory might have some appeal. This particular theory, which is as much a narrative of the Garden of Eden as anything, fails to convince many outside Catholic and Protestant ranks. Such a shortcoming might suggest that the theory is more of an ethnic code than anything else. Even (or especially) ethnic codes can change, as I've indicated: in 2005, the Holy See largely discredited the realm of limbo, where unbaptized babies and virtuous Muslims were supposed to live out eternity. Where these souls rest now is something of a mystery, but it suddenly seems more likely they ended up in heaven. The Fall of Adam and Eve may have happened long ago, but theological interpretations of its implication continue to evolve—and to evolve in ways that brighten humanity's future.

TYPES OF SIN

Just as children can hurt their parents by lashing out at them, so do believing Jews and Christians envision themselves wounding their heavenly father by disobeying him. How extraordinary it is that mere mortals possess the power to affect a being infinitely stronger and wiser than themselves. That he actually cares about the actions of his inferiors makes him vulnerable. In that vulnerability we sense the power of sin and the fearful capacity of a person to scorn the precepts of God.

We can hurt God through various means: the one we fall into will have something to do with our individual personalities. Given the extraordinary variety among human beings, it should come as no surprise that sins also fall into many categories. We find lists of them scattered throughout Hebrew and Christian scriptures. St. Paul even goes so far as to set down what kinds of sinners have virtually no hope of making it to heaven. The Letter to the Galatians contrasts the works of the flesh with the fruit of the Spirit: "Now the works of the flesh are plain: fornication, impurity, licentiousness, idolatry, sorcery, enmity, strife, jealousy, anger, selfishness, dissension, factions, envy, drunkenness, carousing, and the like. I warn you, as I warned you before, that those who do such things shall not inherit the Kingdom of God" (Galatians 5:19–21).[11] We are responsible ultimately for our own downfall—we fall into sin; we bring it upon ourselves; we fail to resist it. Sin issues from our hearts: "For out of the heart come evil thoughts, murder, adultery, fornication, theft, false witness, slander. These are what defile a man." Successive generations of thinkers have provided still other sin distinctions, the more important of which I'll turn to now. Let's take a brief look at (1) sins of commission versus sins of omission, (2) permitted versus committed sins, and (3) venial versus mortal sins.

Sins of commission differ from sins of omission in a straightforward way. The mugger who assaults someone on the street commits a sin; all those witnesses and passersby that do nothing are also guilty. Because they did not intervene or were perhaps too busy to dial the police on their cell phones, bystanders are guilty of a sin of omission. Sins of omission indicate a failure to do one's duty. Telling a lie qualifies as a sin of commission, while "mental reservation"—uttering a partial truth, while keeping the full truth reserved in the mind—might be considered a sin of omission against the virtue of truthfulness. For example, he asks, "Do you think I'm stupid?"; she responds, "No, I don't think you're stupid," and then says silently, "When compared to absolute imbeciles." Roman Catholic moralists have disagreed over how to classify mental reservation.[12] According to legend, Galileo whispered to himself after recanting his celestial hypothesis before a Vatican tribunal, "And still it moves." Galileo was a good Catholic, even in his defiance of the church.

That they defy easy categorization makes sins of omission more interesting. Were "Hitler's willing executioners," those supposedly helpless, "ordinary" Germans who did not work in or near the concentration camps, guilty of a sin of omission (that is, failing to speak out against National Socialists)? Or were those "willing executioners" cowering in healthy fear, trying to survive a regime that threatened them as well? If the ideal resolution of a sticky situation would require you to go beyond the scope of your duty, by giving up your own life to save a stranger's, for example, can you be condemned for opting not to? Jewish and Christian theologians differ here. To the extent that any consensus emerges, it would be to refrain from requiring people to do what philosophers call "supererogatory" acts—deeds above and beyond the call of duty—but to applaud vigorously anyone who does. It is, after all, much easier to articulate what we should not do than what we should. Thus, it is often difficult to hold individuals responsible for neglecting or deliberately avoiding good deeds, particularly when their own lives are at stake. Yet, we find ourselves regularly admiring those heroes who do precisely that.

The next distinction can be summarized as "taking one for the team"; the distinction presupposes that someone must be held accountable for every offense. Heroic people are prepared to sin so that you won't have to.

An enthusiastic focus on our conduct, on avoiding sin, resisting temptation, may make us selfish, stiff prudes and consequently curiously sinful. The distinction between committed and permitted sins underscores that very possibility. Is it better to allow *others* to sin rather than to commit a sin ourselves? In *On Lying*, for example, Augustine argues that it is wrong to lie even if we want to protect someone else from harm. Like Kant after him, Augustine condemns providing false information about an innocent neighbor in order to prevent him from being captured by hostile or enemy forces. But we may disagree, insisting that someone has to lie in order to prevent a neighbor, who's hiding in the attic upstairs, from being captured. Who will lie then—you or someone else? Wouldn't it be virtuous for you to "take one for the team," to lie yourself so that no one else has to incur the penalty? Better love hath no man than to sin so that his neighbor won't have to.

Such thinking would seem to violate St. Paul's prohibition of doing evil so that good may come. Yet many people, on serious reflection, will approve of the lie of the compassionate neighbor. The evil stalker forfeits his right to be told the truth, it might reasonably be thought, by virtue of his decision to harm another or to work for a corrupt organization. Other examples suggest themselves (think of Almodóvar's popular film from 1992, *High Heels*, in which a daughter commits a murder for which her mother quickly accepts the blame). This category of sin brings up the fascinating notion of vicarious suffering, central to Christian theology and an important part of chapter 2 (on atonement).

Much more familiar than the distinction between sins that are committed versus those that are permitted is the distinction between venial and mortal sins. These terms specify degrees of wrongdoing in Catholic culture (which is broader than, but not synonymous with, Catholic theology). Various factors—"extenuating circumstances," lack of full evil intention, or a conflict of duties—can bolster your penance in the confessional or your fate at the Last Judgment. In *On the Good of Marriage*, for example, Augustine argues that although fornication and adultery are both immoral, the latter is more sinful since it breaches marital trust. This judgment relies on the idea that there are degrees of sinfulness.

A crucial verse in the New Testament justifies the Catholic distinction between mortal and venial sins: "All wrongdoing is sin, but there is sin which is not mortal" (1 John 5:17). Subsequent Catholic moral theology refined the distinction between mortal and venial sins. Mortal sins entail three components: (1) a clear knowledge of guilt, (2) full consent of the will, and (3) "grave matter." Although venial sins certainly imperil the soul, they do not deprive the individual of sanctifying grace, which might be described in contemporary parlance as the positive, life-giving energy that God transmits to us (or tries to). Venial sins might show up as tiny cracks in a beautiful vase: after a certain number of cracks, the vase will crumble. Mortal sins, to continue the metaphor, would immediately destroy the vase (think of taking a sledgehammer to the delicate object).

Protestant Reformers not only rejected the distinction, but attacked Catholics for it. The very category of venial sin seemed to Protestant theologians to suggest that some offenses against God weren't all that bad. For them, all sin expressed disloyalty to God—an idolization of sensual pleasure, material wealth, or simply the self. Some contemporary Roman Catholic thinkers have portrayed mortal sin as more than just a discrete act, more the direction of the wind than the snap of a branch.[13] Although times have certainly changed, it is fair to say that the distinction between mortal and venial sin remains an orienting fixture in Roman Catholic culture.

The classification of sins has evolved in fascinating ways. The convictions of earlier moralists could make moderns gasp. Take, for instance, the question of whether a husband might with moral impunity kill his adulterous wife: this matter occupied Christian moralists through the mid–seventeenth century, until Pope Alexander VII condemned the notion in 1665. (Well into the twentieth century, American juries showed leniency to men who killed their wives in "crimes of passion.") As various thinkers have noted, sexual pleasure, either physical or mental, sent up immediate red flags in the church. A moral intention to procreate was to drive sexual intercourse between spouses (no sex outside marriage was permitted). Lust—even for one's spouse—could not count as a moral reason. All sexual sins were mortal; sins of the flesh were not excused as common and therefore venial. Today we may wonder how masturbation, for example, could get you into such trouble; I will explore this question at length in chapter 4. Few educated people today would rank masturbation or premarital sex on a moral par with, say, torture or even racial discrimination, yet our forebears did. This realization reminds us that sin evolves, just as civilizations do.

The availability of the categories "venial" and "mortal" facilitates the moral progress of the West. Few people would insist that income tax cheating demands as much attention as child abuse, and we therefore reserve our most vehement social protests for the battles we consider most urgent. The problem, to the extent we want to call it one, is that more and more sins end up migrating to the category "not urgent right now." The crowding of this category further fuels sin fatigue.

THE PSYCHOLOGY OF SIN

We do not know who was the first to commit any number of sins, but Jews, Christians, and Muslims do know who was the first to sin. It was, of course, Eve. Adam finished a close second. Since then, sin has punctuated human interaction. The inevitability of messing up holds significant psychological implications in an increasingly competitive world.

According to Jewish tradition, everyone is essentially a sinner. "Surely there is no one on earth so righteous as to do good without ever sinning" (Ecclesiastes 7:20). At the same time, it is important to note the countervailing optimism of a verse such as Leviticus 19:2: "You shall be holy, for I the Lord your God am holy," which seems to break with the idea that humans are doomed to utter sinfulness. Hebrew scriptures generally present evil as beginning in man himself. "These people draw near with their mouths and honor me with their lips, while their hearts are far from me" (Isaiah 29:13). From man's evil heart came all sin: "When the Lord saw . . . that man's every thought and all the inclinations of his heart were only evil" (Genesis 6:5). Only when God gave man a new heart would he be able to live by his statutes and carefully observe his decrees (Exodus 36:26–27). For the Israelites, it was the heart, the seat of the understanding and will, that had rebelled against God. They said, "We will follow our own devices: each one of us will behave according to the stubbornness of his evil heart!" (Jeremiah 18:12). This recalls Jesus's subsequent lamentation: "Why is it that you honor me, yet you do not do as I say?" Actions speak louder than words.

For Jews, the notion of sin involved pollution as much as it did disobeying divine commands.[14] One impure individual (e.g., a menstruating woman) could contaminate an entire household or community. Sin as a contagion or epidemic has surfaced in other religions as well. In early modern Spain, for example, purity of the blood became an obsession. Not only did Catholic Spaniards seek to avoid marrying anyone with even a small trace of Jewish or Muslim blood, such Christians also worried about the pedigree of a wet nurse. Christians did not want Jews, Muslims, or, after the Reformation, Protestants nursing their children. What's notable about linking sin to pollution is that God has essentially nothing to do with the problem; people bring sin upon themselves, either by eating unclean food or by touching unclean women. (We might object that menstruation just happens: no woman menstruates because she chooses to. The book of Genesis explains menstruation not so much as sin per se but as a punishment, one visited upon Eve for her disobedience.)

According to a rival view, one set out clearly in the third chapter of Genesis, a superhuman power introduced sin to the world. No mere animal, the serpent masterminded disorder, the source of revolt and insubordinate pride. The serpent represents Satan, Lucifer, or the devil. Elaine Pagels has argued persuasively that ancient Christians came to equate heretics and especially Jews with the demonic power of Satan.[15] It seems harder to take Satan seriously once we realize the cruelty underlying his Christian conception. That realization opens the door a little further to sin fatigue.

How ironic that a Christian majority might consider itself threatened or even persecuted by a tiny Jewish minority—in either Western Europe or North America (we'll see a parallel to white and black Americans in chapter 6, on affirmative action). In any event, it certainly bears noting that hatred of Satan continues to animate some religious believers. We can hardly hope to find a more gripping example of this overflowing hatred than the Muslim hajj (annual pilgrimage) of January 2006, when several hundred pilgrims were trampled to death during the dramatic stoning of Satan (in a hajj in the early 1990s, well over a hundred thousand Muslim pilgrims were stampeded to death during the stoning ceremony).[16] Some three million Muslims journey to Mecca for the hajj. In the stoning ritual, all the pilgrims must pass a series of three "pillars" called al-Jamarat, which represent the devil and which the faithful pelt with stones to purge themselves of sin. Muslim revulsion to Satan has led to terrible fervor, the result of which has been considerable loss of human life.

The idea of an evil genius also underlies hell.[17] Jews disagree among themselves on whether there is such a place. Christians in general roundly agree on the reality and horror of hell. This horror has spawned a whole genre of novels, sermons, and films. Hell is Satan's kingdom, and he rules over it mercilessly. We might wonder how a loving God could ever abandon a beloved creature to such a fate, but the traditional answer—people sentence themselves to that fate, through exercising their free will sinfully—makes some sense.

For Catholics, no single act by itself can merit eternal punishment in hell unless that act constitutes a fundamental rejection of God. Only a mortal sin, Thomas Aquinas concluded, deserves the name "sin" (*Summa Theologica* I–II, q. 88, a. 1). Various Christian thinkers—some of them Catholic—have since disagreed with Thomas.[18] Jews, however, have largely agreed with the logic behind his thinking.

Sin breeds sin; the taste of vice keeps inviting us back. As Alexander Pope once wrote in the *Essays on Man,*

> Vice is a monster of so frightful mien,
> As to be hated needs but to be seen;
> Yet seen too oft, familiar with her face,
> We first endure, then pity, then embrace.

Repetition leads to perverse inclinations. Before we know it, we've fallen off the path, alone with our clouded conscience and compromised ability to discern good and evil. Although sin tends to reproduce and reinforce itself, it cannot destroy the moral sense at its root. Context as well creates a proclivity to sin; theologians have referred to troublesome settings as "occasions of sin." For some it will be slot machines; for others, access to company funds; and for others, the frat house. The two central points to grasp before moving on are, again, that we do ourselves in and that our misdeeds possess the power to wreck God's whole day, as it were.

God's transcendence defies quick conclusions about his human-inflicted wounds. Again, the very idea that people can wound God boggles the mind. Job ponders, "If you sin, what injury do you do to God? Even if your offenses are many, how do you hurt him?" (Job 35:5–6). Saddening God is what we do when we sin. We deprive God of some happiness by indulging in our own. This very thought should vex us, if we love him properly (see 1 Samuel 5:7–9; 6:19–20; 24:7, 11, 13; 2 Samuel 1:14–16). We also risk saddening God when we mistreat other people, for God identifies with other people. A good example of this imaginative identification is the sin of David, who lusts after Bathsheba, the wife of Uria (2 Samuel 11–12). David despises God himself (2 Samuel 12:7, 9–10). David eventually repents, lamenting, "I have sinned against the Lord" (12, 13). King David mistakenly believed he had sinned only against another person, and a relatively insignificant (because non-Israelite) one at that. David learns that God resides even in apparently insignificant strangers.

Arguably the worst consequence of understanding that everyone will sin is learned helplessness, about which much remains to be said in the final chapter.

INTENTION

I find intention the most effective touchstone of sin, the most useful way of gauging wrongdoing. In this I follow Peter Abelard (1079–1142), who argued along these lines roughly a thousand years ago. The focus on intention, for all its good, contributes to the venialization of sin, for an informed individual can always put himself at far remove from the scene of sin. "I never meant to separate myself from God," he can reassure himself later, "only to step out of line briefly, even as I questioned the logic of that line."

Abelard, the first serious moral philosopher of medieval times, went beyond the established traditions of pious moralizing, which usually involved little more than quoting scripture or other religious authorities, and tried to apply rational analysis to the nature of moral goodness.[19] In order to discover exactly what sin and virtue amounted to, he started by distinguishing the different senses in which something may be said to be good or bad. Abelard concluded that moral goodness must be a matter of having the right intentions. Abelard felt confident that God will consider intentions, not acts, when he comes to weigh people in the balance on the Day of Judgment. As for the question of what makes an intention good or bad, Abelard's answer is straightforwardly theological: the difference lies in God's wishes or, rather, in what his wishes are believed to be. A man sins when he scorns what he takes to be God's wishes and acts well when he seeks to embrace them.

Almost all the theologians of the time placed intentionality at the center of morality, but Abelard stood apart from the mainstream. Recognizing the importance of the interior state and the potential danger of sinful thoughts, even those that don't result in action, Abelard focused on *action*. A state of mind alone could neither win people praise nor subject them to shame (in this Abelard resembles Kant, who wrote over six centuries later). A dirty mind or greedy spirit is not straightforwardly a moral fault. And so the husband with the proverbial "wandering eye" would not arouse much blame from someone who thought as Abelard. The point to be taken here is not that a narrow legalistic fact ("he never touched her") makes all the moral difference, but rather that a broader and more vivid moral picture follows from attention to what may initially seem unduly technical distinctions ("there's nothing wrong with continuing to look at the menu, even after you've placed your order"). This broader picture dovetails with Karl Rahner's softening of mortal sin and, moreover, abets sin fatigue.

Abelard's last ethical treatise (*Scito teipsum*) takes sin as its overriding theme. There he argues that actions in themselves are almost entirely indifferent or morally neutral. Moral judgment of any action should center on the root of the intention. The problem here might be easily grasped through the example of a prostitute who sells sex in order to feed her child or finance the medical operation of her mother. The Council of Sens (1140) condemned the view that actions are indifferent in themselves, but I think Abelard had seized on an altogether important distinction. This distinction demotes discrete actions (good or bad) to a rung on the moral pecking order lower than the wishes of the person who acts. This demotion of sin contributes in some positive way to the decision not to worry unduly about sin, understood as a discrete event.

In his letter to the Romans, St. Paul portrays sin as a force capable of dominating human beings. In conjunction with death, sin rules over the entire world (Romans 5:12–21). In 1 Corinthians 15:56, Paul identifies sin as the sting of death. Again, Paul exhorts his followers to die to sin with Christ (Romans 7:1–6). Combining the insights of Abelard with the spirit of Paul's teaching, our overriding intention or ultimate goal should be to die to sin, to live blamelessly, to love God with all of our mind, strength, soul, and heart. In the abstract, Paul's exhortation sounds perfectly noble, but Abelard's attention to intentions will help a great deal more as we negotiate the moral messiness of day-to-day life.

Intention conflicts with tort theory, as taught in American law schools. In American tort law, intention counts for virtually nothing: if someone slips on ice on your property or breaks his neck diving into your swimming pool, you can be sued. It doesn't matter how good your intentions may have been, actions (or inaction) determine culpability. Yet in other aspects of criminal law, intention plays a crucial role: in wrongful deaths, for example, juries take into consideration whether a killer accidentally (involuntary manslaughter) or purposely (homicide) ended the life of another. Invocation of the concept of intentionality requires for its application the acceptance of some prior account of morality; pointing to this acceptance, a lawyer or an individual can make a compelling case for the exculpation of an offender. The difficulty of appeals to intention is that such appeals open the door to interpretation; any act or motive can be interpreted in a variety of ways, and the possibility of bad faith lurks over such interpretations.

No one person can be singled out for credit or blame, when it comes to examining the cause of sin fatigue. Plenty or predatory priests, corrupt politicians, hostile dictators, scandalous rabbis, criminal police officers, hypocritical preachers, larcenous businesspeople, and abusive nuns have individually prevented otherwise-good people from believing that virtue always overcomes vice, and that sin is inevitably punished. Sin fatigue was no one's intention per se, which is not to deny that a group of people may have an intention (e.g., world domination or the unseating of a political incumbent). Many parents intentionally inculcate particular religious beliefs in their children, so it seems clear that intentions are not limited to solitary individuals.

What parents or religious groups or political parties frequently see themselves doing is contributing to a larger, historical movement in which one particular way of describing right and wrong prevails. In fifteenth-century Europe, it must have seemed that the Roman Catholic Church really was what God wanted to favor, just as, a century later, it might have seemed that Protestants were gathering such momentum because God had grown displeased with ruling Catholics. Today we might sidestep the question of God's will and more humbly conclude, along Darwinian lines, that sin fatigue set in sometime during the mid–twentieth century because the old picture of sin no longer fit the West very well. Gradually, like the changes on a coral reef, Westerners readjusted their individual notions of right and wrong along similar lines.

What Abelard offers us is a useful way of explaining away bad things we may have done without meaning to. Traditional believers in the West may not derive much solace from the notion that they themselves deserve no blame for the remarkably eroticized, even pagan, world they now inhabit, but it would behoove them to think in terms of sin's rationality. If sin ceases to make sense broadly, then sin fatigue will set in gradually—perhaps not as a sin of commission, but rather a fruit of omission.

MORAL MOTIVATION

What is it to have a reason for action? What are the connections between having a reason to do a certain thing and being motivated to do that thing? Why do we obey God's law and avoid the sins we sometimes ache to enjoy? Is it (1) to show our love for God, (2) to avoid hell, or (3) to earn God's favor and increase the chances he will grant our wishes? The lesson from the Book of Job would make (1) the correct answer. This answer, as ancient as it may be, kicked into high gear toward the close of the twentieth century and, as it did, robbed sin of its place on center stage of the believer's imagination. Believers of various stripes gradually acknowledged that scaring others into a particular kind of faith (or into faith at all) was ignoble; surely, it was morally preferable to extend love as the motive for following God. Fear seemed to rate very low as a worthwhile motive for worshipping God, who presumably could see through our supposed piety anyway.

The devil cannot be considered the cause of sin in the sense that he directly moves man's will to sin. At most he is able to tempt humans to sin by altering their moods or attitudes, causing them to have momentary thoughts of sinful things or to dwell on the fantasy of illicit pleasure. Not all temptation need be explained in terms of diabolical activity, however; the world and the flesh can account for most of the temptations people experience. In a general sense, nevertheless, because the devil was instrumental in causing Original Sin, which has left men prone to evil, he can be considered an indirect and partial cause of all sin. When a person resists temptation or overcomes sin, he or she does it through sheer force of will. We can be the cause of sin in another to the extent that we induce someone to sin by means of persuasion, suggestion, command, or example. Some religious people would say that the devil (or some analogous negative force) works through sinners who "recruit" teammates.

Satan challenges God in the disturbing Book of Job, as frightening to some believers as any slash-and-burn horror film. Satan declares that the only reason people love God or follow his rules is in order to win favors. It's not God that people love, Satan asserts, but blessings or rewards. Astonishingly, God enters into the conversation, even suggesting a contest. "Have you considered my servant Job?" God challenges Satan in turn. That launches one long slide for poor Job, a veritable living saint. Even after Job loses all his land, cattle, belongings, family, even his health and his wife, Job never ceases to love God. Some readers will marvel at how bold Job becomes, demanding as he does again and again that God explain himself. God never comes through, but he does restore everything Job had lost—even giving Job a new wife. What's even more striking than the misery and despair Job had to endure is the particular effect of Job's questions, which is to silence God, who never again speaks to a human being. (Christians may differ here, offering as a challenging example the verse "Saul, Saul, why do you persecute me?" or St. John of Patmos, the putative author of the Book of Revelation.)

Surely it is preferable to swear off wrongdoing as a way to show love for God than to do so in the name of avoiding hell. A variety of Jewish and Christian theologians agree on this score. It only seems logical to conclude that the omniscient God of Judaism and Christianity can read a believer's heart (or intentions), and that God will prefer acts of love to those of expedience. Proper moral motivation—love, not expediency—demotes sin as well. For love eclipses sin in the mature heart. That fewer and fewer moderns accept the horrific picture of hell depicted in Michelangelo's *Last Judgment* only accelerates the demotion of sin on this front. Jews, Christians, and Muslims who avoid sin in order to demonstrate love for God (as opposed to avoiding nasty consequences) defy sin fatigue. The moral motivation of these believers will keep sin alive; in any event, certain believers may well redouble their motivation to keep sin alive in a world suffused with sin fatigue.

OCCASIONS OF SIN

As the West drops its moral guard, occasions of sin proliferate (think, e.g., of Internet pornography). Their sheer number facilitates the venialization of much sin.

What theologians call "an occasion of sin" is like the springboard a diver uses to get in the air. A diver wants so badly to be in the air that he finds himself drawn to the board, without even realizing it. If you think of diving as something that everyone in the world can do, you'll see the consequence of suddenly or inadvertently finding yourself on a springboard—you will naturally dive. If you define diving as something undesirable or immoral, you'll see why we might describe a springboard as dangerous. It's not sinful in and of itself, but it facilitates sin.

An occasion of sin lures a person to sin and presents an opportunity to sin. An occasion of sin can be a person, place, or thing. An occasion to sin lies outside us; it is not helpful to call inclinations such as greed, anger, or lust an occasion of sin, because we already have useful ways of referring to and categorizing passions and bad habits. Theologians distinguish between remote and proximate occasions of sin, based on the appeal of a given occasion of sin and the probability that a sin will happen. As remote occasions pulsate through our lives, we have no obligation to steer away from them. Even staying home for the rest of our lives might not eliminate occasions of sin. Homeschooling your children, it might be thought, could dramatically reduce such exposure. (Homeschooling likely fails to curb such sins as pride and bigotry, though.)

Living in the West in the twenty-first century almost invariably involves scantily clad people and news of corporate tax fraud—arguably to a greater degree than ever before.[20] The entire public sphere has become an occasion of sin, it might seem to traditional Jews, Christians, or Muslims, who understandably worry about a corresponding neutralization of sin. The head scarf worn by many Muslim women came to symbolize the occasion of sin in the early twenty-first century. Women who expose too much of their flesh exposed the extent to which the occasion of sin had been conceived in masculine terms. The social advances of Western women in the twentieth century contributed to sin fatigue, both by challenging traditional gender roles and by undermining the resistance of men who view women as sexual temptations that ought to stay out of the workplace or even the public sphere.

WHAT FEAR OF SIN CAN DO

Believers try to avoid sin but keep failing. A destructive pattern of guilt and shame can result from this pattern of fallibility. Feelings of worthlessness make perfect sense, but they undermine a believer's resolve to live blamelessly. However, fear of sin does have its benefits: It may encourage people to take responsibility for their own actions. September 11, 2001, itself may go down in history as a watershed moment that challenged the moral laxity of the 1960s, 1970s, 1980s, and 1990s, for 9/11 clarified the notion of moral responsibility in an unforgettable way.

Fear of sin may inspire a resolve to overcome personal limitations, and perhaps of collective limitations as well. For some believers, fear of sin also telegraphs terror of eternal damnation or the sad state of having let down God, who had hoped for better from us. But fear of sin rushes out to seek a boundary—that between virtue and vice, that between the peculiar and the pathological, that between the human and the divine. Today, that boundary shifts faster than ever. Hell seems a distant memory and a film about demonic possession such as *The Exorcist* simple entertainment.[21] At the end of the twentieth century, hell was too unpleasant to think about anymore, too inconvenient to fear.[22] Far preferable was a God who, with paternal patience and boundless long-suffering, would always love us, would always forgive us. No matter what.

How did Catholics come to resemble Jews, for whom the whole idea of hell never held much sway, in this regard?[23] A gradual twentieth-century loss of the sense of sin was already evident in Hannah Arendt's observation of the banality of evil during Adolf Eichmann's trial in Jerusalem, although it had been slowly evolving at least since Thoreau. The gradual death of sin-fear stems in large part from twentieth-century psychoanalytic and pharmacological insights. Since Freud, we see good and evil (or at least the potential for them) in everyone, even Nazis and terrorists. We are loath to blame anyone for alcoholism, depression, attention deficit, or violent tendencies. Biology is the culprit, not us.[24] This heightened sensitivity to ways in which sin can highjack the life of a well-meaning person has further eroded sin's power. By loving the sinner and hating the sin, we simply throw pills and therapy at sin to make it go away.

The diminution of sin-fear also involves the increased opportunities for sexual titillation wrought by the Industrial Revolution, when women went to work in factories, often in close proximity to men. Several decades later, American women entered the workforce in even higher numbers, filling voids created by men who were away fighting in World War II. This transformation of the workplace seems to have led to an increase in premarital and extramarital sex in America.[25] Sexual desire often outran fear of sin.

Why do we need to include sin in our moral vocabulary today? Wouldn't the word *immorality* suffice? And wouldn't the word *immorality*, by erasing an instinctive reference to God, make it easier for people of different religious views to get along and agree with one another? The word *sin*, like the devil and hell generally, was on its way out before 9/11. The word *sin* separates one religious group from another, a regrettable consequence in an ecumenical age. Although fear of sin may improve our behavior, that fear may make the world dangerous, if it prompts us to threaten or assault people who do not share that fear. Furthermore, it could be, as Alasdair MacIntyre asserts in *After Virtue*, that Christianity would collapse without a working sense of sin.

Can you sin if you don't believe in God? It makes no sense to say that you have offended someone you do not know, someone you can't even fathom. What if you don't have faith? Why wouldn't you have faith? By definition, God can't sin, but why would he seem to withhold faith from some? These answers are a mystery. God's ways are not our ways, and only he can explain why he gives faith to some while withholding it from others. Meanwhile, an entire class of people struggles to find faith, to choose belief. Fear of sin, ultimately, seems a mixed blessing. It can hardly be considered excellent moral motivation—obeying God's law only because you worry that he'll send you to hell if you don't. And if those who don't believe in sin (because they don't believe in God) are held by God to a lower standard, then believers are left with a puzzle. It's not so much that ignorance of the law exculpates nonbelievers as it is that God might not hold against nonbelievers a law they wanted to believe in (read: intention) but just couldn't swallow.

September 11 prompted a lazy generation of Americans to find a compelling way to blame Al Qaeda for audacious sins. The task proved quite tricky, but sin emerged as a tool of immeasurable usefulness. The problem was that the enemy of America had the nerve to use that same weapon against Americans. That realization compelled some Americans to dig in their heels even harder, even as it unleashed a simultaneous new wave of sin fatigue.

THE LIMITS OF SIN

Can we trivialize sin so far that we eliminate it altogether? Can we collapse the very concept? The limits of sin, the extent of naughtiness we'll allow or at least tacitly overlook, suggest no predictable end to sin. Although it's possible that all sin will someday be venialized, that day would seem to be at least a century away.

Think of other boundaries and the effect they have on ordinary life. Salary increases almost invariably change our lifestyle. The more money we make, the more money we will spend. Our spending habits seek limits and, if we're lucky, stop there. Teenagers who gain a little freedom from parental authority will often, within a short time, plead for more freedom. The same holds true for potted plants—if we transplant a thriving plant to a larger pot, the roots of the plant will expand until the new pot prevents further growth. The same might also be said about our personal idiosyncrasies or what others may term our "bad attitude." The more power we acquire—in the workplace or on the playing field or at the country club—the more we will allow ourselves to tell others what we think of them, and the less we are likely to be "team players."

It seems only natural for us to want to find our limits and then to expand our human potential. Given the examples just cited, it may seem ultimately prudent to respect boundaries and to avoid becoming the sort of person who regularly walks over them. Like athletes who push personal limits to become the best they can be, so does humanity consciously or unconsciously ache to expand its own dominion—intellectual, technological, and moral. That's not such a bad thing. Indeed, such boldness spurs scientific and artistic explorations (think of stem cell research or erotic art).

Religious people hunger for certainty—they want to know what's right and wrong. Perhaps the answers were never very clear; maybe our forebears, motivated by the same fear of uncertainty that nags at us, just behaved as if right and wrong were brutally obvious. Today, only the most basic moral principles (e.g., cruelty is bad) seem obvious. About the rest we argue incessantly (e.g., by questioning how to define cruelty). Maybe that's not such a bad thing, either.

What's right isn't so much what we can get away with as what we can justify through old-fashioned argument and a newfound sensitivity to moral differences. That newfound sensitivity should respect the Judeo-Christian tradition of anchoring what sin represents in the God of Abraham, Isaac, and Jacob. Sin as a secular metaphor, as shorthand for the message "A penalty is on the way to you," undermines that tradition (even if only inadvertently) while risking confusion. If we forget the religious roots of our contemporary thinking about good and bad, reward and punishment, we can lose our bearings in the West. Beyond that, it is not entirely clear that Judaism, Christianity, or Islam could remain intact without a vivid sense of sin. The philosopher Alasdair MacIntyre, for instance, persuasively asserts in *After Virtue*, "What Christianity requires is a conception not merely of defects of character, or vices, but of breaches of divine laws, of sin."[26]

The Christian account of where sin comes from has helped millions of Westerners find their moral bearings. On this account, sin comes from one or more of three sources: (1) the appeal of desirable things like pleasure, love, or success; (2) the temptations of an almost equal anti-God; and (3) the human possibility of turning away from God. Of the three, the third seems the most compelling in the twenty-first century. Despite the intellectual advances of the Enlightenment, it wasn't really until the twentieth century that we began to consider questions such as "Can you sin if you don't believe in God?" This question begs others, such as how religious believers will categorize people who lack faith. Such nonbelievers might ask believers why a good God would deny anyone the gift of faith. By definition, God can't sin, but why would he apparently choose to exclude some from the guest list of the best party ever? The answer is a mystery.

The limits of sin parallel the limits of humanity. We may fear and/or loathe the AIDS virus, tornadoes, or the desert, but we don't call them sinful. The more we learn about the world, the richer our stock of metaphors for sin becomes. Disease has been a popular stand-in, but now cortisol strikes a more contemporary chord. The chemical given off by our fears and worries, cortisol ages our skin, grays our hair, and reduces our memory capacity. Although cortisol does not sin, it may seem as noxious as sin. In cortisol we see a glimmer of how sin might affect bodily health.

What is most interesting about the recent scientific understanding of cortisol is the way it leaves us with a rosier picture of self-control. Plenty of people think that we are at the mercy of our genes and bodies. Matt Ridley has cogently concluded that far from behavior being at the mercy of our biology, our biology is often at the mercy of our behavior.[27] It is the body that switches on genes when it needs them, often in response to a more or less cerebral, or even conscious, response to external events. You can raise your cortisol levels just by thinking about stressful eventualities—even fictional ones. Likewise, the dispute between those who believe that a certain suffering is purely psychiatric and those who insist it has a physical cause (consider chronic fatigue syndrome) misses the point entirely. The brain and the body are part of the same system. If the brain, responding to psychological stress, stimulates the release of cortisol and cortisol suppresses the reactivity of the immune system, then a dormant viral infection may well flare up or a new one catch hold. The symptoms may indeed be physical and the causes psychological. If a disease affects the brain and alters the mood, the causes may be physical and the symptoms psychological. Believers who consider sin a spiritual disease may make themselves literally sick by their compulsive bad behavior. Sin may have spilt over into the realm of the corporal, exceeding previously imagined boundaries and making its baleful power evident in and on human organs. Of course, only people who worry about their sinfulness would be affected by cortisol in this way.

Recent scientific discoveries about mind-body interaction yield noteworthy implications for sin research. One aspect of Christian thinking about sin has not changed: Jesus died for humans' sins. The angel announced to Joseph: "You shall call his name Jesus, for he will save people from their sins." Catholics believe the same is true of the Eucharist, the sacrament of redemption: "This is my blood of the covenant, which is poured out for many for the forgiveness of sins." If there is no such thing as sin, then Jesus died in vain. Christians are unlikely ever to discard this limit and will instead insist that we can't ever overthrow the idea of sin without betraying Christ.

Another thing that hasn't changed is fear's ability to dictate action and inhibit risk taking. Believers in the West seem to fear God's wrath a little less today than, say, the eighteenth century, when Jonathan Edwards delivered perhaps the most famous American sermon ever: "Sinners in the Hands of an Angry God." With the rapid advancement of science and medicine in the twentieth century, Westerners feel the fear of God less frequently. That said, we Westerners have developed a new and special way of fearing for the survival of both the human species and the planet Earth. It would be a sin to waste either, a broad spectrum of Western believers would surely agree. That consensus, though it seems to ignore God, points to something quite important for people of different faiths.

With few exceptions (exceptions that modern psychiatry has illuminated), no one intends to be a monster. No one wants to fail either, and believers who "buy in" to a more or less codified moral system do not intend to fall short of it. Through intention, we see the creative mind at work. "I may have done something you consider sinful," a believer can cogently contend to a critic, "but I did not intend to do something sinful. I don't consider what I did a sin." We see flawed human beings making sense of their own illegal desires, their own problematic biological drives. Through intention we see not so much hypocrisy or thinly veiled rationalization as genuine, if put upon, love for God. More than any other factor, intention highlights the inappropriateness of sin as the be-all and end-all of morality. Love for God and neighbor counts for more and allows appropriate leeway for the intrinsic slipperiness of sin—a category that keeps running away from us, even after we seem finally to have it in our grasp.

The contemporary West has glorified private experience, at the expense of erstwhile virtues like obedience and humility. The will to believe has surpassed emotional conviction in many religious North Americans and Europeans, such that believers hold on to a hope (eternal life with a father who loves us regardless of what we've done) while letting go of many of its conditions. Even the modern reader who may feel he has outgrown biblical religion will understand the former importance of sin, that is, a fear through which our forebears imposed order on whispering, indefatigable desires. These desires no longer seem to frighten us quite so much. Poets such as Dante, Milton, and Baudelaire demonstrated their originality in the reworking of traditional themes involving moral conduct. In a sense, we're all poets now, using the traditional themes as we see fit, working out our salvation in occasional fear and trembling, while discounting the reputed link between Genesis and the modern world, between transgressive instincts and universal experience.

Transgression seems less powerful the closer we get to it, and we've gotten pretty close, thanks to contemporary artists and performers. Fatigue has set in, as we discover that sin might not set a fire under our feet after all. We'll see that atoning for our sins also gets boring in a world in which sin doesn't arouse much interest.

2

ATONEMENT FATIGUE

A tonement no longer functions as a Zamboni, the slow truck that purrs down an ice skating rink and magically erases all scuff marks. Today, atonement seems to leave plenty behind. What we have to do to prove we're sorry, what good we can expect our apology to do, and whether others can do this work for us—the answers to these questions are up for grabs.

If Judaism and Catholicism teach that every sin can be forgiven, why would Jews or Catholics worry about sin at all? Why wouldn't they just do whatever they pleased and wait for God to forgive them? We'll see that atonement—heartfelt contrition coupled with a genuine intention to avoid sin, along with some sacrifice and prayer—was necessary for forgiveness. Once you atoned, you might look forward to the sort of fresh start a Zamboni can give to ice. We'll also see that at least one Christian thinker, Jean Calvin, denied that humans can redeem themselves through atonement (even though he still believed asking for forgiveness and making amends were imperative). Calvin's view would seem to be in ascendancy today, despite the reasons on which he based that view.

Today atonement stretches on indefinitely (in which case, it doesn't really work) or meets with refusal (both by Calvin and reality show contestants, although in different ways). Forgiveness is no longer the remission of sins; forgiveness is now the masked determination to "come on, get over it!"—the psychological realization that bearing grudges distracts us from achieving other goals. Forgiveness now often amounts to a weary resignation that what's done is done. Both of these psychological responses indicate sin fatigue. If we weren't tired of sin (or of trying to

---

33

figure it out), we wouldn't bend atonement to fit our busy schedules or scoff at it altogether. Sin fatigue has ushered in atonement fatigue.

ATONEMENT FATIGUE

Before embarking on a brief overview of Western atonement, I'll rush to the end of the story in order to explain what I mean by atonement fatigue. Just as comfortable white people may have tired of hearing about the struggles of black people, just as heterosexual people may have tired of hearing about the plight of homosexual people, and just as upstanding Americans have tired of televised images of suffering in the developing world, so have many good souls tired of the apologies of those who have gone astray. This is atonement fatigue.[1] We're never quite certain of the sincerity of someone who slipped off the path—into social disfavor, adultery, prison, or worse. We maintain high expectations of atonement.

As an example of someone who overcame atonement fatigue, we can usefully focus on a man whose fall from grace was well publicized by the Western media. The British politician John Profumo (1915–2006) represents the kind of sinner we forgive. Like an ancient prostitute driven to live ascetically in the desert, he never stopped repenting. In one of the most publicized sex scandals of the twentieth century, Her Majesty's secretary of state for war resigned his post after having lied to the House of Commons about his relationship with a showgirl (Christine Keeler), who consorted with a KGB officer. (Sir Ian McKellen starred as Profumo in the 1989 motion picture *Scandal.*) Shortly after a spectacular fall from grace in 1963, Profumo began volunteering at Toynbee Hall, a charitable mission in the East End of London. For forty years, Profumo performed works of charity, never speaking publicly, never trying to take advantage of previous professional contacts or his own family wealth. Profumo set a very high standard of atonement, right up there with Mary Magdalene. It is this kind of atonement we want to see today; anything short of the utter contrition Profumo mustered may leave us wondering about a sinner's sincerity. People like John Profumo can rouse us out of our atonement fatigue, but people like John Profumo are few and far between.

A bodily analogy will drive home both the importance of atonement to those who seek it and the reservations of those who would grant it.

The North American organization Born Again Virgins of America! (BAVAM!) exists to help all those (mostly women) who regret having lost their virginity before marriage (another organization, True Love Waits, urges "Waiters" to sign pledge cards, vowing to withhold sex from a lover until marriage in order to avoid the kind of regret that fuels interest in BAVAM!). Young people who join BAVAM! claim that they not only renounce previous instances of fornication but also, in the process, get their virginity back. (The Tony Award–winning play *Avenue Q* from 2004 features a character named "Lucy the Slut" who eventually claims to have recovered her virginity.) Even some Orthodox Jews will insist today that the slate of a sexually experienced woman is wiped clean on her wedding day, thus validating her decision to wear a white dress. The ritual of the wedding cleanses the bride of her carnal transgressions.[2]

Critics may hasten to point out that such a process can be at best metaphorical or symbolic, as the state of virginity, once lost, can never be reclaimed. We should remember, though, that many Christians claim to be reborn through the experience of baptism; following the logic of St. Paul, some Christians will insist that they die to sin and are reborn in the Holy Spirit as new people. Religious people should be the last to pooh-pooh metaphors and symbols. A further complication with the BAVAM! example illustrates the consequences of sin fatigue. An ever-decreasing number of North Americans view the premarital loss of virginity as particularly remarkable; even old-fashioned sorts may hold that deflowering is certainly not important enough to justify the formation of a support group.

Those of us who deny that virginity can be reclaimed may not show sufficient sympathy to those who earnestly believe they have done just that. We are guilty of atonement fatigue, insofar as we decline to wipe the slate clean for penitents who ask that of us. When it's our turn to atone for something, we may find it increasingly difficult to muster the emotional energy needed to turn the tide.

Now let's start at the beginning, with a summary of Jewish and Christian histories of atonement.

JUDAISM

Jews and Christians both profess that everyone sins, and so everyone needs to atone for sin. Judaism of course predates Christianity, which sprang from its parent awkwardly. Looking for the most part only at broad brushstrokes, we'll see more similarity than dissimilarity between Judaism and Christianity.

Hebrew scriptures provide conflicting details about God, and some readers are left wondering whether he is more punitive than merciful. It is certainly possible to locate in Hebrew scriptures a merciful God who regularly forgives iniquity, transgression, and sin (Exodus 34:6–7 uses three different words for the same thing).[3] Certain conditions apply to this forgiveness: confession, repentance, and the resolution to swear off the transgression. Man's power to sin can never exceed God's power to forgive, we read in the book of Exodus (34:6–7), so people have good reason to feel optimistic after wrongdoing.[4] Psalm 103:10 fuels the fire of optimism that God will not only forgive but also forget (much like a Zamboni): "He does not deal with us according to our sin." In Isaiah, chapter 6, we see an angel take a hot coal from the altar and fly toward Isaiah. When the angel places the coal onto Isaiah's lips, we see the Zamboni ride. We hear the angel say, "Your sin is wiped out," and we see Isaiah's joy.[5]

So much for our relationship to God—what about our relationship to other people? Since we are to imitate the attributes of God, we are to forgive freely those who injure us. This idea may ruffle feathers today, when Westerners place a high premium on self-respect. Why should Jews, gays, and blacks, for example, readily forgive the hateful people who oppose them? Why should we forgive anyone who isn't in fact sorry? Actually, Judaism permits its followers to withhold forgiveness in some instances. Until the culprit has properly made up to a wronged Jew (through rectifying any wrong and appeasing him), the Jew may morally withhold forgiveness. In other words, the offender must atone for the offense against the Jew, just as the Jew must atone for his sins against God.

Atonement, the precondition for forgiveness, shouldn't scare believers. Instead, it should buoy their spirits as a small price to pay for a jewel beyond worth. God can and will give us a second chance. Atonement rests on the belief that God watches us lovingly and hopes for our well-being. When we defy God's will, we rupture his love. That's not to say that God will then strike us down for having strayed. Consider this passage from Jewish scriptures: "As I live, says the Lord, I have no pleasure in the death of the wicked but that the wicked turn from his way and live. Turn you, turn you from your evil ways" (Ezekiel 33:11). God wants us to mend fences; through forgiveness, he shows his willingness to meet us halfway. Through atonement, we do what we can to earn forgiveness (which is not to say that we can ever repay our debt or that we can *make* God forgive us). Forgiveness depends on expiation of your sin, and it is that expiation that constitutes atonement.

Atonement offers various paths to forgiveness: (1) payment of compensation for wrong committed, (2) suffering, or (3) the performance of certain rituals. All of these presuppose repentance and correcting errant ways. The Hebrew word for atonement (*kapparah*) is derived from a legal term signifying "ransom" or "compensation" (e.g., paid by the owner of an ox that has gored a man). Atonement then passed into ritual and theological use. The Talmud insists that sacrifices were accepted as atonement only for those sins committed inadvertently or in ignorance. For those sins committed deliberately, no sacrifice could avail.

In the Ashkenazi folk ceremony of *tashlikh* on Yom Kippur, Jews go to water, preferably a river or a sea full of fish, and shake their clothes as if to cast off every trace of sin (think Zamboni), while reciting appropriate biblical verses, such as Micah 7:18–20, which contains the words "and you shall cast [tashlikh] into the depths of the sea all their sins." The origin of this practice is unknown, and there is no mention of it before the fifteenth century; it may represent a Jewish adaptation of a pagan ritual.[6] Pious Jews also bathe in the *mikveh* on the eve of the fast, perhaps as a symbol of the washing away of sins, or in recollection of a celebrated play on words ascribed to Rabbi Akiva: the prophet Jeremiah (17:13) calls God the mikveh (meaning "hope") of Israel. "As the mikveh cleanses the unclean, so does the Holy One, blessed be He, cleanse Israel."

Not surprisingly, theologians and ordinary Jews understood repentance in different, more and less nuanced, ways. Among the masses, a tendency developed to regard the propitiatory sacrifice (e.g., a burnt offering) as the very thing that would undo divine wrath for a sin committed deliberately. People came to believe that sacrificing could atone for all sins. The prophets inveighed sharply against this belief, stressing instead the moral aspects in such passages as "Shall I come before him with burnt offerings, with calves a year old? He has showed you, O man, what is good, and what does the Lord require of you, but to do justly, and love mercy and walk humbly with your God" (Micah 6:6–8) or the statement of Hosea, "Instead of bulls we will pay [the offering of] our lips" (Hosea 14:3). The destruction of the Temple (70 c.e.) automatically abolished the sacrificial system. Alternatives to the sacrificial system had to be devised, because one couldn't make sacrifices at the Temple any longer.[7] Although Jews might have ruled that it was all right to sacrifice animals elsewhere (instead of at the Temple), they did not in fact.

Repentance must always include oral confession—Jews can't simply profess "I'm sorry" silently. The effectiveness of Yom Kippur, the holiest day of the year, depends on sincere repentance, to which a preparatory ten-day period is devoted. It bears noting once again that sins committed against God require a different kind of atonement than sins against people. Apologizing to people is arguably harder than apologizing to God, as people require not only words of regret but material restitution for any harm you've caused. This restitution could be to the specific individual wronged or, in certain instances, to humanity in general (as in works of charity). Again, behavior modification must accompany repentance, which of course hinges on sincerity. Jews do not tend to believe that we can make restitution for someone else's sins, although other religious groups do (e.g., Roman Catholics—more on this later).

Yom Kippur is the only fast never postponed, even if it falls on a Sabbath. Although strictly observed from sunset as a twenty-five-hour fast in accordance with the biblical injunction "and you shall afflict yourselves," it formally belongs to the category of festivals. The biblical commandment regulating its observance is found in the book of Leviticus (23:26–32). On Rosh Hashanah, the Jewish New Year, the fate of every individual for the coming year is decreed, and on Yom Kippur it is sealed. An unfavorable decree can be averted by repentance, prayer, and charity. The rabbis insist that a worshipper's contrite behavior on Yom Kippur itself will not unleash forgiveness unless that piety is accompanied by sincere repentance. Judaism places in the hands of an individual the power to transform a dreary fate.

The scapegoat, familiar to us now as a metaphor for an unjustly punished individual, used to be more than a figure of speech. In early Judaism, Yom Kippur was the occasion for an elaborate sacrificial ceremony based on Leviticus 16. This ceremony consisted of two parts. The first was the sacrificial service in the Temple, at which the high priest pronounced the threefold confession of sins on behalf of himself, the priests, and all Israel. The climax came when, clothed in white linen, he entered the Holy of Holies (the one occasion during the year when this was permitted) to sprinkle the blood of the sacrifice there and to offer incense. The second part of the ceremony consisted of hurling the scapegoat to its probable death in the wilderness. Jews symbolically transferred to the animal the sins of the community. In early Christianity, some of Jesus's followers saw Christ as quite literally the ultimate scapegoat: he took upon himself the sins of all humanity. Even though Christian scriptures do not explicitly liken Christ to the scapegoat, the scapegoat became an apparent intersection point between Christianity and Judaism.

One's proper observance of Yom Kippur atones for transgressions against God.[8] Sins committed against others require their forgiveness prior to the day. Five "mortifications" are prescribed for the day: abstention from food, drink, and marital intercourse; anointing with oil; and wearing leather shoes. All Sabbath work prohibitions govern Yom Kippur. The prayers of the day stress confession for sins and supplications for forgiveness. Like all congregational prayers, these petitions seek forgiveness on behalf of "the whole congregation of Israel." Many worshippers remain in the synagogue for the entire day (some Orthodox Jews for the entire twenty-five hours), and the four services stretch prayer (hymns, litanies, and confessions) throughout the day.

A special feature of the Afternoon Service on Yom Kippur is the reading of the Book of Jonah as the Haftarah. The message of the book is that repentance averts the evil decree, even for a whole city of wrongdoers like Nineveh. Then as now, the peremptory stance that no sacrifice could undo sins deliberately committed must motivate plenty of Jewish believers to tell themselves that they hadn't *really* meant to do wrong in any number of specific instances. In a moving contemporary context, we see that denial of wrongdoing, such as domestic abuse, can lead to toleration of future wrongdoing. The same frustration with traditional marriage roles that lead to violence illustrates disenchantment with atonement. For no matter how often or earnestly you atone, you still falter and you still feel inadequate. Sometimes it seems easier to forget than to forgive; weariness brings about this resignation.

Beginning in the late 1990s, the American media, especially the *New York Times*, brought to public attention reports on the problem of wife beating within Orthodox Jewish households.[9] Orthodox Jewish women struggled to obtain divorces from husbands who denied wrongdoing, from husbands who subsequently would not atone for alleged wrongdoing.[10] According to Jewish belief, God will not forgive trespasses committed against other people. For that damage, Jews must ask forgiveness from the person(s) hurt. Jewish scriptures acknowledge "sins of omission": "Do not stand idly by the blood of your neighbor," intones the Torah in Leviticus 19:16. It would be shortsighted to dismiss such examples of domestic violence as pure denial of wrongdoing; knowledge of the difficulty of preventing such behavior, much less of losing a ready outlet for venting anger over perceived powerlessness, surely plays a role as well.

Under Orthodox Jewish law, only the husband can grant a religious divorce decree, or get, to his wife. Without a get, a woman cannot remarry within Orthodoxy. But with a Heter Meah Rabonim, a rare religious decree that resembles a Roman Catholic annulment, a man is allowed to remarry after a rabbinical court finds his wife to be "recalcitrant or incapacitated," according to the judge's opinion. Atonement in a system that strongly favors men over women would seem to be fraught with frustration; not just women but men as well might grow tired of fighting a mind-set that appears ever more outdated and downright cruel. As the secular world grows increasingly supportive of the rights of women, it becomes increasingly difficult for the old guard to admit it was wrong and to update its stance. When people compel us to change our minds about them, we may hold the effort required very much against them. A moral order that admits its past immorality loses some purchase among followers struggling with their own shortcomings.

We might generally expect sin fatigue to have surfaced earlier in Judaism than in Christianity, because Jews tend to focus on this world; although Jews may think occasionally of the afterlife, their thoughts wander to that realm much less often than either Protestant or Catholic Christians. Although less explicitly than in Christianity, the culmination of atonement in Judaism is the attainment of heaven—as Jews sometimes put it, having your name written in the Book of Life.[11] The fact that Jews have institutionalized atonement on a specific day every year speaks not to the ineffectiveness of forgiveness but to the inevitability of human transgression. It's not that Jews necessarily keep committing the same sin over and over again (which might indicate the futility of repentance) but that Jews keep failing morally in any number of different ways.

What Jews seem to accomplish on Yom Kippur is to reconcile themselves to a future of moral disappointment, even as they celebrate God's willingness to forgive moral shortcomings. Aware that their particular understanding of scriptures may be mistaken, Jews may feel ambivalent about atonement. And because so many Jews disagree with one another about scriptures, wholehearted atonement may require a great deal of effort to tune out dissonant voices.[12] There is no end to the interpretation of scriptures, and yesterday's commended or permitted practices (stoning, polygamy, patriarchy, slaughtering infidels) can become today's sin, and today's sin may become tomorrow's virtue or at least accepted behavior (supporting the professional ambitions of women who wish to work outside the home, defending the right of gay and lesbian people to dignity, speaking out against the lavish salaries of corporate executives). While holding on to the value of atonement in the abstract, it is possible to doubt the worth of atonement in a specific instance. Meanwhile, fatigue can set in.

CHRISTIANITY

Christianity begins in Judaism. Various Christian beliefs, instincts, and attitudes grow out of Judaism. From Yom Kippur Christians took the cues for public penance, a practice of enormous public and spiritual significance.[13] If a virtuous Jew refuses to forgive a Jew who has wronged him, then the sin of the confessing Jew becomes the sin of the wronged Jew. Jesus likewise exhorts his followers to forgive and forgive and forgive. We'll see that atonement fatigue has set in among Christians, especially Catholics.

Like Jews, early Christians believed that God could remove the stain of sin and, in so doing, restore a broken relationship between God and man. To humanity, God's forgiveness of sin is both a gift and a responsibility. God forgives sins (Colossians 1:14; Ephesians 1:17), but he requires of us repentance (Mark 1:4; Luke 24:47; Acts 2:38; 5:31; 13:38; 26:18), confession (James 5:15f; I John 1:9), and the forgiveness of others (Matthew 6:12, 14f; Luke 11:4; 17:4). We've seen in Judaism a dark underside to the good news that sins can be forgiven (three sins one must never commit, even if faced with death, are idolatry, murder, and adultery),[14] and this darkness hovers over Christianity as well: the blasphemy of the Holy Spirit is beyond forgiveness (Mark 3:28).[15] Theologians argue over precisely what "sins against the Holy Spirit" might mean. To the extent there is consensus, it rests on the idea of despair, on turning one's back on God in some permanent way. In other words, the only way we can lose forgiveness is if we choose to. Our forgiveness of others is related both to devotion to God (Luke 17:3; Matthew 18:15–35; Ephesians 4:32) and to the discipline of the fellowship of the Spirit (John 20:22).[16]

Can Christians atone for someone else's sins—say, a cruel dictator's or a ferocious teenager's? Not exactly, but they can petition God to have mercy on the dictator or wayward teenager. Christians can also try to harness the power of prayer to compel a sinner to change his ways. And so a Stalin, a Hitler, a Saddam Hussein—are they beyond the help of concerned Christians? Not really, provided the Christian has faith. And along similar lines, can the suffering of an innocent person—say, a child dying of cancer—benefit others? Yes, according to some Christians.

The idea of vicarious atonement returns us to the discussion of human community begun in the discussion of Original Sin. That the sufferings of an innocent person can benefit others was already well accepted in the Judaism of Jesus's day. In the Servant songs of "Deutero (Second) Isaiah" (42:1–4; 49:1–6; 50:4–9; 52:13; 53:12), the Servant, probably Israel itself, becomes an instrument of divine salvation through his/its passion and death.

The Acts of the Apostles identify Jesus himself with the Servant of the Lord (3:13, 26; 4:27, 30). This identification colors several Gospel accounts (e.g., Matthew 8:17; 12:18–21; Luke 22:37). The imagery of an innocent scapegoat runs through 1 Peter 2:22–25 as well:

> He did no wrong; no deceit was found in
>   his mouth.
> When he was insulted, he returned no
>   insult.
> When he was made to suffer, he did not
>   counter with threats.
> Instead, he delivered himself up to the One
>   who judges justly.
> In his own body he brought your sins to the
>   cross,
>   so that all of us, dead to sin, could live in
>   accord with God's will.
> By his wounds you were healed.
> At one time you were straying like sheep,
>   but now you have returned to the Shepherd,
>   the Guardian of your souls.

But the Servant role, at first eagerly attributed to Jesus, was later abandoned as being too Jewish and, therefore, not readily understandable within the Gentile world.[17] The notion of ransom and the associated idea of redemption moved to the center of Christian thinking. On the basis of selected Gospel passages (e.g., Mark 10:45 and Matthew 20:28 and 1 Timothy 2:6), Christians came to believe that Jesus understood his own death as a ransom for many. In this way, the sufferings of an innocent person (the "lamb of God") benefited the rest of humanity.[18] Long after the death of Jesus, some Christians continue to think in such terms. It's as though God demands a certain amount of suffering from us, and he doesn't care who does it. (This is one of the principal objections to the philosophical doctrine of utilitarianism: whether the culprit or some substitute for him suffers makes no difference, provided that *someone* suffer for the offense.)

In the ancient Greek world, a god or goddess would sometimes call for the sacrifice of an innocent human. This very event drives the tragedy of Euripedes' *Iphigenia at Aulis*. In the New Testament world, the ancients paid a ransom to buy back a pawned object or to liberate a slave. Christ signifies the ransom given to liberate us all from the slavery of sin. God did not demand this payment. On the contrary, "the redemption wrought by Christ" is itself "the gift of God" (Romans 3:24). We do not pay a ransom to God (Psalm 49:8) and thereby redeem ourselves; it is God who redeems us (Psalm 78:35; see also Psalm 19:14; Isaiah 63:5). Far from a casual or arbitrary act, God's forgiveness signifies boundless love. It "costs" God much to forgive, as we owe him something, and he agrees not to collect payment. Otherwise put, he does not give us what we deserve. Catholic and Protestant theologians have argued over the extent to which we can earn God's forgiveness. Educated believers might reasonably confess to atonement fatigue, as no one has managed to unpack the mysterious nature of sin. How can you atone for something you don't really understand? Protestants argue among themselves, just as Catholics do. This infighting can breed skepticism and fatigue within a believer.

Another example of Jewish influence in Christian practice surfaces in the Last Supper, which replicates the Jewish Sabbath meal: the words over the bread, followed by its breaking and sharing, and the blessing over the wine. Whereas earlier Jesus was identified with the Servant of the Lord, here Jesus identifies himself with the bread and wine. It is his body that is broken and his blood that is poured out in atonement for sin and for the establishment of a new Covenant. The four Gospels agree on this. Because Jews linked every death, but particularly the death of an innocent, to atonement, Jesus could easily have seen his own innocent suffering as atonement. The final answer to the question of whether Jesus already atoned for the sins of all Christians, though, remains up for grabs. Because Christians cannot agree on the extent to which Jesus atoned for human sin, the mystery of forgiveness persists and sin fatigue finds room to deepen.

HISTORY OF CHRISTIAN CONFESSION I

Desert Fathers

A history of confession in Christianity begins with the Desert Fathers of antiquity, who hoped that atonement could do for sin what the Zamboni did for ice. It is just as easy to argue that the Desert Fathers were psychologically tortured as it is that they sincerely believed Jesus, who once said, "See, mother, I make all things new again!" The Zamboni effect, as I call it, amounts to a washing away, a baptism, a rebirth.[19] John Profumo's renunciation of the world and devotion to works of charity followed an ancient path.

The Desert Fathers made atonement more difficult than the New Testament did, but late antiquity and the Middle Ages made it easier by formalizing it, mechanizing it through penitentials, or reducing it to an economic exchange (indulgences). Ecclesiastical development after the Desert Fathers can be described as a shift away from atonement as *something done for being a sinner* to *something done for sinful acts*. Perhaps most important is the contrast between the hope that atonement could wipe the slate clean (Desert Fathers) and the belief that the slate would never be wiped clean (various subsequent Christians). Calvin's protest against wiping the slate clean marks something of a return to the Desert Fathers, but only insofar as both camps agreed that virtue relied on a constant, even ascetic, vigilance.

The Desert Fathers elevated asceticism to the status of "stairway to heaven": if you wanted to wipe the slate clean more than anything in the world, you would opt for self-denial. Asceticism, or radical self-denial, made sense in the same way that the saying "An ounce of prevention is worth a pound of cure" does. Early Christians adopted practices that would demonstrate the depth of their gratitude for Jesus's self-sacrifice and the seriousness of their intention to emulate him. The Desert Fathers focused on sex as something special to beware of and celibacy as a herculean sacrifice in the quest for atonement. The asceticism of the Desert Fathers inspired and influenced ordinary Christians living in villages and cities and drove home the importance of bewaring the *occasions* of particular sins.

Jesus had already reinforced the importance of atonement. The Desert Fathers subsequently ushered in a new age of contrition. The hermits of Egypt, circa 250–500, developed the institution of monasticism. Although Paul of Thebes (c. 227–340) likely inaugurated the Desert tradition, Anthony of Egypt (c. 250–356) is usually regarded as the prototype of the Desert Fathers. It wasn't as though Christians knew nothing about asceticism—they had the examples of Jesus and John the Baptist to contemplate, as well as resources in the Jewish tradition. From the end of the third century, increasing numbers of Fathers, many of them simple Coptic peasants, drew thousands to permanent discipleship in their desert retreats through the force of their single-minded search for God and the freshness and vigor of their teachings. As these teachings came to be recorded in sermons, monastic rules, and spiritual sayings, they shaped subsequent Christian instincts and views of atonement.

St. Anthony of the Desert stands as the best known of the Desert Fathers. He took to the Egyptian desert as a young man around the year 270. The desert, which held no women, seemed a logical place for a man worried about lust. Part of atoning for sin is what has come to be known as "removing yourself from the occasion of sin" (as discussed in chapter 1). This is what St. Anthony did with respect to both sex and food. According to the historian Peter Brown, food exceeded even sex in worth in the economy of sacrifice. Worse than the lust for human flesh that flared up in the city, where people were everywhere, was the desire for food, according to Brown. The desert ascetic's greatest worry was with his stomach (as opposed to his penis), for hunger could bring on hallucinations in the desert. Hallucinations intensified temptation.

All Christians were expected to fast for Lent. Doing so would undo a little of the fateful sin of Adam. The Desert Fathers resolved to do better than ordinary fasting. To fast heroically, eating nothing beyond the bare minimum for survival, was to relive Adam's first temptation and to overcome it. (This assumes that Adam's temptation was hunger, not curiosity.) The monks hoped to transform themselves through self-mortification. The ascetic had to learn, over the years of taxing life in the desert, to sand down his very will. (This is precisely what we hear Augustine struggling to do in the *Confessions*.) Steadfast focus on a lofty goal brought about "singleness of heart" or modern-day integrity. The Egyptian struggle included acute dependence on others—of disciples on their masters, of cell mates on each other. All too often, though, the company of one's fellows presented yet another strenuous trial to endure.

Especially ardent Christians would eventually follow St. Anthony's example, finding in the desert a glimpse of the world to come. Peter Brown has explained, "The myth of the desert was one of the most abiding creations of late antiquity. It was, above all, a myth of liberating precision. It delimited the towering presence of 'the world,' from which the Christian must be set free, by emphasizing a clear ecological frontier."[20] To flee "the world" for the desert was to enter a "counterworld," a place where an alternative "city" could grow. In that city, as in heaven, all trace of sin would be removed. Although you might remember your own mistakes, a Zamboni would have erased all incriminating evidence of them.

All of this Christian asceticism focuses on God, and pleasing him, as opposed to the self and aiming for the satisfaction of perfection. Alas, the focus on God increases the stakes for guilt and shame. Sadness or frustration over having missed a goal can easily lead to self-defeating behavior. An unconscious desire to punish oneself in an effort to show solidarity with God can bring on self-sabotage and masochism. It seems reasonable to assume that desert monks atoned in large part through guilt and shame. Guilt and shame can burn for an awfully long time; a true believer may find, however, that his guilt turns to gratitude the moment he believes God has wiped the slate clean.

The monks uplifted and supported one another during times of weakness. They could band together to locate food. The loosely woven community of monks in the desert brought to life the demons and the angels whose evanescent presences registered in the heart and in stirring trains of thought. The desert became the powerhouse of a new culture, a forerunner to the present-day Olympic Training Camp for the most serious athletes (and the ascetics were even regarded as spiritual athletes).

Why did the Desert Fathers stay out there? Why didn't they eventually trickle back to the cities they had fled? Part of the frustration of the

Desert Fathers must have been the unyielding power of sexual desire and physical hunger. All the atoning in the world couldn't quench those fires, at least not for good. This realization might explain in part why committed Christians in the contemporary West don't follow the example of the Desert Fathers and flee civilization.[21] St. Gregory the Great gave city dwellers the idea of spiritual martyrdom in the late sixth century with the exhortation: "Even though we do not bend our bodily neck to the sword, nevertheless with the spiritual sword we slay in our soul carnal desires," and "if, with the help of the Lord, we strive to observe the virtue of patience, even though we live in the peace of the Church, nevertheless we bear the palm of martyrdom."[22] Brilliant idea: if you don't have time to go to the desert, you can bring the desert to you. It was then only a small step from the idea that you *could* do this to the idea that you *should* do this. The extent to which Christians in the twenty-first century hunger for martyrdom—literal or metaphorical—as an opportunity to prove one's faith can be gauged in ongoing Western horror at suicide bombers in the Middle East. One of the consequences of sin fatigue is having to strain to understand the motivation of a suicide bomber or a Desert Father.

HISTORY OF CHRISTIAN CONFESSION II

Theological and Practical Evolution

Over time, Christians formalized atonement, much in the way that Romans had formalized laws and government. In a way, the early Christian church made codification and standardization its business. Ordinary believers couldn't live as desert hermits, no, nor could they consistently rely on making spiritual martyrs of themselves. But that's not to say that the Desert Fathers were considered simply exceptional. On the contrary, their example may have inspired and delighted ordinary believers. This section will link early Christian asceticism to later canonical penance. We'll see that, over the course of centuries, forgiveness of sin gradually gave way to "reconciliation." Reconciliation (by which I do not mean specifically the Truth and Reconciliation Commission in South Africa) didn't necessarily forgive a transgressor but rather smoothed over his return to a community he had offended or threatened. The subtle difference between forgiveness and reconciliation illuminates the atonement fatigue that lies at the heart of this chapter. Within a few centuries of the passing of the Desert Fathers, Christians largely rejected the Zamboni ideal of a forgiveness so deep that it verged on willful forgetting.

Thomas Tentler has argued that penance, the ecclesiastical ritual to restore baptized Christians who have committed serious sins, remained roughly constant from the earliest centuries of the church through the eve of the Reformation.[23] The success of the ritual rested on four criteria governing the sinner: (1) he had to feel sorrow at having failed, (2) he had to make a confession of sins, (3) he had to undergo penance, and (4) he had to rely on a priest to make a full recovery from his fall from grace. In the requirement to confess one's sins to a priest, we see a signal innovation. This stipulation certainly did not hold in Judaism, nor would it later hold in Lutheranism, Calvinism, or the other Protestant communions. This innovation ushered in the era of canonical penance. Note that Tentler speaks of a "full recovery" even though, as we'll see, recovering sinners could never expect to regain certain privileges (e.g., serving in the military).

Historians seem to concur that between the ninth and the thirteenth centuries, four further, highly significant, changes occurred in the theology and practice of confession: (1) penances were lightened and made arbitrary; (2) contrition became the essential element for the penitent and pushed penitential exercises into a subservient position; (3) private confession, already accepted as a necessary part of the forgiveness of sins, was declared universally obligatory by the Fourth Lateran Council of 1215; and (4) the meaning of the priest's role was more carefully defined and its importance in the process of forgiveness robustly expanded.[24]

The break between the penitential exercises of various Christian communities and canonical penance cannot be established in sharp chronological terms. That said, Tentler finds that a formal system of forgiveness of serious sins and reconciliation with the body of the faithful began to emerge in the middle of the second century (about a century before the Desert Fathers fled their cities). This system developed into "canonical" penance, which predominated until the middle of the seventh. And so, the Desert Fathers were practicing a new form of piety while canonical penance started to take formal shape. The most striking features of canonical penance were its extreme severity and utter lack of privacy. Exclusion from the community of faithful was public, just as the ceremony of return was. Furthermore, for some sins (adultery, murder, and idolatry), atonement was allowed only gradually and with reluctance. Certain sins preempted the atonement Zamboni, if you will. For reasons that will become obvious, the public admission of guilt (along with the routine exclusion from the body of the faithful, performance of arduous penitential exercises, and reconciliation with the body of the faithful), was allowed a Christian only once in a lifetime. Gradually, Christians would judge their own atonement culture too severe and then soften it—most notably in the rise of casuistry and then once again in the twentieth century.

Tentler writes that canonical penance, with its austere public performance, became the norm in much of Europe. In Rome, a formal ceremony that included the laying on of hands, signified the sinner's entrance into an order of penitents, a third class of Christians distinct from catechumens (who were on their way into the body of the faithful) and the faithful (who were members in good standing). Penitents privately gave alms and fasted; they also endured public humiliation (think Hester Prynne in *The Scarlet Letter*) before being admitted back into the community by a ceremony that again included the laying on of hands. Once reintegrated into the community, the penitent's life was forever compromised. The readmitted Christian could never enter the clergy, nor could he marry. If he was already married, he could not expect sex from his spouse. He was to forgo worldly affairs as much as possible in order to focus on his spiritual life. He was barred from military service. Atonement did not restore sinners to pristine condition, then, if we take the Zamboni as our model. For even after properly atoning for his sins, scuff marks and restrictions remained all over a "reconciled" believer.

During the first centuries of the medieval church, Christians increasingly deferred penance until the last possible moment. This delay stemmed in part from a natural aversion to the severity of penance and in part from a two-strikes-and-you're-out rule. Even without the benefit of formal education, people could tell they were in a high-stakes game that required strategizing. And if atonement wasn't going to give you everything you wanted (i.e., a fresh start with a blank slate), then it was less attractive to you. If you only get one shot at redemption, you'd do well not to squander that shot. When Pope Leo the Great directed in the fifth century that dying Christians be reconciled without the imposition of penitential exercises, an easy way out presented itself. Alas, even the easy way out came with risk: you may die before you got the chance to confess your sins. In a society without sin fatigue, the pressure to die with a clear conscience was surely enormous.

Since deathbed penances, performed without ascetic exercises, seemed to get you the same reward as severe sacrifices, two contrary practices developed: doing penance and receiving penance. While some zealots disagreed, Pope Leo insisted that the dying should not be penalized because they are unable to perform the requisite harsh tasks. Augustine later expressed grave reservations about deathbed penances. Although Augustine did not oppose Pope Leo's policy, he nonetheless deplored deathbed conversions. Augustine would not say whether the man who is reconciled at the end is damned or saved; he simply expressed fear and consternation. He advised that those who wanted to live without nagging doubts should do penance while healthy. Augustine could be sure of the sincerity of such a penance because you do it while it is still possible to sin. But if you perform penance when you no longer are able to sin, the sins abandon you more than you abandon them, Augustine reasoned. This makes eminent sense. It is all too easy to swear off sex as an aged, perhaps infirm man. Much more courageous and demanding is the task of giving up sex when you still crave it and when you are attractive enough to stir carnal enthusiasm in others. (Against Augustine, we might caution against underrating carnal attraction among unattractive people.)

We should notice here the great ecclesiastical control the church exerted over its followers. Far from derisively rolling their eyes in discussions of eternal salvation, Christians of the past struggled painfully over their behavior and their escape plan (from sin). Not unlike a game of musical chairs, you never knew when the music would suddenly stop. If death caught you suddenly, before you had a chance to repent properly, you lost everything. Unlike musical chairs, the Day of Judgment was not a game. Consequently, ordinary Christians accepted the control over their day-to-day lives exerted by the church. Many early Christians ached for the Zamboni effect: Jesus, their savior, could make all things new again, and they prayed for him to do so.

This brief history of confession will move next to the Penitentials, then to casuistry, indulgences, and, finally, to television. Over time, people became more comfortable denying forgiveness to sinners (with occasional and notable exceptions such as Linda Lovelace). Child molesters, mass murderers, racists, dictators, abortion doctors, abusive parents, and various other classes of problem people justify our withholding forgiveness in certain circumstances.[25] Such circumstances should compel us to reconsider the very point of atonement. Although there is some historical precedent for pooh-poohing atonement, it is also possible to marshal the support of earlier Jews and Christians who avowed a forgiveness so thorough as to make the Zamboni metaphor perfectly apt.

Penitentials

The next great innovation in formalizing atonement was the Penitentials. A problem had arisen: Why might lying or stealing earn you a more severe penance in one region than another? Surely, the penalty ought to be the same everywhere. Right? Not only would uniformity increase the integrity of the organization (i.e., Christianity), but a book outlining atonement could cut down on the tortured guesswork of individual priests who heard confessions. Late in the twentieth century, sentencing guidelines in American courts reflected the same concern.[26]

Short manuals that classified sins and directed a priest to condign penance for a specific sin had begun to appear in Ireland by the end of the sixth century. Their popularity undoubtedly had to do with a useful innovation: canonical penance was thoroughly public, whereas the Penitentials instituted a system that was essentially private.[27] Sinners preferred to make amends far from the madding crowd. How doubly sweet the forgiveness that did not require public humiliation (think again of Hester Prynne wearing the scarlet letter and grimly enduring the contempt of her neighbors).

John McNeill and Helena Gamer have pointed out that with the collapse of the Western Roman Empire, "the conquests of the Visigoths and Franks fundamentally transformed the West. . . . The new barbarized society could not be subjected to the old discipline which had already proved too severe for the Roman Christians."[28] McNeill and Gamer conclude, "An effective reform of ecclesiastical penance was only possible if there was a retreat from the rigid principle that forbade its repetition." This made sense, as an all-or-nothing approach forfeited too many otherwise-willing participants in the system. Having fallen off the wagon a second time (with regard to the same sin), a sinner had no motivation to keep trying; he might turn to a dangerous life of crime or abandon himself to hedonism. Contemporary Westerners might recognize the utility of a criminal justice system that simply killed people who committed the same crime twice (or perhaps any crime twice), yet the reason we don't find such systems in place must be a pervasive belief that a more forgiving schema will be more effective, socially and morally.

The major retreat from a system of once-only penance gave way to a more workable system of atonement, a system that mimicked the monastic tradition of spiritual direction of individual monks by an older monk or a superior. Repeated private confession, with its reassuringly confidential penitent-confessor relationship, structured the pastoral work of monasteries and itinerant monks. What fast-food restaurants do for hunger today, the Penitentials did for the contrite Christian soul centuries ago.

The terse and practical Penitentials served to "connect the dots" from sin to penance, thus simplifying life for priests considerably. Over time, some Penitentials also included instruction on how confession of sins was to be made. Detailed lists of questions that the confessor should put to the penitent man, woman, or child helped the priest avoid conveying salacious new ideas about sins not yet tried. Advice on how to counsel penitents according to their social status and the circumstances of their case personalized confession, helping avoid a cookie-cutter approach to this obviously intimate ritual.

Penitential books may have originated in Welsh synods held in the sixth century, before proliferating in Ireland and then spreading with Celtic missionaries to the Frankish lands, England, Italy, and Spain.[29] The Penitentials evolved gradually over the course of centuries, not unlike a coral reef. Those who shaped them often saw their goal as healing or medicinal. Likely inspired by Aristotle's Golden Mean, they believed in curing vices by the application of their contrary virtues. The suffering imposed by the Penitentials helped achieve social order, to be sure, and helped ordinary believers approach the overwhelmingly complicated mystery of God. The expectations of the heavenly father seemed less distant, slightly more concrete, and certainly more urgent because of the Penitentials. When no one but your priest knew of your specific sins, it was sometimes easier to imagine the Zamboni effect of total forgiveness.

Casuistry

Several centuries after the Penitentials, casuistry evolved as a methodology, a response to unusually tricky moral questions. Casuistry promised

carefully measured, nuanced solutions. Casuistry has always had its opponents. Particular moral decisions should apply universal ethical rules to
particular cases, hard-liners maintain, and casuistry or "situational ethics"
undermine universal moral rules (e.g., the prohibition of murder).

As a discernible moral innovation, casuistry followed roughly on the
election of Hildebrand to the papacy in 1073 as Gregory VII.[30] Gregory
deliberately transformed the Church of Rome from the loose spiritual
association that it had been for centuries into a centralized ecclesiastical force. The church asserted itself beyond personal ethics as a reliable
authority in resolving intellectual questions such as collective jurispru-
dence, mercantile propriety, and political sovereignty. If the Zamboni
were to roll, it would only be with the approval of the hierarchy. Precisely the opposite happened, though, as individual priests took atonement plans into their own hands (presumably with an eye to carrying
out the hierarchy's wishes).

The church's canon law subsequently absorbed the informal rulings
of the bishops and abbots, often articulated in penitential contexts. Ecclesiastical courts adjudicated moral, legal, and political issues, and
they could reprimand individuals with private penance, public punishment, or both. Take, for example, King Henry II of England. His
penance for the assassination of Thomas à Becket necessitated walking
barefoot to the cathedral at Canterbury in 1172, making public submis-
sion to the papal legate in Normandy. His penance also required re-
nouncing those parts of the "Constitutions of Clarendon" in which he
had reasserted royal power over the English church. The powerful
church could and would humiliate even a king, whose public penance
naturally strengthened the ecclesiastical power of the institution that issued it. Again, we see that the break from penitential exercises of early
Christian communities to canonical penance defies a sharp chronological boundary, as public humiliation continued to play a role, however
sporadic. When we get to televised confessions later in this chapter,
we'll see that public humiliation continues to pack a real punch.

The rediscovery in 1070 of the great text of Roman civil law, the *Di-
gest* of Justinian, stimulated the classical age of canon law, which
opened in 1140 with the appearance of Gratian's highly influential *Decretum*. The confluence of ideas from Christian theology, Roman ju-
risprudence, and Greek philosophy in canon law made casuistry intelli-
gently supple, with considerable depth and breadth. The teaching of
canon law employed the case method and contributed a technique to

moral casuistry. Common to both casuistry and canon law was a practical need to streamline diverse legal sources (some of which might be quite obscure) into elegant coherence.

These formulas of belief helped Christians negotiate the practical difficulties of day-to-day life outside the church. The gospels rarely offered such practical information. Furthermore, much of what the gospels did offer required interpretation. The generality and rigor of law found in casuistry an acknowledgment of the necessity for interpretation and a sensitivity to the uniqueness of situations. This is where priests came in handy.

As we'll see in the upcoming discussion of indulgences, casuistry did not weather the Reformation well. Martin Luther cast the *Summa Diabolica* into the flames and his followers inherited his strong dislike of casuistry.[31] The subsequent fervor of the Counter-Reformation helped casuistry, as Catholics united in the struggle against emergent Protestantism gave casuistry a shot in the arm. In the face of Protestant denial, the sixteenth-century Council of Trent reiterated the canons of the Fourth Lateran Council and insisted on the validity and necessity of personal and private confession. In addition, it required the penitent to confess sins according to species, number, and circumstances (theologians had long agreed on the importance of this stipulation). This decree flew in the face of reformers who had insisted that confession to a priest was not necessary and that repentance was for sinfulness in general rather than for particular sins.

That casuistry still holds sway in Roman Catholicism today is hardly shocking; anyone remotely familiar with televised criminal cases (e.g., O. J. Simpson) understands the importance of landing on just the right defense attorney, notably in the case of annulments and end-of-life dramas involving medical technology.

Indulgences

Originally, an indulgence seems to have been a gift of money to charity as an expression of gratitude for forgiveness. Gradually, the idea developed into a sort of marketing plan: Johannes Tetzel of Germany (d. 1519) held that for a mere three German marks, a sinner could be released from all punishments he would otherwise have faced in purgatory. Under such a plan, you could enjoy your venial sins without losing sleep at night over fear of divine punishment. Even more appealing to Christians was the idea that they could release the soul of a loved one from its sufferings in purgatory through a similar payment (read: vicarious atonement).

In 1095, Pope Urban II and the Council of Clermont decreed that all Christians who died in a crusade automatically received a plenary indulgence. If you were killed while trying to convert a Muslim, all your sins were immediately forgiven. The idea of indulgences continued to evolve until the sixteenth century. In 1517, a scandal associated with an indulgence offered for the rebuilding of St. Peter's in Rome prompted Martin Luther to criticize the preaching of indulgences and eventually to reject the underlying doctrine (he was not alone—Eastern Orthodox theologians had also criticized the notions of purgatory and indulgences). Reflecting on the implications of justification by faith alone, Luther reached the conclusion that indulgences undermine the total trust in divine forgiveness (due to Christ's sacrifice) that is essential to the Christian faith.[32] Furthermore, Luther viewed purgatory as a fiction, one without basis in scripture.

In its last session (1563), the Council of Trent endorsed the right of the church to grant indulgences. In the same decree, the council deplored the abuses that had taken place and ordered the bishops to correct them and to fight the superstitious use of indulgences. Nearly four centuries later, Pope Paul VI issued the apostolic constitution *Indulgentiarum doctrina* (1967). There he referred to sin as "disobedience to divine law" and "contempt for the friendship of God" and stressed that *sin deserves punishment*. He reiterated the traditional Catholic belief that expiation takes place in purgatory unless penance had already been performed before death. The expiation of the temporal penalty due to sin is precisely the domain of indulgences, and Catholics may still rely on them in good faith.

By the end of the Council of Trent on December 4, 1563, the church had succeeded in setting the basis for the reorientation and renewal of Roman Catholicism. The new Counter-Reformation piety would stress individual rather than institutional expressions of faith. It would be driven by the development of new forms of mental prayer and an urge toward good works as a way of attaining grace. Above all, the Counter-Reformation placed renewed stress on the sacramental system, which had been seriously undermined by Luther's doctrines of justification by faith alone and the priesthood of all believers.

Within the context of this new sacramentalism, it would be difficult to exaggerate the importance of the role given to sacramental confession. The more the old order was threatened by Protestants, the more the church appreciated the importance of confession as the forum of conscience. With a revived and better-educated clergy, ready to administer the sacrament and with a restored episcopacy now able to impose discipline, it had become possible to make the confessional the first line of defense against religious doubt, immorality, and disrespect for the sacred. Furthermore, the result of the Trent decrees regarding the sacrament of penance was to change significantly the relationship between priest and penitent. In demanding that penitents render an exact and detailed accounting of their sins and the circumstances under which they were committed, the church also required the confessor to carry out a more searching interrogation and to judge the relative gravity of sins.[33]

One of the most striking characteristics of Catholicism after Trent was the way in which sacramental penance emerged as a defining element of the new Christian order.[34] In a very real sense, Catholic Europe became a confessionally oriented society with a heightened awareness of sin, increased frequency of confession, and a greatly enhanced role for the priest-confessor as the "doctor of souls." Atonement had become a performance, a story through which one persuaded a confessor that one had done one's all to amend for mistakes made.

The heavy penances prescribed in penitential books could be replaced, in part or in whole, by prayers and other pious works, such as fasting or almsgiving. Serving the poor or denying oneself food were substitute penances rather than conditions for gaining an indulgence. Thanks to indulgences in the form of material and monetary gifts, great cathedrals and monastic houses were built and kept up, schools and universities were founded and endowed, hospitals were maintained, and bridges were built. Indulgences ultimately provided another path to the Zamboni effect: people—wealthy or not—would never have coughed up money to purchase an indulgence unless they believed in the Zamboni effect. New churches, financed in part by penitent sinners, wiped many slates clean. The edifices would spend centuries reaching up to the sky, begging God for forgiveness for sins once shamefully whispered in a dark confessional. The money subsequently sacrificed by rich and poor alike attested to the sincerity of countless penitents and to the gnawing fear of sin in which it was rooted.

HISTORY OF CHRISTIAN CONFESSION III

Calvin

A chapter on atonement would fall flat without mention of a theology that challenged the very concept of forgiveness (not to mention indulgences). Not everyone agreed (or agrees) on how sins could be forgiven or even whether they eventually would be. Martin Luther objected strenuously to the practice of buying indulgences, or paying money for atonement, as we have seen. He still believed in the forgiveness of sin, though. Shortly after him, Calvin preached that some unlucky Christians were simply stuck with their sinfulness forever—there was nothing to be done for those passed over for salvation. Like Lutheranism and Anglicanism, Calvinism was one of the three dominant magisterial reformations of the sixteenth century. Although Calvin came to differ with Luther over predestination, they shared an abiding belief in the (very un-Catholic) doctrine of justification by faith alone.

Calvin's *Institutes of the Christian Religion*, which first appeared in 1536, is early Protestantism's greatest theological work. There has been a tendency to reduce all of Calvin's theology to predestination; even though various scholars have warned against such abridgment, the centrality of the idea that some are born lucky and others not remains popular in the West.[35] In Calvin's theology, some people are justly excluded from the operation of God's saving grace and naturally suffer the consequences of their sin. Justification is by faith alone, which means there's nothing an individual can do to deserve or earn forgiveness. Calvin explains in the *Institutes* (3.21.5), "We call predestination God's eternal decree, by which he determined with himself what he willed to become of each man. For all are not created in equal condition; rather, eternal life is foreordained for some, eternal damnation for others." If Calvin were right, atonement might seem a waste of time. Nothing could help the damned. To the extent that anyone can legitimately hope for the Zamboni effect, Catholic theology is infinitely more optimistic here (as are, e.g., Mormon and Muslim theologies).

Calvin affirmed what he termed the doctrine of reprobation, even though it appalled him. The reprobate is condemned justly (*Institutes* 3.21.7), which is to say that he has no moral claim to the Zamboni effect. The *decretum horribile* manifests God's glory by virtue of its very mystery.[36] Calvin's insistence that reprobation or election proceeds from a mysterious decision of God may well lead to sin fatigue, specifically by sapping a would-be saint of the motivation to reverse a possibly negative judgment. Prayer, atonement, and works of charity in and of themselves can't necessarily get the contrite sinner what he wants.

Calvinism took root principally in France, Switzerland, Holland, and subsequently in Scotland. In his 1902 classic *The Protestant Ethic and the Spirit of Capitalism*, however, the German sociologist Max Weber identified Calvinism as a fundamentally important development in the creation of the modern West. Weber argued that Calvinism's emphasis on divine election produced a culture of "innerwordly asceticism" in which Calvinists hoped to demonstrate the fruits of their election through worldly involvement and enterprise. This mentality contrasts with Catholic culture, which has long celebrated parties, carnivals, and wedding blowouts. Since anything can be forgiven, Catholics may reassure themselves, why not eat, drink, and be merry? The fatality of Calvin's theology would seem to prompt those destined for hell to make all sorts of mischief while on Earth (because you're going to hell anyway). The brilliance of Calvin (if we may call it that) is that, according to his theology, you cannot figure out before death whether you are one of the elect or not. "Why bother?" contemporary Westerners might conclude; even people contemptuous of Pascal's wager analogy might find more reason to bother in the idea that you at least have a chance of improving your fate.

Intrinsic to Calvinism is the idea that God is the cause of a lost soul's problems. Let's fast-forward to the late twentieth century now, where we'll witness a different conviction: a lost soul's problems stem largely from social conditions outside the individual. Inner conflicts and sinful actions reflect environmental tensions or injustices, such that society is to be blamed for thieves and drug dealers (and not the sinners themselves). Television audiences came to relish public confession and self-criticism, even as they failed to grasp that they were allegedly part of the problem (because audience members were part of the society that caused the sinner to step out of bounds).

TELEVISED CONFESSIONS

Some fashions fade only to return. Centuries after public contrition for sins fell out of fashion, television brought it back. We'll see that the reality television shows that began to claim vast American audiences in the late 1990s frequently involved refusals to forgive. Only time will tell whether in fact the popularity of these programs conditioned a new generation of Americans to withhold forgiveness in good conscience. In any event, we've seen some precedent for such withholding.

The TV talk shows trumpet confessions and, as I've said, return us to the day when atonement was very public (e.g., stoning the adulteress or making a king crawl on his knees through city streets to earn forgiveness). Both talk shows (e.g., Oprah Winfrey or Geraldo Rivera) and "reality shows" (e.g., *Survivor*) draw crucial energy from the confessional sideshow. MTV's popular offering *The Real World*, one of the first of this genre, regularly interrupted the narrative to showcase "confessionals," as the producers of the program called them. Cast members would retreat into a separate room to offer a more frank commentary on the day's public events; MTV would either show the confession as it unfolded or use the content of the confession as a voice-over. Subsequent reality shows such as *The Apprentice* (2004) continued to rely on this crowd-pleasing technique.[37]

That said, it is important to realize that talk shows and reality shows feature an important political aspect as well, one that contrasts with religious confession. For disabled people, gay people, or socially deviant people not only reveal information about themselves but also, frequently, insist that they are not sorry for who they are or what they do. Ordinary people, noncelebrities, have often succeeded before television audiences precisely because nonpowerful people can plead for sympathy in a way powerful people cannot generally. The general public can punish the rich, the famous, the powerful by withholding attention. Since ordinary people live largely anonymous lives, they stand to lose less. And so social status determines public-confession strategy.

Two televised confessions, both of them involving sexual misconduct, link recent history to the early and medieval Christian periods. Jimmy Swaggart and Bill Clinton both admitted wrongdoing and expressed remorse to large crowds. Both Protestant, each admitted to carnal sins. Both must have realized that the sexual sins they repudiated were much more common than Americans were prepared to admit. The point of their respective confessions was either to bolster or simply to pay lip service to reigning public morality even as the emotional depth of the confessions attested to the difficulty of prying forgiveness from the hearts of tough customers.

On February 21, 1988, Jimmy Swaggart, then America's leading television evangelist, resigned from his ministry amid revelations that he had paid a prostitute for services rendered. Vengeance played a prominent role on the road to this confession. Just a few years before Swaggart's "outing," he had brought down another successful evangelist (one Martin Gorman), who had hired a prostitute. Beyond that, Swaggart had quite recently excoriated in the national press another prominent television evangelist, James Bakker, who had once conducted an affair with a female church secretary and with at least one man as well.

In front of a congregation of seven thousand in Baton Rouge, Louisiana, Swaggart sobbed and confessed to "moral failure" without going into any detail: "I do not plan in any way to whitewash my sin or call it a mistake," he told shocked members of his Family Worship Center. What even jaded readers may find fascinating is the testimony of the prostitute. Four days later Debra Murphree, the woman in question, told a New Orleans TV show audience that she and Swaggart had not had sex, despite their multiple meetings. She said he liked to watch her undress. Only a few years later, a presidential candidate would claim that he had held marijuana cigarettes to his mouth while a young man but that he had never inhaled. This same candidate would later confess to sexual misconduct with a female intern, but he would stake his personal defense on the fact that his penis had never entered the intern's vagina.

On August 17, 1998, President Clinton took to the national airwaves to confess that he had in fact consorted with Monica Lewinsky, as widely suspected. He stated:

As you know, in a deposition in January, I was asked questions about my relationship with Monica Lewinsky. While my answers were legally accurate, I did not volunteer information. Indeed, I did have a relationship with Ms. Lewinsky that was not appropriate. In fact, it was wrong. It constituted a critical lapse in judgment and a personal failure on my part for which I am solely and completely responsible.

Remarkably, the American public not only forgave Clinton but then also indicated that the media coverage of the Lewinsky affair had been too invasive (of course, not everyone forgave him, and not everyone thought the coverage had been too invasive).

Initially, when word emerged that President Clinton might have had a sexual relationship with the former White House intern Monica S. Lewinsky, public reaction to the news coverage was overwhelmingly negative.[38] The American public seemed outraged (but not disgusted: Clinton's lowest approval ratings came in his first term, shortly after he moved to end discrimination against gays serving in the military).

After Clinton's admission that he did have an "inappropriate" relationship with Lewinsky, however, the public's opinion of both their president and the media covering him improved measurably. A national poll found that more Americans believed that Clinton and Lewinsky had been treated unfairly and did not deserve the public humiliation they received. The public confession had worked wonders for the president's popularity rating.

Ten days after the televised confession, Clinton made his first public appearance and received a strong vote of confidence for professional competency. The review of his personal conduct, however, was mixed. Clinton had flown to the Democratic stronghold of Worcester, Massachusetts, to deliver a speech on school safety. His advisers hoped the speech would distract the nation from its preoccupation with the president's sex life. An audience of 1,200 people gave him sustained applause and standing ovations.[39] The *New York Times* concluded that behind the resounding applause, many in the crowd managed to distinguish between the president's policies and his personal conduct. While some placards read, "We support you," "We're proud of you, Mr. President," or "We're still with you, Mr. President," others ordered him to "Resign now!" or simply said, "Liar!" One placard offered a "Scarlet A."

Distinguishing between the sinner and the sin, a majority of Americans eventually responded favorably to Clinton's confession. Swaggart fared worse, perhaps because America was younger in 1988, or perhaps because he seemed less skilled at making a confession (Swaggart gurgled through tears and threw the towel in without bringing to the public's attention the absence of actual sexual intercourse), or perhaps because money had changed hands. He may have suspected that the public would have deplored him even more for not having actual intercourse. Kinky would have been the verdict or, even worse, impotence.

Television "worked" for Clinton in a way that it didn't for Swaggart. Yet television might seem to be a poor venue for confession, unlike the church's carefully constructed confessional or the psychoanalyst's couch. The real work of Clinton's and Swaggart's confessions (to their respective wives, that is) took place far from the prying ears of the outside world, in the privacy conducive to consolation and healing. The trick to succeeding at public confession would seem to come down to mixing a personalized message with a balanced delivery. Show some tears if you like, but appeal to the audience's sense of solidarity: let those without sin cast the first stone.

The third example of a dramatic confession transmitted via television centers on New Jersey governor James McGreevey, a committed, if divorced, Catholic. The good people of the United States witnessed the (married) governor's televised resignation on August 13, 2004. Although generally familiar with talk show confessions, American audiences placed the confession in a pattern established by Swaggart and Clinton.[40] That is, audiences immediately understood that the sinner on trial stood more to lose than the sad guests on television talk shows. Unlike Clinton, McGreevey chose not to save himself through confession. The governor seemed determined to punish himself instead, perhaps in an effort to save his political party or to earn forgiveness in the old-fashioned, Catholic way.

In a dramatic and sudden announcement, the governor publicly regretted his actions, which involved an affair with a man on his payroll. (Apparently McGreevey's office had called the FBI shortly before the announcement and complained that the governor's lover had requested $5 million to keep quiet.) With his wife by his side, he reflected on a life of tortured identity. "My truth is that I am a gay American," the forty-seven-year-old governor confessed in an emotional voice. He revealed to a live audience that he had engaged "shamefully" in an adult consensual affair with another man and said it had violated his "bonds of matrimony."[41] He continued, as if doing penance with the sincerity required by medieval Penitentials, "It was wrong. It was foolish. It was inexcusable." The governor reasoned that, since the affair had compromised his ability to lead the state of New Jersey, he should step down—more than a year before his term was scheduled to end.

His humiliation palpable, McGreevey nonetheless left questions about the point of his penance. Unlike Swaggart and Clinton, the New Jersey governor knew that he would not return to office and likely knew as well that his marriage would end (it did, shortly thereafter). McGreevey seemed concerned about the future of his party in the state; his motivation for the confession may have been altruistic. It's not clear whether the people of New Jersey forgave him before they forgot him; in any event, McGreevey quickly vanished from the public eye (only to reappear briefly in late 2006, when he published his autobiography as an openly gay man). As a Catholic (albeit a twice-divorced one), Mc-

Greevey was eligible for the Zamboni effect in his tradition; as a politician, he probably was not—only politicians as consummately skilled as Bill Clinton can hope for that.

CRIME, PUNISHMENT, AND FORGIVENESS

The gradual venialization of sin—that is, its dilution and demotion—stems in part from an unusually high level of familiarity with sin. Of course, Westerners have long known what gossip is, but not until radio and television were our forebears bombarded with reports of sin on a daily, or perhaps even hourly, basis. That sin fatigue gradually led to an atonement fatigue. Skepticism about whether people can really train themselves to be good, especially after having done something particularly bad, might naturally lead to reconciling us to the "cold, hard truth" of a "real world" in which atonement just doesn't work.

A brief examination of prison rehabilitation will indicate the reluctance of some Westerners to honor the atonement of those who have transgressed. Civil reformers in the West have justified incarceration on the basis of its purported mission to strengthen a weak character, and to deepen a criminal's respect for civil laws. In this section we'll see the high cost of civil atonement in comparison with the astonishingly low cost of atonement in, say, contemporary Christianity (think of a Catholic's penance of five Hail Mary's). Most Americans who end up in prison are troubled to begin with (they tend to lack much formal education and to suffer from substance abuse problems). On exiting prison, though, ex-convicts carry the added burden of a prison record, which evokes distrust and even fear in many potential employers and neighbors. Ex-cons have no chance for the Zamboni effect—at least not in a social sense.

Do societies forgive secular sinners, criminals? It's not clear that we Americans do—think of the fate of first-time drug offenders in the United States, who face obstacles we used to associate with murderers and child molesters.[42] The slate is never wiped clean, in the way some Christians have understood; the Zamboni effect may refresh ice but not souls. The highly influential French philosopher Michel Foucault argues that social authorities have used punishment (essentially a synonym for atonement in his work) to control citizens. He would have us believe that we are all in the grip of a prison system we can't see. Few

Jews or Christians would describe God's expectations as anything like a prison system, yet contemporary Americans may vacillate between legitimate fear of an ex-convict's recidivism and suspicion that all citizens live on the brink of a prison sentence. The case of the pornographic actress Linda Lovelace, to which I'll turn shortly, indicates the high price of secular atonement.

Foucault begins *Discipline and Punish* with the horrifying account of one Damiens's public torture and eventual execution in 1757 (Damiens had attacked Louis XV). Foucault argues that centuries of Catholic penance had molded the secular culture not only in France but throughout Europe. Foucault asserts that torture forms part of a ritual, much as Christian atonement had done. Torture is an element in the liturgy of punishment. To be effective, torture must scar the victim and must cross emotional boundaries, revolting and terrifying those who witness the spectacle. The victim would suffer so much as to cry out for mercy, confessing to anything and agreeing with his torturers that they were right to take such action against him. Formerly an enemy, the victim becomes a good guy, falling quickly into ranks behind his oppressors. The sputtering victim now represented living truth, with its holy and supernatural aura. He had seen the light. "If torture was so strongly embedded in legal practice, it was because it revealed truth and showed the operation of power."[43] Committed Christians were already quite familiar with the notions of truth and power, thinking of them in terms of the confessional and God's majesty.

At the end of the eighteenth century, torture was denounced as a survival of the barbarities of another age. Why did this brutality last so long? Foucault answers plausibly that ordinary citizens believed that the cruelty of the earthly punishment would be deducted from the punishment to come after death; in it was glimpsed the promise of forgiveness. "There was something of the ordeal and something of God's judgment that was still undecipherable in the ceremony of the execution."[44] The savage violence of premodern societies found a compelling parallel in Christian expectations of the Last Judgment and the unspeakable horrors of hell. What's interesting is that many Christian denominations (but by no means all of them) have softened the apocalyptic line,[45] whereas former prisoners in America report widespread social impediments to their quests to forge a new life (most commonly, in attempts to gain employment). Social distrust of a wrongdoer's atonement conflicts with religious rhetoric, such that an ex-con can find more support and

encouragement from groups that have learned to accept a vastly reduced price for mercy. If ecclesiastical forgiveness is now easier to obtain
than ever, social redemption should be easier to get.[46]

After the execution of the regicide Damiens, Foucault focuses on a
document from a Paris reformatory, roughly eighty years later. The
timetable he analyzes sets out in minute detail how the prisoner's day
was to be structured. Like modern confession, the punishment of the
Paris reformatory of the mid–nineteenth century took place in silence
and in private. Foucault's aim is to describe how the ritual of punishment changed in Europe between the torture of Damiens in 1757 and
the birth of the modern prison around 1840. Whereas authorities (secular and religious) had long targeted the body for punishment, they began in the late eighteenth century to target the soul. By the sheer volume of references to the soul, Foucault believes that authorities were
able to conjure it into existence, at least in the minds of the masses. For
Foucault, the metaphor of the soul represents the power of a ruling
class to dominate and subordinate social inferiors (who are led to consider any ill will directed at the ruling class as an affront to God).

Writing at the end of the nineteenth century, Nietzsche had claimed
that there was very little difference between the bloodthirsty desire for
vengeance in primitive societies and what goes on in modern courtrooms. Foucault adds nuance to Nietzsche's insight by focusing on how
closely legal torture was regulated (as in the execution of Damiens) and
by arguing that the modern prison dehumanizes and tortures human
beings in a primitive way. The climax of Foucault's book comes in the
insight that modern penal systems do not forgive transgressors in the
way that early Christian models of penance did. For once a sinner was
readmitted to the body of the faithful in the early centuries of Christianity, the slate was largely wiped clean. Given that certain restrictions
still applied to former sinners, though—no military service, no conjugal
rights—it may be that the modern prison, at least as Foucault interprets
it, lies closer to the original Christian model than Foucault let on.

In the modern network of penal institutions and bureaucracies,
"punishment" has come to approximate a rational form of action, conducted in routine, matter-of-fact ways, and represented in morally
neutral, bureaucratic terms. Of course, underlying these "objective"
practices and discourses, there is a range of values and beyond that a
series of emotional forces and moral judgments. Resentment, outrage,
hatred—as well as mercy, justice, and forgiveness—continue to fester

within these rationalized measures. But they do so in a vaguely religious way, relying on institutional discipline to describe punitive actions in beneficial terms, which will conjure up the relief of having been forgiven, redeemed.

Foucault's *Discipline and Punish* stresses that, in the modern era, punitive sentiments have come to be judged as shameful, negative, and irrational and that, more and more, punishment has been redefined in positive, administrative terms as a form of correction and normalization. Does this mean that modern Western societies are becoming more Christian, more forgiving? Not really. It means that we fool ourselves when we call prison rehabilitation; it looks more like vengeance. In the secular sphere, atonement rarely ends, and the Zamboni seldom rides.

For Foucault, the world still needs atonement, but now for a different reason. We aim to placate a ruling elite, not a heavenly father. The implications of Foucault's work, itself a culmination of earlier thinkers' insights, underscore not only the futility of longing for the Zamboni but also the personal difficulty of extinguishing such hope.

THE SACRED AND THE PROFANE

Punishment in secular states has waxed and waned, just as atonement in religious communities has done. One of the best ways of tracing the demise of atonement in the sacred realm is by examining the secular sphere during times of stricter religious authority. Civil punishment for crimes has lightened over the past three centuries, which is a good thing, insofar as it indicates less corruption on the part of vindictive rulers. But civil punishment carries a half-life that fades slowly. The slate has not been wiped clean on the day we leave prison: another prison sentence is just beginning.

In *The Spirit of the Laws* (1748), Montesquieu pointed to the connections of structure and of belief that tied forms of punishing to forms of governing: "It would be an easy matter," he wrote, "to prove that in all, or almost all, of the governments of Europe, punishments have increased or diminished in proportion as these governments favoured or discouraged liberty."[47] From there he went on to sketch the political and psychological dynamics that produce these connections, thus giving a sociological as well as a normative quality to his conclusion that "the severity of punishment is fitter for despotic governments, whose principle is terror, than for a monarchy or republic, whose spring is honour and virtue."[48]

Roughly a century later, Durkheim articulated a crucial difference between "religious criminality" and "human criminality." Virtually all offenses against the *conscience collective* of a simple society have the status of "religious criminality." As such, these offenses provoke a veritable horror among the reverential onlookers, whose revulsion at this abomination, and whose fear of its consequences, drive them to take violent measures against the criminal. Religious passions are thus the source of atrocious punishments, and indeed it is precisely because a deity has been attacked that such punishments seem to show little concern for the offender's suffering, "for what is an individual's suffering when it is a question of appeasing a God?"[49] By contrast, the criminality typical of secular, modern societies is "human criminality"—that is, offenses against persons and their property. Such crimes still provoke strong reactions and still give rise to a public demand for punishment, but the sentiments involved in this reaction are qualitatively different, since "the offense of man against man cannot arouse the same indignation as an offense of man against God."[50] The rise of humanism and individualism transformed punishment. According to Durkheim, the same people who express outrage when an individual suffers unjustly find themselves concerned with proportionality when an individual suffers for his sins. The consequence is that "the same cause which sets in motion the repressive apparatus tends also to halt it. The same mental state drives us to punish and to moderate the punishment. Hence an extenuating influence cannot fail to make itself felt."[51] The combined result of these interlinked changes is to make the average intensity of punishments in modern societies much less than was formerly the case. The most repressive secular punishments are to be found in an absolute monarchy, Durkheim argued.[52]

Several decades after Durkheim, another Frenchman picked up the ball and carried it even further. According to Foucault, our governing predecessors used to punish the body but now punish the "soul." In other words, contemporary punishment has gone psychological; this psychological turn dovetails beautifully with fear of eternal punishment, Foucault observed.[53] Like Durkheim, Foucault insisted on a vital nexus between religious thinking and secular expectations. Also like Durkheim, Foucault takes great interest (most notably in *Discipline and Punish*) in the intensity and quantity of punishment doled out by a secular court. While Foucault holds that modern punishment can be quite insidious, he, like Montesquieu, sees a gradual diminution in the intensity and quantity of punishment in the West. Although Foucault does not mention this specifically, it seems reasonable to argue that Westerners no longer view natural disasters or epidemics as God's revenge.[54] Nor do Christians today show much willingness to inflict physical pain on themselves in the name of earning God's favor or making up for sins committed.[55] Martyrdom more likely than not leaves most twenty-first-century Christians cold.[56]

Foucault on balance argues, as I do, that transgressors are never really forgiven in the modern West. Whereas even severe punishments used to end after a predetermined limit, today atonement stretches on forever (particularly for ex-convicts, who often cannot vote or serve on juries after release from prison). This prolongation owes something to the religious influence of Christianity, which in turn took its theological cues from Judaism. Prisons gave up on the Zamboni effect; Calvin's mind-set seemed more convenient in the case of secular criminals.

SERIOUS SINNERS OF THE 1970S

To flesh out and apply the insights of Montesquieu, Durkheim, and Foucault, let's turn back to modern America. The first half of the 1970s gave America three notorious sinners, each of whom eventually became a born-again Christian (i.e., an Evangelical Protestant). These three vignettes tell us as much about the stratification of American culture as they do about the Judeo-Christian belief in God's infinite powers of forgiveness. Each of these three sinners, guilty of sexual transgressions, reached for the Zamboni effect away from the glare of television cameras. One woman failed, one woman arguably would not let herself succeed, and one man arguably triumphed. If his slate can be wiped clean, anyone's can. Like Bill Clinton, Harry Reems beat the social odds and earned the kind of redemption supposedly still available to all Christians.

The pornographic film *Deep Throat* seized the attention of the United States in 1972 and revolutionized the adult entertainment industry. The two stars of the international classic, Linda Lovelace and Harry Reems, became household names. Lovelace had grown up in Yonkers, the daughter of a New York City cop and a domineering mother who believed in frequent corporal punishment. At Catholic school, Lovelace ended up with the nickname "Miss Holy Holy" because she wouldn't let boys near her.

An automobile accident led to a chance meeting with the man who would become her husband and manager. Under his influence, she began having sex on camera. Her experience in smaller films led to her infamous role in *Deep Throat*, reputedly the highest-grossing film of all time. She later divorced her husband and failed to make a go of a legitimate career as an actress. By 1976, when *Linda Lovelace for President* ended her career, she had called it quits with her postmarriage boyfriend and run straight into the arms of yet another man, a construction worker named Larry Marchiano. By 1980, she had become a born-again Christian crusader against pornography, a feminist, and the mother of two children. She was living on welfare as her husband tried to make ends meet as a cable installer on Long Island.

Feminists quickly embraced Lovelace, who publicly claimed that she had been forced at gunpoint by her husband to act in *Deep Throat* and other films. She preached about the demeaning effects of pornography and turned up in Andrea Dworkin's 1979 book *Pornography: Men Possessing Women*. She proceeded to write three books about her own life and the terrible abuse she had suffered at the hands of racketeering men. She was on the straight and narrow, having thoroughly repudiated her past and focused her life on Jesus.

In 1986, she wrote her last autobiography, *Out of Bondage*, with an introduction by Gloria Steinem. She described her life of poverty and discussed health problems wrought by ritual beatings while a pornographic actress. She lamented the attacks on her credibility, the reports from other actors that she had never been forced to do anything on sets and that she had always seemed to enjoy her work. Likening herself to a rape victim who gets raped all over again in the court of public opinion, she insisted she was telling the truth. God had forgiven her, and she wanted Americans to forgive her as well. She asked for sympathy, not the leering fascination Americans still seemed to feel for her. Despite the fact they had film footage to hold on to, Americans seemed determined to keep Linda Lovelace the actress around, too. They would not let the Zamboni take her away.

The porn industry spawned the term "The Linda Syndrome" to describe porn stars like Angel Kelly and Samantha Fox, who rise to fame and then disavow their sexual (and cinematic) history in order to embrace feminism and, in some instances, to become born-again Christians.[57] This syndrome, such as it is, underscores the social difficulty of making amends for youthful indiscretions (admittedly, a career in pornography might be considered somewhat more serious than a "youthful indiscretion"). But even if you believe that God forgave Linda Lovelace, you might still wonder at the lengths to which she went to convince the American public of her sincerity.

Lovelace's leading man in *Deep Throat* had been Herbert Streicher, a twenty-five-year-old Jewish man from Westchester County (New York) who had done television commercials and off-Broadway theater but who was still struggling to make it as a legitimate actor. Raised by Orthodox Jewish parents, he claims that his parents largely lost interest in their faith and, apart from giving their sons a bar mitzvah, provided no religious education.

Streicher had turned to porn, both behind and in front of the camera, to pay the bills and had even made a couple of short films with Lovelace. On the trip to Miami for the filming of *Deep Throat*, he had been hired strictly as a production assistant. Last-minute circumstances resulted in Streicher's casting in the leading role. Streicher, whose screen name was Harry Reems, donned a white coat and then made film history. Streicher liked Lovelace and would always defend her as a sweet person, even though he waved away her accounts of being forced into porn.

Later Streicher suffered through alcohol and drug addictions. He became a born-again Christian, married, and had two sons in a conventional marriage. He did all this in Utah, where he became a successful real estate developer. The religious conversion transformed his life. Streicher became a living testimony to the Zamboni effect (in part because of a different name, no doubt). He had wiped the slate clean, which is not to say he was his own Zamboni: he gives Jesus most of the credit and his long-suffering wife the rest.

Not long after *Deep Throat* competed with the Watergate scandal for the imagination of Americans, the Supreme Court handed down *Roe v. Wade* (1973). At the heart of the case was a woman who testified that she had been raped and demanded the right to a legal abortion. Whereas Lovelace had been raised a Catholic and Streicher a Jew, Norma McCorvey came from the Bible Belt of Texas. Like Lovelace and Streicher, she repudiated her un-Christian past and joyfully became born again.

She was a pregnant twenty-one-year-old with a tenth-grade education, too poor to obtain an illegal abortion in Texas or a legal one in California. The landmark decision to which her case led held that a woman's right to an abortion falls within the right to privacy protected by the Fourteenth Amendment. In awarding a woman the right to an abortion, the Court defined criteria by which states could regulate abortion in the second and third trimesters.

McCorvey later publicly regretted her action. She explained in an autobiography that, at the time in question, she had been pregnant for the third time. Having previously placed one child in adoption, she knew she could not part with another child. Abortion seemed the sensible option. Even though she never went through with the abortion herself, she helped to secure a woman's legal right to one in the United States. That is the sin for which she never stopped repenting.

Long after *Roe v. Wade* became the law, Norma McCorvey admitted that her testimony had been false. In 1987, she confessed her lie to *Washington Times* columnist Carl Rowan. She admitted that her account of being raped in 1969 was a fabrication designed to invalidate the law. She admitted that she had become pregnant by her boyfriend. Far from feeling proud of her role of helping American women earn the legal right to an abortion, McCorvey has said that her actions caused her unrelenting misery. She has reported more than one attempt at suicide and that she has never overcome the shame of her deed (again, she herself never actually had an abortion—she only helped American women win the right to one). She questioned not only whether God could ever forgive her but also whether she could forgive herself. Presumably, God will only run the Zamboni if you ask him to, and McCorvey seems incapable of asking him. Instead, she seems grimly determined to prolong her atonement indefinitely, much as John Profumo did. Perhaps she understands the atonement fatigue that has settled over America. McCorvey eventually converted to Roman Catholicism (in 1998), a faith wedded to and still enchanted by the Zamboni effect (and also a faith dead set against abortion rights).

Even as we laud the therapeutic effect of identity as a born-again Christian for these three serious sinners of the 1970s, we might wonder what it takes for public sinners to gain widespread social acceptance. Without an easy answer, we can nonetheless see the mounting social and political power of conservative Protestant groups in the 1970s and 1980s. Becoming a born-again Christian was a clear way to signal one's readiness to enter the mainstream on sober terms.

Just as antipornography feminists seized on Lovelace as their poster child, so did antiabortion Christian groups relish the chance to brandish

McCorvey as an ally in the struggle to overturn *Roe v. Wade*. As McCorvey fought to forgive herself, the forgiveness of her fellow Christians helped her regain the will to live. What is perhaps most remarkable about McCorvey is that Evangelical Protestants unleashed the Zamboni for her (raising a curious parallel to vicarious atonement).

It could just be a coincidence that a Jew, a Catholic, and a lukewarm Protestant ended up fervent Christian Evangelicals. Or it could be that character rehabilitation in America is best accomplished through identifying oneself with a particular kind of religiosity. Either way, we can see that religious atonement carries with it immediate and obvious social implications, just as Foucault had argued. If you want to reintegrate yourself back into the American heartland, conservative Protestantism could be your best bet. That is, if you want to ignite the Zamboni of the social sphere, you have to tell the people what they want to hear.

THE SOMETIMES HIGH COST OF FORGIVENESS

Religious Jews, Christians, and Muslims alike cringe at the idea that God may refuse to forgive some or all of their sins. You couldn't be more out of luck if God turns his back on you. The parable of the unforgiving servant in the New Testament (Matthew 18:23–35) reinforces the expectation that humans will forgive one another, because that is what God is doing for people. God may be trying to get us to see that our judgments of others often turn out to be plain wrong; once humbled by this recognition, we will judge others less frequently, and certainly more reluctantly when forced to take some position. In Romans 12:19 we read, "Vengeance is mine; I will repay, saith the Lord"; in John 8:7, we read, "He that is without sin among you, let him first cast a stone at her." We are no better than the woman caught in adultery, which gives us one reason to draw back. Another powerful reason may be that our minds may sometimes fail to grasp the context of a particular sin and therefore leave us ill equipped to draw important conclusions about appropriate punishment.

Despite divine exhortations, some believers may find the cost of forgiveness prohibitively high. In fact, believers may see good reason to refuse to forgive their neighbors altogether. People trying to please—indeed, imitate—God may invoke him as the reason for this refusal. A particularly gruesome example of using God to refuse forgiveness to people surfaces in the Irish Magdalene Asylums, where "fallen" women were sent well into the twentieth century to perform slave labor supervised by the Sisters of Mercy.[58]

At other times, the reason will be either self-esteem or the limits of the forgivable. Whether it's African Americans demanding reparations from the U.S. government for the centuries their ancestors worked as slaves or Jews demanding reparations from the German government for the torture, enslavement, and brutal deaths of their forebears, the past sometimes refuses to recede into the distance. In a purely personal (as opposed to a racial or religious) context, we may sometimes feel that someone else has insulted us so deeply that we are justified in denying forgiveness—particularly if we suspect or know that that other person isn't sorry. In the terrorist bombings that plagued London in the summer of 2005, an Anglican priest lost her daughter. Several months later, the priest resigned her position, citing an inability to forgive the bombers. She explained that she could no longer preach the necessity of forgiveness.[59] Perhaps the best philosophical justification for withholding forgiveness can be found in David Novitz's essay "Forgiveness and Self-Respect."[60] Novitz wants to protect self-esteem and worries about damaging it in the act of forgiveness.

The Truth and Reconciliation Commission of South Africa took bold steps to heal the emotional wounds of apartheid. The media have reported at considerable length on the work of this commission, and scholars are sure to parse through the work of this commission for some time to come.[61] Part of what made the work of this commission newsworthy was the great reluctance of some blacks to forgive and the considerable work required to surmount that quite rational unwillingness.

Another unusual attempt at atonement took place in November 2002. Five Americans who had lost relatives in the 9/11 attacks met secretly with Aicha al-Wafi, the mother of the alleged twentieth hijacker, Zacarias Moussaoui.[62] Mrs. al-Wafi had asked to meet the relatives in order to seek forgiveness and gain support from Americans opposed to the death penalty. Andrew Rice, who lost his brother that day in the World Trade Center, said that the meeting with Mrs. al-Wafi would be viewed as treachery by both public and government—"no different to meeting and consoling bin Laden's own mother." Insisting that he had not "gone soft," Rice said, "Of course I'm angry, but there's a spiritual supremacy. I'm protecting my brother's spirit by putting a barricade around him. I'm refusing to fall in line with what 'they' want, which is visceral hatred between two sides. This gives me permission to reconcile." Interestingly, the meeting went unreported in the American media.

Whether one believes in God or not, a compelling reason for forgiving those who atone is the feeling of well-being. For some, *sorry* is the hardest word. For many others, though, saying sorry, "getting it off your chest," brings welcome relief from anxiety. Those who choose to forgive will similarly report relief.[63] Instead of holding on to bitterness and anger, the wronged sometimes feel purged when they choose to forgive. The wronged may also feel a little more virtuous as well, "a bigger person," as Americans sometimes say. Even more often, the wronged may feel they lack the power to do anything about their lot: forgiveness often amounts to resignation.

The events of 9/11 do not threaten the venialization thesis I have advanced, for responses to 9/11 point up the diminution of sin's power—if only because Americans have a hard time classifying the attacks as unilaterally sinful. Certainly the friends and families of 9/11 victims will still maintain, will always maintain, that the attacks were evil, sinful. But these friends and families will increasingly emphasize the practical necessity of letting go of their anger in order to get on with their lives. Most Americans did not personally know any of the 9/11 victims, yet many Americans felt themselves victims as well, through a kind of imaginative identification with the bona fide victims. Even more important, many Americans have learned to place the 9/11 attacks within the context of a complex struggle between two forces, each of which vilifies the other. Media coverage of 9/11 drove home to some Americans the extent to which many foreigners believed Americans had brought the attacks on themselves. Those who died in the 9/11 attacks were not at fault, but those who supported and planned the attacks can be seen as confused individuals expressing their religious enthusiasm in a hateful, terribly misguided way.

When it comes to obtaining forgiveness, part of the challenge seems to be gaining the sympathy of others. To do this, you might swear off what you did and insist you'll never do it again. More difficult but more effective is convincing, ever so subtly, those you've offended, and perhaps an entire audience, that anyone would have done the same in your place. You have to learn to show how and why sinners run amok in the first place. Think here of the British play *Talking to Terrorists* (2005) or the best-selling novel *The Reader* (1997), in which readers are cleverly induced to sympathize with an illiterate Nazi prison guard named Hannah.[64] That people trapped in desperate circumstances choose to do evil does not excuse their acts; however, the context in which the decision to perform an evil act was made bears on our moral evaluation of the person. We can exploit that insight to our own ends, or we can push on it to get self-righteous critics to yield ever so slightly in the course of their rage against us.

Two contemporary films usefully dramatize the refusal to forgive and drive home the terrible consequences of such decisions. Lars von Trier's *Breaking the Waves* (2000) and Michael Tolkin's *The Rapture* (1990) take up the moral impasse from different angles. Von Trier, a Danish atheist who converted to Roman Catholicism in adulthood, depicts a deeply religious Protestant woman named Bess rejected by her family and community for having acceded to the admittedly bizarre sexual requests of her paralyzed husband, and Tolkin offers an account of another Protestant woman, Sharon, who murders her own child in an effort to help the little girl experience the joy of union with Jesus in heaven. Sharon later regrets the murder and refuses to forgive God for having allowed her to carry through with the act. Sharon lives to see the end of the world and tells God that she'd rather spend eternity in hell than forgive him. Her decision is surely not in her own best interest, but then believers will likely argue that sin never lies in our best interest.

But whereas Sharon might strike viewers as embittered and self-pitying, von Trier's Bess is another story altogether. Full of hope and love for God, Bess gladly accepts physical brutality, humiliation, and ultimately the shunning of her parents and pious community in order to redeem her husband. Bess believes that she bears the blame for her husband's paralysis, for she had beseeched God to bring her husband home from his distant work on an oil rig. The terrible accident that returned him to her once and for all was her own fault—for God had given her what she asked (meanwhile, her family worries that she has lost her senses). To please her immobile husband, she agrees to begin having sex with strange men and reporting back to him the sordid details. When she allows men to use her sexually, she brings happiness to her frustrated husband but forfeits her place in both a family and a community that will not forgive her "sacrifices." Bess believes in atonement; she stakes her personal safety on redemption, the Zamboni effect. Bess has learned—as her neighbors have not—that there is something more important than law. That is love. Bess prompts us to ask whether love might even surpass in importance our own self-esteem. It seems that Bess could forgive anything, even people who did not understand love.

Both films leave viewers aching for forgiveness and bristling at the destructive consequences of denying it. Both films place viewers in an all-knowing position, a position from which it makes sense to conclude "Tout comprendre, c'est tout pardonner." Far from encouraging simplistic answers to life's sometimes vexing problems, these films depict both the dramatic simplicity and the high cost of making the mental move to forgive someone. It should come as no surprise that the Zamboni is not free—God can run it in one realm without charge, but you've got to pay to move it in this realm, the world of people who do not want to forgive us.

MUSICAL CHAIRS

In conclusion, you can get terrified people to do just about anything. For many centuries, Christians feared dying while in a state of sin, for they would be punished with eternal damnation or a lengthy stay in purgatory.[65] Today, much of this fear has disappeared. The penalties for sin still apply, nonetheless. When you really think about it, a good death comes down to luck as much as virtue. For if a Catholic has made a proper confession to a priest just before he dies, he's in good shape. If you're a Protestant, the situation is considerably easier: you make an earnest petition to God to forgive your transgressions (all by yourself), and you gain forgiveness. Either way, death and salvation for Christians can resemble a game of musical chairs: when the music suddenly stops, you'd better be sure you know how to find the ground beneath you quickly.[66]

You can also rationalize just about anything. This exercise in excusing or erasing personal wrongdoing works more smoothly in a culture in which "everyone's doing it" or "the rat race at the office demands it." The goal of atonement overlaps with the goal of rationalization: to absolve ourselves from nagging feelings of guilt or worthlessness. An increase in the frequency of rationalization might indicate an increase in our ability to forgive ourselves (as opposed to obtaining forgiveness from someone else). The reason so many American Catholics lost interest in confession in the mid-1970s might have something important to do with an enhanced ability to forgive themselves.[67]

People who don't believe in God have a considerably easier time with atonement. God is cut out of the equation, and a spiritual Zamboni is unnecessary. God can hardly blame people who don't believe in him for damaging their relationship with him. Beyond that, overcoming guilty feelings (e.g., using birth control or engaging in gay sex) may diminish the intensity of belief in God. It may be that nonbelievers hold themselves in spiritual prison: they don't expect God's mercy because they just can't bring themselves to. Hamlet's uncle Claudius famously cries, "My words to heaven fly," but understands that God will not hear his prayers (Act III, Scene iii). In his soliloquy, Claudius admits to killing his brother and tries to atone for his sins by praying. It dawns on him that although he can find the words to ask for forgiveness, he doesn't believe what he is saying. Meanwhile, Hamlet stealthily enters the scene and then forfeits a perfect opportunity to kill his uncle. Spying on the praying Claudius, Hamlet fears that killing his uncle while he prays will result in the instant forgiveness of Claudius's sins; Hamlet fears that killing the praying Claudius will send his uncle's soul directly to heaven.

Claudius knew that his contrition was not genuine and suspected that he would not be forgiven. It wasn't really God who had turned his back on Claudius; it was Claudius who had turned his back on God. Through atonement, then, believers help themselves turn toward God. Believers refresh their own faith.

Roman Catholic confession is much easier today than old-fashioned penance or self-flagellation, but many American Catholics cannot be bothered to go. It could be that a return to harshness would increase the rate of Catholic confessions. When Galileo sinned against the church in the late sixteenth century, he was publicly forced to undergo a trial and perform penance before living out the rest of his life under house arrest. Some Catholics will say they believe they are largely forgiven because they are generally willing to perform penitential exercises outlined by the church. After penances had become lighter and more arbitrary, the answer to the question "How do I know I am forgiven?" had to be found elsewhere than in the willing performance of frightful penitential exercises. After the Council of Trent, penance became one of the most distinctive aspects of Roman Catholicism. Catholicism lost a good deal of its distinctiveness in the 1970s, when atonement fatigue largely displaced confession.

It is difficult to gauge the frequency of Protestant penance, because it is almost always conducted in private. Catholic confessions, which entail a priest, can be counted. Despite the changes from a public and quite harsh system of penance to a modern and essentially private one (of course, a priest hears the confession), prayer and a resolve to change for the better bridge the two forms. The rigor of arduous penances no doubt sharpened and revivified a sinner's faith. Guilt may be harder to dislodge in a penitential system that asks little of the contrite. Guilt, of course, remains a serious, psychological consequence of sin: it was the condition of divine disfavor that meant the sinner had fallen from grace, lost heaven, and become liable to eternal punishment. An appealing alternative to arduous penances might be the old-fashioned pilgrimage (Protestant theme parks and resorts are booming and may serve a role analogous to Rome, Lourdes, and Fatima, destinations popular with Catholic pilgrims). An interesting form of penance that would repay further study is that of exile: for centuries, political leaders would choose not to kill a problem person such as Seneca or Napoleon but to send him far away. The separation from home endured might resonate with the painful narratives found in Dante's *Purgatory*. Today, Americans still maintain forms of "virtual" exile such as voting disenfranchisement and running for political office.

Secular vestiges of older religious sensibilities persist in the twelve-step programs of groups such as Alcoholics Anonymous and Gamblers Anonymous.[68] Fear of or revulsion to sin encourages us away from a narcissistically self-reflective state of mind. Twelve-step programs develop a sense of human vulnerability that serves much the same end. The self-help movement of the 1970s proclaimed that we are not to blame for our compulsions and addictions; in the process, this new culture took the sting out of sin and gave us confidence to reject our own responsibility for what we do.[69] People who cannot be held fully responsible for their actions have an easier time arguing for forgiveness. Meanwhile, neurotic Jews and guilty Catholics are constantly atoning for their sins, at least according to stereotype or cultural profiles. Even this kind of easily recognizable neurosis, though, can lead to narcissism—and cynicism as well, for various authors have questioned the moral responsibility of people who "hide" behind their disability.[70]

Today the legal literature on remedies reveals the same kind of mental effort required to dispense an appropriate penance. How can a court decide how much to compensate a victim for the loss of an eye, an arm, a car, or a career? Christian theologians had been trying to "connect the dots" between sin and penance for centuries when modern juries took up a similar moral struggle. Damages and rewards are the flip side of sin and penance. Religious people couldn't expect to get much sympathy from secular juries by invoking the parable of the Prodigal Son, but Christian audiences might well extend sympathy after such a comparison had been made (think of President George W. Bush and his erstwhile drinking problem). Atonement in the religious sphere requires less of a wrongdoer than atonement in the penal system. This is perhaps as it should be, yet it bears noticing how remarkable it is that Christians have moved beyond an insistence on public penance. Or had moved—television may be reinstating an ancient tradition.

Generally speaking, we see more and more fatigue with atonement. In exploring apocalyptic communities in the ancient world, Harvard Business School professor Rosabeth Kanter found that the stronger and more difficult the conversion experience, the stronger and more unshakable the resulting beliefs. If a group is made up largely or entirely of converts, its cohesiveness tends to be much greater than a group whose membership is filled by casual affiliation with no decisive rejection of other choices.[71] If the prize hardly seems worth the fight, people repenting of their sins may lose interest in atonement, which comes too cheaply. From an organizational standpoint, setting the price of atonement higher would increase its worth, even as the price rise would reduce the number of people willing to pay for it. Atonement fatigue comes down to a variety of factors, factors that are each in an important way psychological. With atonement fatigue has come a decrease in the sense of mystery and magic that once pervaded much of religious experience in North America and Western Europe.[72]

Adulterers—at least, female ones—used to live a stone's throw away from punishment. They no longer do. Rending your garments in the town square, beating your breast convulsively, or spreading ashes on your forehead has gone out of fashion. Today Jews and Christians apologize to God more discreetly, perhaps less stirringly: the Zamboni responds even to the demure, though. Christians who reflect on Jesus's words "Ye shall not be let out until the last penny has been paid" or on the frightening images of the Last Judgment may still quake on their knees. Other Christians will more casually reassure themselves that the God they worship can forgive anything.

Meanwhile, the news media delight in exposing the hypocrisy of sin hunters. Aversion to this hypocrisy, coupled with the reassuring notion that God can forgive anything, fuels atonement fatigue. We're not sure God really demands it, and we're not sure we really believe atonement works today. If porn stars and corporate thieves can mainstream themselves through atonement, then it may seem that anyone can get away with anything. Ultimately, atonement fatigue emerges as a primary symptom of sin fatigue.

II

LOST SINS, CASUALTIES OF FATIGUE

3

CATHOLIC MASTURBATION AND MODERN SCIENCE

In part because sexual sins must be the most common of all, the very idea of sexual propriety is dissolving into fodder for stand-up comedy acts. Surely one of the clearest arenas in which to isolate sin fatigue lies in masturbation. Not only does almost everyone do it, but some scientists now claim it can prolong a man's life. When talking about science and sin generally, we might think of epidurals (remember that God told Adam and Eve that childbirth would henceforth involve pain), the abortion of defective fetuses, or face transplants. Science can tempt us away from old views of sin, and masturbation is no exception here. How a religious group will respond to perceived attacks on an arguably trivial sin can tell us a lot about how that religious group will negotiate meatier issues.

Various sexual sinners in Dante's *Inferno* insisted they hadn't done anything terribly bad, and that was long before scientists invented the birth control pill. The availability of a reliable, oral contraceptive in the 1960s has utterly transformed thinking about sex in the West and, arguably, increased the frequency of sexual transgressions. Attitudes and mores may be more relaxed, but the rules have not changed—indeed, in vitro fertilization (IVF) is sometimes condemned on the grounds that it necessitates masturbation. If rule changes are to begin anywhere, we might reasonably expect the relaxation of regulations to commence in solitary sex.

The three major faith traditions have condemned masturbation as a particularly grievous sin, yet a medical study has praised the health benefits for men of frequent masturbation.[1] It is impossible to quantify how many men over the centuries have curbed the urge to masturbate in an effort to honor religious convictions, but surely some have succeeded, and it is these cases that interest me. For these victors, winning might be losing. Forgoing male masturbation may be enabling prostate cancer.

Once again, Catholicism will serve as a useful case study. If the church has overstated its case against masturbation, then the church may be wrong about issues such as IVF, which it has forbidden in part because the process requires masturbation, and contraception. Roman Catholic opposition to contraception is well known; such opposition reduces contraceptive sex to masturbation (despite the fact that the birth control pill does not come between sperm and egg but rather prevents ovulation). If the Catholic world were to smile on contraception in some official way, then masturbation would raise its puzzling head anew. In the early twenty-first century, when adolescent oral sex seemed to supersede masturbation (although not eliminate it entirely), masturbation seemed even less capable of arousing moral concern.[2] A religion genuinely intent on curbing adolescent sex (which is frequently unsafe) or adultery might find good reason to turn a blind eye to masturbation or at least move to a "don't ask, don't tell" policy. Moreover, the religious group responsible for the Galileo embarrassment might find another reason for fearing the effects of scientific advancement, insofar as scientific discoveries might come up with new ways of honoring the "sanctity of life" trumpeted by Catholic leaders.

A SIN DYING ON THE VINE

Doubts about the sinfulness of masturbation were already rampant before the American television show *Seinfeld* captivated millions of viewers and normalized the practice on a prize-winning episode in the early 1990s that featured a competition among the main characters to see who could go the longest without masturbating.[3] Roman Catholics are far from alone in exhorting men (and women) not to masturbate. Indeed, some of the strongest voices in the chorus of condemnation have been Protestant (e.g., Rousseau, Tissot, and Sylvester Graham). For the sake of convenience, though, I will focus on Catholics here. As late as the mid-1970s, as we'll see, a pope would still claim publicly that those who masturbate forfeit the love of God.

Given the extraordinary medical advances of the twentieth century, it does not seem prudent for any religion to insist it can ignore or automatically override troublesome medical discoveries. Stem cell research, for example, has enraged various religious factions not because of potential outcomes (which seem uniformly positive) but rather the cost of those outcomes, specifically, the destruction of human embryos. Despite governmental obstacles strewn in its way, science will forge ahead and likely find cures for diseases (perhaps Parkinson's) through stem cell research anyway. And no small number of protesting believers will later avail themselves of the cures wrought by stem cell research, thereby raising the question of the point of religious or moral opposition.

What interests me here is the possibility that subsequent medical studies will prove that masturbation cleanses the prostate gland and reduces the frequency of cancer. Can Catholicism officially reverse its position on masturbation without losing face? How could a religion knowingly recommend that its followers disregard medical insights that could preserve good health? This chapter points to an emerging Catholic problem without solving it: thinking believers need a way to adjudicate between competing religious and medical claims, just as Catholic theologians need a way of protecting moral truths from competing claims. This discussion of the dying sin of masturbation raises a much larger question, that of the power of science to squelch sin (this broader topic, treated properly, would require a separate book).

Although the masturbation question may be novel, the apparent conflict of science and religion is certainly not. Geologists, astronomer, and biologists since Darwin have undermined the central tenet of creationism, for example. To take another: Scientists have now managed to breed pigs capable of secreting the omega-3 fatty acids found in salmon.[4] These salubrious acids are unavailable to many people who cannot rely on finding salmon nearby or in the grocery store. Yet many Jews and Muslims eschew pork products; as such, these Jews and Muslims would forgo certain health benefits in the name of their religious beliefs. Other examples suggest themselves. Christian Scientists refuse all medical treatment and consequently put themselves at higher risk of early (and medically unnecessary) death. Roman Catholics claim to eschew physician-assisted suicide, a position that may prolong a terribly painful death. The list continues.

Followers of religions that eschew the consumption of alcohol would seem to forgo certain health benefits as well. Not just Mormons and

Muslims but also Protestants of various stripes swear off wine. Clinical tests, however, seem to prove the salubrious effects of wine (which include lowering the risk for heart disease).[5] Other tests have apparently established the salubrious effects of coffee, which can reduce the incidence of liver cancer.[6] Mormons, however, will not drink beverages containing caffeine. Of course, the faithful of any religious group may retort that salvation concerns them more than bodily health, even as others from their own ranks may wonder why the two need be pitted against one another. Catholics now find themselves in the same boat as antialcohol and anticaffeine sects (again, Muslims and Jews have also condemned masturbation as an important sin).

As contemporary believers struggle to reconcile what they read in the newspaper with what they believe about God, masturbation jokes proliferate on television and in popular films.

CATHOLIC MASTURBATION: FORBIDDEN?

In this section, we'll see that Roman Catholic moral theology is not so immutable as might be thought, at least not with respect to masturbation. Lingering disapproval, though, raises a bioethical problem.

Garry Wills, perhaps the most energetic intellectual in America today and certainly one of the most creative of contemporary Catholic thinkers, has taken his church to task for its stance on masturbation. That an otherwise-good Catholic would be kept out of heaven for having masturbated strikes him as a singularly ridiculous idea, one that must be defused once and for all. (He is not alone here, especially among Catholic intellectuals.) Although masturbation remains officially forbidden, the Catholic position started to soften in the 1950s. Outside of Catholicism, serious academic interest in masturbation has taken off.[7] Academic research, like jokes in movies and television sitcoms, has eased discussion of the subject.

Like Evangelical Christians generally, Catholics continue to disapprove of masturbation. In *Christian Courtship in an Oversexed World*, a committed Catholic author warns:

> Since the appetite listens to the senses, you must be careful about what you look at or watch. Viewing sexually explicit movies of pornography or even focusing on provocatively dressed members of the opposite sex is

poison if you are seeking chastity. The worst of these is viewing porno-graphic web sites or materials, since pornography depicts sex as merely recreational and women (or men) as mere objects of enjoyment.[8]

The danger of masturbation or hanky-panky with another is clear: "To freely and knowingly violate chastity is to destroy that relationship with the Lord, a relationship which is our source of happiness and our only way to salvation. To destroy that is a huge price to pay for a few mo-ments of pleasure." The verb *destroy* (as opposed to, say, *compromise* or *harm*) sounds dangerously permanent. Although the book does not bear an imprimatur (an official sign that the teaching authority of the church approves of the book's contents), it hardly needs one, insofar as it raises no challenge to tradition. Protestants generally see eye-to-eye here; Lauren Winner's exhortation to chastity in *Real Sex: The Naked Truth about Chastity* endorses a similar conservative objection.[9] Part of the traditional Protestant objection to Catholic clergy is the likelihood that celibacy will lead to frequent masturbation (or, almost inevitably, at least to occasional masturbation).

The larger question to which this section will lead is whether medical proof (which the Australian study hasn't yet established) of a therapeu-tic benefit could throw the balance in favor of definitively reversing the Catholic position. If so, then we are left to ponder what other moral po-sitions the Catholic Church might eventually find itself compelled to re-verse by scientific advances, as well as the possibility that science de-serves more reverence than theology. The risk is clear: a medically related reversal might undermine the authority of the church's position on what may have once seemed a purely moral (that is, nonmedical) position.

In his best-selling book *Papal Sin*, Garry Wills writes:

Take the matter of masturbation. Until very recently, young boys were taught that every act of masturbation was a mortal sin, one that drained the soul of grace and sent it to hell if one died before repenting and con-fessing it. They were even given weighty arguments in theology. In mat-ters of the Sixth Commandment (in the Catholic numbering), there is "no parvity of matter"—every sexual act but that between marital partners not practicing contraception is "grave" (i.e., every such sin is a mortal sin). This made young teenagers hardened sinners, who were blackening their souls time after time, all through adolescence. Yet they were often confessing to men who, without the excuse of adolescence, were mastur-bating themselves.[10]

Wills asks what kind of a religion will send people to hell simply for masturbating. He bemoans the fact that the official masturbation policy has not changed in his own religion (he acknowledges that Catholic culture is moving away from the official Vatican position) and blames the impossibility of changing doctrine in Catholicism. As I've indicated, one of the reasons why Roman Catholicism forbids artificial insemination is that it requires masturbation of a man (some Catholics had proposed using a punctured condom in sexual intercourse, a condom that could be mined for residual sperm immediately after coition, but this suggestion was condemned).[11]

Bernard Häring, the most influential Roman Catholic moral theologian of the twentieth century, turned to masturbation in several works. He tried hard to include "wiggle room" in his theology: "Wherefore what authors in another age or area rightly condemn as gravely immodest might justly be judged more leniently in other times or areas. And since the converse is likewise true, this must be borne in mind in appraising the casuistry of earlier moralists as, for instance, Saint Alphonse."[12] While alerting all faithful Catholics to the dangers of lust, Häring carefully acknowledges the shifting sands on which moral values rest. He cautions, "All that we say in the following discussion on modesty or immodesty in looks, touches, and reading (lectures) must always be understood in the light of the reservations indicated above. We are dealing primarily with directive prudential norms corresponding to the current sentiment of the middle European (i.e. of Western Man) of the twentieth century. Hence these pronouncements are not unqualified or absolute." He offers as an example primitive tribes that simultaneously enforce high moral standards and allow (perhaps expect) women in the tribe to go about naked. Häring writes with unusual self-awareness.

In a later work, Häring ties masturbation to narcissism, "an imprisonment in the selfish youth."[13] He allows that adults may bear the responsibility for the masturbation of an adolescent who has not received the love and attention he is due. He agrees that educators must be warned that "immense mischief has been done by grossly overemphasizing the harm done by masturbation." By the end, Häring seems a sympathetic soul indeed, clearly opposed to damning masturbators. "But if it is a case of persons who are generous and sincerely striving, the presumption is that it is subjectively not a great sin but, rather, can be a mixture of suffering and not-yet-overcome egotism."[14] This represents a real departure from Thomas Aquinas, one of the lynchpins of the Catholic moral position, who listed masturbation as an "unnatural vice," along with sodomy and bestiality (*Summa Theologica* II-II, q. 154).

Häring was not the only Catholic theologian to address masturbation in the 1970s. On December 29, 1975, the Congregation for the Doctrine of the Faith issued a declaration on sexual ethics bearing the pedestrian title "Declaration on Certain Questions Concerning Sexual Ethics." In addition to reaffirming the highly divisive and controversial teaching of *Humanae Vitae* (often referred to as "the birth control encyclical"), it touched on masturbation. The 1975 document attacked the grave sin of onanism. The pope explained that the masturbator forfeits the love of God. Beyond that, he maintained that masturbation qualifies as a mortal sin, "even though it is not possible to prove unequivocally that Holy Scripture expressly repudiates this sin as such."[15]

As we saw in chapter 1, though, full knowledge of the sinfulness of any mortal sin stands as a prerequisite for the category. Given the astonishment many Catholic men express when they learn about their church's stance on masturbation, it seems safe to presume that fewer and fewer of the faithful consider this common practice gravely sinful. The sin of masturbation is not only foundering but also threatening the reputations of other mortal sins, such as murder and blasphemy.

THE AUSTRALIAN STUDY

Roughly a decade after *Seinfeld* mainstreamed masturbation, a team of Australian researchers pitted the bodily health of a nonmasturbating man against his spiritual well-being. Science now challenges religion in a new way.

No one would deny that prostate cancer merits sustained study. It has become one of the leading killers of men in the Western Hemisphere. Prostate cancer is now the most common disease among males, with around twenty thousand new cases a year in Britain. Despite the fact that it was diagnosed in an estimated 189,000 men in the United States in 2002 and led to the death of over 30,000, there is no universally agreed-on strategic plan for its diagnosis and management.

In July 2003, a group of Australian scientists claimed that frequent masturbation could protect men from prostate cancer.[16] These researchers reasoned that ejaculation can flush cancer-triggering agents from the prostate gland and can also induce prostate cells to mature fully. Consequently, these researchers encouraged men between the ages of twenty and fifty to masturbate regularly, at least once a day. Frequent masturbation, particularly when a man is in his twenties, will supposedly make him less susceptible to carcinogens.

Working in concert with the seminal vesicles, the prostate produces most of the fluid in semen, a fluid rich in potassium, zinc, fructose, and citric acid. Some experts think this buildup of chemicals helps to trigger cancer in vulnerable men; ejaculation seems to have a protective effect because the prostate secretes the bulk of the fluid in semen, and ejaculation cleans and clears the prostate gland.

Few experts had considered masturbation as a weapon against prostate cancer. Australian scientists discovered the link after questioning 1,079 men with prostate cancer about their sexual habits. Their responses were compared with those of 1,259 healthy men of the same age. Men who had ejaculated more than five times a week in their twenties were a third less likely to develop aggressive prostate cancer later in life.

The most likely explanation for preferring ejaculations from masturbation over ejaculations from sexual intercourse is that infections caused by intercourse promote prostate cancer, say the scientists. Previous studies had suggested that frequent sexual activity can increase the risk of prostate cancer by up to 40 percent. This is because some sexual infections may act as a trigger for prostate cancer, which is clearly not a risk in masturbation. But ejaculations without intercourse appear to be protective. Graham Giles of the Cancer Council of Victoria in Melbourne believes that the association would be even more striking if masturbation were studied on its own.

The key to preventing prostate cancer lies in a man's own hands, so to speak, and a Catholic man who follows Rome would seem to be subjecting himself to greater physical risk. Anthony Smith, of the Australian Research Centre in Sex, Health and Society at La Trobe University in Melbourne, recommends male masturbation on medical grounds.

Overlooking the possibility that men may not need any such encouragement, the question under consideration now is: To what lengths may a man go to reduce the threat of death by prostate cancer—forfeiting his eternal salvation? This question returns us to a conflict that the twentieth century may have detonated but did not eliminate. Today, it is worthwhile to gauge the state of that scientific/religious conflict from the vantage point of a single medical advance (or the promise of one). A breakthrough in masturbation research should not be dismissed too quickly as trivial, given the prevalence of the underlying practice and the therapeutic promise that practice holds. Even though American doctors concluded in the summer of 2006 that drinking pomegranate juice could significantly decrease the likelihood that a man would suffer from prostate cancer, still it remains that the Australian study deserves to be considered carefully.[17] The UCLA study found pomegranate juice to be effective in reducing prostate cancer in men who were already suffering from the disease; it was not clear that the juice could help prevent the disease, although subsequent tests may show as much and consequently displace any medical benefits of masturbation.

EVOLVING RELIGIOUS ETHICS

We've seen that the Catholic ethic of masturbation was already evolving before news of the Australian study splashed over newspapers. The reasons for this evolution were largely unscientific (earlier belief that the homunculus, or live man, inhabited the sperm had already been discredited by science in the eighteenth century). What role will a *scientific* reason play in a religious ethic? Do we already privilege science over law, culture, and art? I think so, particularly with regard to forensic evidence in courtrooms (DNA has become many an attorney's focus, as either trump card or bogeyman).

Galenus, the great medical authority of antiquity, had justified masturbation on medical grounds when necessary for the release of tension (he allowed only one ejaculation per month, however). Roman Catholics have ignored this secondary therapeutic benefit of masturbation, calling the practice instead intrinsically evil.

The notion of intrinsic evil at work in the 1975 document involves the conviction that some acts are wrong in spite of circumstances. Catholic tradition has maintained that adultery, unjust killing of the innocent, and the use of contraception are intrinsically wrong. Probing the sin of masturbation pays off in a better understanding of contraception, a topic of interest to a larger number of people. The norms against these actions are believed to share the same characteristic insofar as the types of action they identify are specifiable, as potential objects of choice, without reliance on any evaluative term that presupposes a moral judgment of the action. Richard McCormick, among other Catholic ethicists, has argued that what had been regarded as exceptionless norms in traditional theology were in fact based on teleological grounds; hence, calculation of consequences is vital to establishing which norms are virtually exceptionless and which depend on a given situation.

The masturbation policy would seem to expose a conflict: new knowledge might show that the traditional policy conflicts with one of Catholicism's professed principles, to cherish life and protect one's health.

Consequentialists claim that the right thing to do in any situation is the act that delivers the best consequences. (One prominent form of consequentialism is utilitarianism, according to which the value to be maximized is human happiness.) Only those who are predisposed toward consequentialism will be concerned to discover its limits. But given that life is what hangs in the balance, wouldn't the Magisterium, or teaching authority of the Catholic Church, be compelled to agree that this particular consequence demands sympathy? Perhaps not; given the reverence for martyrdom in Roman Catholicism, and given that prostate cancer generally afflicts older if not elderly men, the Magisterium might stick to its guns.

Given masturbation's remoteness from the core of the faith, the church ought to forget about masturbation as it proceeds with its mission of offering moral guidance. This sin should be sacrificed, both to physiology and to psychiatry. If medical studies can indeed prove the efficacy of male masturbation as an anticancer agent, then the very norm itself should change in Catholicism (one thinks here of the Catholic position on slavery or on Galileo). Further clinical tests linking frequent masturbation to lower incidence of prostate cancer may demonstrate that the Catholic list of sins needs updating.

TAKING MATTERS INTO ONE'S OWN HANDS

Georges Simenon (d. 1989), the great Belgian detective novelist, reports a collision of personal hope and Catholic policy in his *Intimate Memoirs*. Before the birth of their son Jean, he and his wife, Denise, then very far along in her pregnancy, visited a gynecological clinic in Arizona, which had been strongly recommended to them. But they left it immediately upon seeing a notice that "in accordance with the decision of the chief physician and the mother superior, in grave situations the fate of the child would take precedence over that of the mother." Simenon writes, "A cold shudder ran down our backs, and we tiptoed back out." Their son was born in a hospital that was less authentically Catholic.[18]

It seems inconceivable that Roman Catholic hospitals might post signs in patient rooms forbidding masturbation or explaining that spiritual concern for a patient will override physical or emotional ones in the instance of patients caught masturbating furtively. And yet as long as religious disapproval of masturbation remains, some men will avoid a practice that might benefit their health.

The Australian scientist Graham Giles has positioned himself as the Galileo of masturbation, it seems. He has heralded a significant problem for some Roman Catholics. In the clash between medical progress and religious values, medical solutions will likely prevail, particularly with regard to masturbation, which young men are inclined to do anyway. What does the avoidance of sin have to do with the avoidance of disease? In the past, steering away from promiscuous sex (a sin) reduced or eliminated the likelihood of contracting a sexually transmitted disease or needing an abortion. With regard to masturbation, avoidance might signal a problem for men. Believers looking forward to heaven understand that prostate cancer would never count as a strike against them on Judgment Day. And so, absent explicit approval from Rome, some Catholic men will decide to risk prostate cancer instead of heaven. In this, Catholic men will likely behave as non-Catholic men. Science will not exactly have begun a masturbation revolution, only further undermined the foundation of a sin whose time had come.

The Catholic Church could respond to the alleged therapeutic benefits of masturbation along four primary lines: (1) admitting fault and amending their relevant moral theology (much as they did with respect to Galileo and slavery), (2) denying fault and digging in their heels (much as the Vatican has done with regard to the questions of female priests and gay marriage), (3) ignoring the problem altogether, and (4) taking the *via media* by appropriating certain insights from medical studies.

While option 1 might seem most prudent, it would entail certain refutations. For example, Augustine, the lynchpin of Roman Catholic theology, once asserted that masturbation poses such a grave moral danger that a man would be better off copulating with his mother than wasting his precious seed alone. This mentality would fall off the table as an appropriate response to the moral question of masturbation (as it effectively already has). Option 3, ignoring the problem, would buy the Vatican some time but eventually lead to a Freudian "return of the repressed" if medical authorities definitively affirm the therapeutic benefits of masturbation. In the meantime, another generation of devout men would have been subjected to undue risk of prostate cancer. Option 4 seems the most likely: while applauding the renewed attention given to a growing medical problem, the Vatican could urge earlier and more frequent prostate examinations (say, an annual checkup, beginning at the age of thirty-five). Option 4 avoids the embarrassment of admitting a mistake, but it, too, entails certain costs. Other medical breakthroughs of this sort could pop up. Then the church would once again find itself trying to backpedal.

I have focused on Roman Catholicism here in part because of its size (over a billion members worldwide) and in part because of its power. Doth the Catholic Church protest too much? Today, it seems so. Science will never put religion out of business, for science can never scientifically establish whether life begins at the moment of conception, why people suffer, or whether there's life after death. Consequently, religion will actually encourage science by creating a healthy rivalry to moral authority. In the turf war for control of human conscience, religion can never lose definitively, but religion thwarts science at its peril. A religion that prizes the physical health of its followers and its own reputation as a coherent doctrine should pay close attention to ways in which science might someday undermine its own credibility. AIDS seems so much more important than masturbation, but Catholics have lifted the sin of masturbation to an equivalent moral level. The future of the planet (principally in Africa now, but once in the United States as well, under the Comstock Laws of the twentieth century), and the health of children and mothers hinges on the availability of condoms. Sex with a condom qualifies as a sin in part because such nonprocreative sex is considered essentially masturbation.

Perhaps most important of all is the question of hypocrisy—not of the church but of the good people who would like to belong to it. Anyone who feels it dishonest to join a group that forbids what he or she does with some regularity might walk away wistfully. It's not necessarily the case that "lapsed Catholics" don't care about their faith but rather that they feel dishonest when they practice it. The contemporary world seems to dislike the stark choice between spirituality and sensuality, not so much because it is difficult, but because it is wrong-headed. James

Joyce's biographer indicates that the reason Joyce left the church had to do with sex, not theology (on some level, of course, the two are linked). In 1904, Joyce wrote to his fiancée (and eventual wife) Nora, "Six years ago I left the Catholic Church, hating it most fervently. I found it impossible for me to remain in it on account of the impulses of my nature." Elsewhere in the biography of one of the greatest writers of the twentieth century, Ellmann underscores Joyce's sense of the Roman either/or: "It was also true, as he declared flatly some time afterwards to a friend, that sexual continence was impossible for him. He felt he must choose between continual guilt and some heretical exoneration of the senses."[19] Sexual liberation in Roman Catholicism would start in masturbation.

THE FAILURE OF MASTURBATION TO REMAIN ON THE SIN LIST

It is not difficult to understand the moral struggle over fetal testing. Even women who claimed to be staunchly opposed to abortion find themselves electing to have an abortion when they learn from doctors that the fetus they are carrying is defective in some significant way.[20] Unhappy consequences (in this life, not in any world to come) can undermine previous decisions about sin. If we think of the defective fetus as a potential child who could perhaps manage to find happiness, even in a brutally competitive and body-conscious world, then we may naturally cringe at the idea of aborting the fetus. Masturbation would seem to pale in importance when compared to such a complicated example as fetal testing.

The lost sin of masturbation combines incredulity with science in a particularly compelling way. Very few may know of the putative health benefits of male masturbation, yet many men and women, on reflection, marvel that so universal and vigorously repeated an act could be branded a sin. In the case of male masturbation, the science simply enlarges the incredulity, which had already essentially succeeded in undermining the sinfulness of the practice. Of course, the mere frequency of inclination does not render an act morally acceptable—think here of the human propensity to lying and stealing. Masturbation does not deserve moral defense because of its frequency but because of its salubrious effects and because of faulty assumptions about human reproduction that resulted in the condemnation of male masturbation.

In a world in which sexual austerity appears increasingly anachro-nistic, other, arguably much bolder sins inch forward on the horizon. Teen pregnancy, STDs, the "morning after" pill all speak to the gnawing conviction that much more than solitary masturbation is going on in the modern West. (In fact, given the prevalence of other sins, it might seem that less masturbation is going on today than generations ago.) And seemingly everywhere, gay marriage works its way into discussions of social justice. Sexual austerity and masturbation both have largely fallen by the wayside.

Other sins may soon face a similar end. Vanity and pride figure among the list of Christian sins (in fact, pride is the worst of them all), yet a growing number of Westerners turn to plastic surgery. It is one thing to object to the rich going in for cosmetic enhancements, but it is another to object to burn victims or cancer survivors turning to them. French doctors aroused ethical objections in 2005, when they success-fully transplanted a face for the first time. The woman who received the face of someone else (who had recently died) had lost most of her self-esteem after a vicious dog attacked and disfigured her face beyond recognition.[21] It may be objected that such an example has nothing to do with masturbation, for the desire for sexual release cannot compare to the desire to go out in public without frightening others. Even here, though, critics will have to explain again why something so private and prevalent as masturbation can be considered morally intolerable. The same people who object to abortion even when the mother's life is in danger may also argue that face transplants cross a forbidden ethical line, that we must be prepared to accept certain risks, certain kinds of suffering. Although male masturbation may prolong a man's life, anal-ogously, men should be prepared to accept the risk of a shorter, but less sinful, life and forego masturbation.

Other critics will object that masturbation is a frivolous matter, one not worthy of moral debate. These critics will fail to do justice to the Ro-man Catholic position, a position that underlies powerful opposition to stem cell research, one of the greatest hopes on our scientific horizon. The sacredness of life involves male masturbation in a crucial way. It is only a matter of time before families, intent on honoring the wish of a dying son to leave progeny in the world, will instruct doctors to extract semen from the testicles of the dying man, to be inserted into a willing woman at a later date. The Catholic Church will not bless such a pro-cedure, despite its position on the moral good of having children. Life is sacred, but within certain parameters. Catholics (but not only Catholics) rally behind the banner that all life is sacred, even the life of a "brain-dead" person. In the summer of 2005, the slow death of a Florida woman named Terri Schiavo, a Catholic, dramatized the public battle over how to deploy the power of science to keep alive brain-dead people, people who might be brought back to life by a miracle.[22]

Other criticism of the Catholic condemnation of masturbation may take unexpected forms. The French literary critic Hélène Cixous (b. 1937) has lamented in an influential essay "The Laugh of the Medusa" that too many women have obeyed the cultural edict to forgo masturbation.[23] Looking back over several centuries of philosophical and literary tracts in the West, she wonders why women have written so little, compared with the output of men. The answer, Cixous opines, may have something to do with masturbation. If women would allow themselves to do what they want, to masturbate, they will likely unleash a powerful wave of literary creativity that could benefit Western culture, even as that wave liberates women from patriarchal domination. Quite apart from scientific considerations, Cixous recommends masturbation as a means of improving human life.

According to the Law of the Conservation of Matter, matter is neither created nor destroyed under ordinary circumstances. Matter may get displaced, but it does not vanish. No one has ever tried to argue that sin is like matter, although plenty of religious people have insisted that God does not change his mind about sin (because doing so would presumably mean that God was wrong in the first place, and God can never be wrong). Science has arguably taught us that we were wrong about semen, because no such thing as the homunculus lives in it; wasting semen does not automatically kill a human being, in the way that theologians (and scientists!) used to insist. Science has taught us that we were also wrong about the "sins" of depression and alcoholism. Some predilections arise as a consequence of genetic predisposition, not character flaws.

Why would we hold on to the sinfulness of masturbation when we know that there is no homunculus living inside semen? The idea that your body is your temple invites other ways of caring for the body (e.g., staying slim, having massages done, and taking a daily multivitamin). The idea that masturbation demeans the body no longer strikes many

Westerners as plausible. Other religions would appear to have an advantage over Catholicism here, for Catholicism has codified its revulsion to masturbation, a supposed mortal sin. Catholic moral teaching denies a hierarchy within the category of mortal sin; this means that one mortal sin is as bad as another (e.g., rape or murder).

Science fuels sin fatigue. As few other forces can, science compels us to reevaluate our commitment to sin. Science could feasibly deal a mortal blow to mortal sin. Only time will tell.

4

VIRGINITY:
ALMOST A SIN?

Why do we care about virginity? Why do we care about marital fidelity? Could there be any internal connection between the two? Westerners care less and less about both virginity and the infidelity of strangers (the infidelity that happens to them is another story) and for largely the same reason: Puritanical ideals inspire less awe. Sex outside marriage remains sinful in the three major faith traditions of the West, but you might never know it, at least in certain parts of North America and Europe. As much infidelity as might be going on, there's even more premarital coitus. It's as if sex before marriage weren't even a sin anymore. This erstwhile sin slid into the realm of sin fatigue in the 1970s. Atonement fatigue also factors into the loss of reverence for virginity, as declining enthusiasm for wiping clean the slate of a sinner resembles wilting enthusiasm for the clean slate of a virgin.

How would we know if this or any value were disappearing? Would a sociological survey prove it?[1] Or a memoir from a well-placed young American who claimed to speak for her generation? Would reports of American teens having sex in the high school auditorium after an assembly tip the scales in either direction?[2] A Supreme Court decision? Films or music videos celebrating teen promiscuity? Even if we couldn't prove definitively that a given value had died (say, dating only within your own race), we could still ask how a culture would change if the value were to recede so far into the background as to resemble, say, a dim recollection of a gripping novel read a year ago. Someone may object that conservative Protestant schools stand as an exception to the culture propagated by music videos and Hollywood films. Anyone who tried to argue that the Hollywood ethos of sexual expression captures only a small demographic would have a hard time arguing that conservative Protestant colleges capture more of a demographic.

Freud asserts in *Civilization and Its Discontents* that no single person, institution, or idea has influenced Western civilization more than Christianity. Although virginity was certainly not a Christian invention, virginity lies at the heart of this world religion. The virgin son miraculously born of a virgin mother continues to fascinate many. Although the reasons for celebrating virginity may have more to do with disease or reputation today, the state itself still invites comparisons to holiness. And then there is market value to consider: the very word *deflower* suggests a reduction of one's worth in a culture that prefers the opposite.

Most of us will nod readily when we hear a television commentator or college professor claim that holiness has its degrees. Holiness is not an all-or-nothing state; it admits of varying hues. Virginity is the same. More and more of us will nod in agreement when we hear that someone can be "a virgin, sort of." Still, we're already redefining virginity. Just as we're redefining virginity, so are we redefining fidelity. In the process, we're highlighting sin fatigue. To talk about sins the West has tired of almost begs mention of sex before marriage.

TAMPING DOWN NAUGHTY THOUGHTS

This section sets out to demonstrate that early Christians valued not just female sexual purity but also male. Virginity as a category demanded such pervasive purity that the label could never have applied to many women, if any noncomatose, nonretarded men.

The Hebrew Bible celebrates procreation through various stories (e.g., Abraham, Adam and Eve, Rachel and Lia) and references to the lucky future of the Israelites. Not surprisingly, Hebrew scriptures show little enthusiasm for permanent virginity. Shun sex before marriage, yes, but get married soon. Only Jeremiah (16:2) chooses to remain unmarried (and presumably celibate). Hebrew scriptures lack a word for *bachelor*.[3] For Jews, virginity was good only if it was temporary.

The Christian teaching on virginity represented a radical break from the Hebrew scriptures. Jesus speaks admiringly of those who have "made themselves eunuchs for the kingdom of heaven" and urges, "Let him take it who can take it" (Matthew 19:12).[4] Although a dictionary can provide a definition of *virginity* ("the state of maidenhood, chastity, spinsterhood," according to Webster's), a dictionary cannot begin to indicate the emotional investment many ancient and medieval Christians placed in virginity, especially permanent virginity.

Extramarital sex spans various theological and moral categories. Extramarital sex has included in its category sexual fantasies about someone other than your spouse. Fantasies take us right to the knotty heart of both extramarital sex and virginity. For it might be thought that virginity is a purely physical state—either you have had sexual intercourse, or you haven't. A virgin hasn't.

Yet, the question would seem to be more complicated than that. In an attempt to highlight the prevalence of adultery, Laura Kipnis separated the wheat from the chaff with the following exhortation in her popular book *Against Love*: "Will all the adulterers in the room please stand up? This means all you cheating wives, philandering husbands, and straying domestic partners, past present, and future. Those who find themselves fantasizing a lot, please rise also."[5] Implicating mere fantasies in adultery might seem unfair, yet the instinct has a long, if often overlooked, history in the Christian tradition. This history holds implications for virginity.

Jesus told his disciples that the man who lusted after a woman had already committed adultery in his heart (Matthew 19:9). By the fourth century, Christians widely believed that unity with Christ was optimally achieved through celibacy and purity of thoughts. Great figures such as St. Anthony of the Desert and St. Jerome retreated from human contact in order to cleanse themselves of lust, among other social evils. The task was not easy. St. Jerome, for example, struggled:

> There was I, therefore, who from fear of hell had condemned myself to such a prison, with only scorpions and wild beasts as companions. Yet I was often surrounded by dancing girls. My face was pale from fasting, and my mind was hot with desire in a body as cold as ice. Though my flesh, before its tenant, was already as good as dead, the fires of the passions kept boiling within me.
>
> And so, destitute of all help, I used to lie at Jesus' feet. I bathed them with my tears. I wiped them with my hair. When my flesh rebelled, I subdued it with weeks of fasting.[6]

If heroic efforts such as these fail, what hope can ordinary mortals hold out? Lust often overcomes our best efforts to suffocate it.

CHAPTER 4

Augustine struggled over repeated failures to control his erections. He eventually took his stubborn penis as an apt metaphor for sin—indeed, for the fallenness of humanity after Adam and Eve. Augustine's failures suggest that any healthy young man who tries to keep sexual contact at the door will betray himself in his own pants. Augustine and other early church fathers worried about nocturnal emissions, usually referred to as "wet dreams." A boy or man who overcomes the urge to masturbate will sometimes find himself awakened by a pool of his own semen. The question of how to classify such occurrences morally exercised several theologians. In general, theologians blamed men even for what they experienced (or *did*, depending on your viewpoint) while deep in sleep. Ascetic Christian moralists linked the nocturnal emissions to sexual fantasies men had indulged in during the day. "The Fathers concluded that if one observed a truly ascetic lifestyle one should not ejaculate in one's sleep more than once every two months or even every four months."[7] And so we see evidence of moralists questioning the very idea of male chastity. But even they redoubled their enthusiasm for it.

John Cassian, another early Christian ascetic, distinguished between six degrees of chastity:

1. The monk avoids succumbing to the assaults of the flesh while conscious and awake.
2. The monk rejects voluptuous thoughts.
3. The sight of a woman does not move the monk any longer.
4. The monk no longer gets erections while awake.
5. No reference to the sexual act in the holy texts affects the monk any more than if he were thinking about the process of making bricks.
6. The seduction of female fantasies does not delude him while he sleeps.

Cassian gently allowed that the fantasy itself is not a sin, yet the presence of the fantasy indicates that "lust is still hiding in the marrow."[8] Cassian breaks down the state of chastity to small steps one can take gradually. The largeness of the goal thus becomes less daunting, more realistic.

Keeping sexual thoughts at bay has traditionally found help in the efforts of the censor and the mullah. Banning sexually explicit films, plays, and music makes it easier to avoid involuntary arousal.[9] Forcing women to veil themselves, for example, makes it easier for (heterosexual) men to avoid lust. Dressing conservatively in general sends a signal to others that you are not sexually available. It may be that we do our neighbors and colleagues a big favor by making it difficult to see our bodies through clothing, yet the idea of "dressing for success" has taken off in the American workplace. Just try to get a promotion in corporate America wearing baggy, unfashionable clothes. The goal in the streets of America now seems to be to encourage lust, not tamp it down.

Who knows how many Christian children have grown up dreading the lust they felt. Countless generations of Catholic schoolchildren likely have, so I'll focus on the Catholic tradition once again. Catholic children learn to expel dirty thoughts from their minds, just as you would turn away an unwelcome guest at the door (albeit an unwelcome guest who knocks every hour of the day). An age-old strategy calls for visualizing the object of your lust as a skeleton, the skeleton he or she will become after death, when the inevitable decay has robbed the body of its sexiness.

Bernard Häring, the most influential Roman Catholic theologian of the twentieth century, states explicitly in his magnum opus *The Law of Christ* (1956) that it is a mortal sin to fantasize about someone else while having sex with your spouse.[10] And so the mental ploys children learn in Catholic school come in handy later in life, for temptation never ends. Better to strengthen the muscles of repression in childhood than to have to start from scratch in adulthood. Shunning masturbation can help children develop those spiritual muscles as well.

The forbidden, like the impossible, calls out to us throughout life. The sexual realm is no exception. And so the moment you forbid something, you create a fantasy for a large class of people (sexual harassment laws in the United States have fanned the flames of corporate lust as perhaps nothing else could). Take, for example, Straightcollegemen.com, an American Web site that invites gay men to indulge their fantasy of seducing a man who is *totally straight*! The producer of the Web site goes to great lengths in each new interview to "prove" that the young man about to strip, shower, and masturbate is *heterosexual*, as opposed to a mere actor pretending. Some gay men find excitement in the idea of invading territory presumably off-limits to them.

Whether a particular experience is forbidden or practically unobtainable, men and women may continue to differ over desires. Old profiles

103

of gender differences bear themselves out in sex surveys: men seek sex for pleasure and physical release, whereas women seek sex for love and long-term commitment. Men's daydreams, psychologists and psychiatrists tell us, will generally be rougher and more adventurous than women's (which is not to say that women never fantasize about rough or even forced sex).[11]

Philosophically, an ethics of fidelity would seem to require an ethics of fantasy.[12] Western morality has long focused on actions, leaving thoughts, desires, and inclinations largely up in the air (here we see the influence of Kant). For sexual assault and rape must have some relation, however tenuous, to fantasies. More to the point here, virtually no one over the age of five (if we believe Freud) could be construed a virgin. Given the advertising industry today, the goal of keeping one's thoughts pure would seem hopeless. Billboards, radios, television programs, films, and music videos seem intent on luring us into lustful thoughts.

Perhaps it's not so surprising, then, to read a book such as *The Day America Told the Truth*, in which the overwhelming majority of those polled confessed to sexual fantasies (married people, too).[13] We should take with a grain of salt the findings of this book, for 91 percent of Americans confessed to lying habitually. Yet few will debate the shocking finding that Americans regularly lose the battle to tamp down their erotic reveries. The sad underside of a book such as *The Day America Told the Truth* will offend those who, like Häring, only want to keep our minds clean. For in the course of notifying us that Americans fantasize, the authors list twenty-three sexual fantasies. The danger of educating anyone about sex is that you toss your audience new ideas.

The point to be taken here is that you lose your virginity if you indulge in sexual fantasies (or so it has been argued by some theologians). Early Christians conceived of virginity in a way that was doomed to fail. Because of the physiological tendency of nonmasturbating boys to experience nocturnal emissions, virginity amounted essentially to an impossibility. If erotic dreams and nocturnal emissions made you impure (this point is implicit, rather than explicit, in the literature), disqualified you from the ranks of "virgin," then no one could enjoy the honor. The ideal was inhuman. It might also have been somewhat unappealing, as anyone who had heard of the joy of sex would perhaps feel a tinge of pity in the company of a (supposed) virgin.

ORAL SEX

I have nodded to a clear-cut distinction between acting and thinking. Jesus and Bernard Häring didn't so much blur the distinction between these two areas as tie virginity to both of them. Today, moderns might reasonably limit virginity to the realm of *action*. According to this logic, virginity is exclusively a function of penetrating (if you're a man) or being penetrated (if you're a woman or a man in a submissive position). However, the ground is shifting beneath us. A new generation sees oral sex as irrelevant to the determination of virginity. According to this new way of thinking, all that matters is penile-vaginal penetration. Nothing else counts. (An important exception here would be the legal category of sexual harassment.)

According to a lengthy exposé in the *Washington Post*, many teenage American girls in 2003 insisted that oral sex doesn't "count" and that a girl remains a virgin after having performed fellatio.[14] What can these teenagers possibly be thinking when they confess to engaging in mutual oral sex while insisting on the innocence of the act? It's not that they also view sex (proper words slip away from us here—i.e., accurate descriptions of what used to pass as sex) as innocent, too. They don't. They just don't see fellatio as an instance of sex (which would make the term *oral sex* a misnomer). By 2006, the American media could reasonably write of "the blowjob's emergence as the nation's signature sex act."[15] It's not just teenage girls, of course.

Think of Bill Clinton. Think of Senator Chuck Robb. These teenage girls may not be right to deny that fellatio qualifies as sex, but they're not exactly alone in their thinking, either. Meanwhile, a generational divide widens. In 1999, a female psychotherapist wrote in the popular online journal *Salon* of the great difficulty of understanding young women who talk to her about sex while insisting that the fellatio they perform on men is not sex.[16] Shari Thurer explains that women of her generation (having grown up in the 1960s) tended to regard oral-genital contact as the *most* intimate form of sexual encounter; the new idea that such activity should qualify as the *least* intimate form baffled her, as did the idea that a girl who stops at oral-genital contact can still legitimately consider herself a virgin.[17] Perhaps even more difficult to understand are young women who allow anal but not vaginal sex, all in order to keep intact their reputation as a virgin. At base, these apparently novel arguments rely on an old premise—that certain acts and attitudes just don't "count." It was by this logic that generations of married European men could write off the sex they were having with their (female) housekeepers.[18] What's old is new again.

WHY IT MATTERED THEN, AND DOES IT MATTER NOW?

Proponents of abstinence-only education in the United States labor to keep "sex ed" classes out of public schools in part, no doubt, to keep America safe for virgins.[19] Meanwhile, many American high school students come to disagree with their elders over the value of virginity, which to them seems more of an embarrassment than anything else. Young virgins may find themselves in a very difficult market: the jewel they stand to bestow on an eventual beloved may command less interest than the owner had expected. (Students at Evangelical and conservative Protestant schools can safeguard themselves against this negative outcome more easily, no doubt.) Heartbreak can ensue; parents will struggle to help them then and to reassure themselves that the battle to keep sex ed out of school had been worthwhile.

In the ancient world, female virginity excited Romans and Greeks. Although they may not have freely chosen their virginity, priestesses demonstrated the marvelous ability of the human will to withstand what seemed for all intents and purposes inevitable: sexual activity. The vestal virgins of Rome were free to marry later in life; even if they did, though, they could always savor the memory of a heroic deed. "What had mattered, in their case, was an elaborately contrived suspension of the normal process, by which a girl moved with little interruption from puberty to childbearing. By not marrying until they were thirty, the Vestal Virgins stood out as glaring anomalies. They were the exceptions that reinforced the rule."[20] By focusing on the oddity of a woman who wasn't having sex and bearing children, a culture could redouble the force of the idea that women naturally had sex and bore children. Self-control had a lot to do with the practical value attached to virginity: losing your virginity before marriage worried suitors who reasoned that naughty pursuits and bad habits might die hard.

Although devotees of modern movements such as BAVAM! (see chapter 1) and True Love Waits may cherish the notion that virginity lost may be reclaimed, it seems the idea found no home in ancient

Rome. Curious as it may seem today, ancient Romans fastened on the marital bed as a symbol of virginity, perhaps because that bed may have marked the geographic site at which something valuable was lost forever, sacrificed in the name of generation. According to Rebecca Langlands: "The sign of a woman's *pudicitia* [sexual virtue] is her commitment to the bed itself in which her virginity was lost and her sexual life first developed, even when that bed can no longer provide her with sex (after her husband is dead). The marital bed as a physical representation of the marriage itself is a notion deeply engrained in ancient cultures."[21] Using a relevant passage from Valerius to make her point, Langlands writes, "Valerius' passage suggests that a girl's first sexual experience, through which a change is effected in her that can never be undone or repeated, should bind her in a particularly strong and admirable bond with her sexual partner and the bed where it took place." Although the marital bed itself may have lost most, if not all, of its significance, still it remains that contemporary Westerners may remember with particular fondness the specific location in which they first lost their virginity. By the same token, court records might just prove that cuckolded spouses react more emotionally when they discover that a spouse has betrayed the marriage in the marital bed itself, as opposed to, say, a hotel room.

Fast-forward to 1999. Just before the dawn of a new century, a young woman graduated from an elite New England college and then wrote a book about her experience, claiming that experience as largely representative of mainstream American culture. Specifically, she wrote about the jeering she endured because of her virginity. Whether Wendy Shalit's *A Return to Modesty* amounted to more than an amusing curiosity in an age of sexual gorging is hard to say, but the earnest young author exhorted her fellow Americans to celebrate virginity.[22] Success in such a venture is naturally hard to gauge, but the media hasn't noticeably cut back on the sexual imagery of advertisements, nor have television sitcoms heeded Shalit's plea. This is hardly surprising.

At about the same time that Shalit lamented the decline in American mores, another young author wrote a different kind of book about chastity. In *Been There, Haven't Done That*, a woman who had recently graduated from Harvard claimed to be a virgin, despite having been "licked, bitten, felt up, sucked, you name it."[23] Many readers might disagree with Tara McCarthy, but the really interesting question is, Why does she care? Why is it so important to her to call herself a virgin?

In part, the answer centers on her religion, her culture. McCarthy grew up a Roman Catholic, and Roman Catholics have long prized virginity. The most recent edition of the *New Catholic Encyclopedia* claims that "although it [virginity] is not the highest of virtues . . . it is more excellent than marriage, since it has as its object a superior good. Marriage is ordered to the multiplication of the human race, but virginity is ordered to a divine good and enjoys special fecundity."[24] Waves of Catholic immigrants reached the American shores in the nineteenth and twentieth centuries. The virginity of their daughters carried a high value. "Extraordinarily low illegitimacy rates among Italian-Americans through the 1930s testify to the success of community pressures in preserving female chastity before marriage."[25] Catholics from other countries no doubt earned similar statistical distinction.

Various Catholic memoirs convey the importance of purity, chastity, and virginity; these memoirs provide context for McCarthy's pride at having graduated from college a virgin. In *Occasions of Sin*, for example, Sandra Scofield writes of profound excitement while preparing for her First Holy Communion: "I had a beautiful white dress and veil, short lace gloves, and a crown that curved like a halo. The white stood for my virginity, which I thought was a special kind of goodness, something I had not lived long enough to soil; and I knew, from the saints' lives, that virgins were God's favorites. I even remember that I felt a little sorry for my mother, who when I asked said no, she wasn't a virgin anymore."[26] Some three decades after Scofield made her First Holy Communion in the 1950s, Pope John Paul II went so far as to say, "Virginity as a deliberately chosen vocation, based on a vow of chastity, and in combination with vows of poverty and obedience, creates particularly favorable conditions for the attainment of perfection in the New Testament sense."[27] Here John Paul II seems to be recommending the traditional religious life for Roman Catholic priests, brothers, and nuns. But the importance of virginity is unmistakable. (Some Protestant sects, such as the United Church of Christ and the Amish, do not celebrate virginity with much enthusiasm, if at all.)

The traditional reasons for prizing virginity—assuring a woman's purity for purposes of cementing the deal with a would-be husband—would seem to hold in China as well, to take one very different example.[28] Xiao Zhou has asserted that only female virginity matters in China and that whatever power a woman can claim stems directly from her virginity. Suffice it to say that emancipated women, particularly those in the West, generally resist this idea. Yet a significant percentage of well-educated Western women still yearn for a "white wedding" in which the color of their gown will, as they well know, supposedly symbolize their sexual purity. Some ideals die hard.

The simple fact of tradition no doubt holds some explanatory power as well. Because your family, group, or culture has always done something in a certain way, you feel somehow inclined to fall in line. Discussing sex education in metropolitan Washington, D.C., high schools, a Roman Catholic educator explained in 2003, "Abstinence is still the best choice. For Catholics kids, we believe it's part of their vocation."[29] When you come across narratives of people losing their virginity (and only women and gay men seem to write these accounts), those written by Catholics will almost invariably include mention of what they understood to be "their vocation." Sandra Cisneros, a well-known Hispanic author writing in the United States, has even gone so far as to state that she understood her "vocation" as a Catholic girl to include hiding her naked body from other girls in the high school locker room.[30]

The media turned frequently to the religiously sensitive topic of female circumcision in the 1990s and early 2000s. This practice still takes place in Muslim countries in Africa.[31] As immigrants from these countries make their way to places like the United States, the practice of female circumcision they bring with them generates controversy. The reasons for circumcising female infants seem to stem from the twin hopes of curbing lust: curbing lust will make it less likely that a woman will succumb to lust before marriage and less likely that she will betray her husband after marriage. (I will discuss female circumcision in the context of a "modern sin" in the following chapter.)

The "deflowering" of a woman (a curious metaphor) surely had something to do with purity, but likely a lot more with childbearing.[32] In a world in which women did not have jobs of their own and did not have an education to fall back on, a pregnant woman without a husband culturally bound to care for her children was in trouble. The birth control pill hit the American market in the mid-1960s and has transformed the sexual landscape, especially for women. The Roman Catholic hierarchy has consistently condemned the pill, on the reasoning that sex divorced from love and marriage degrades not only women but men as well. According to various polls, Roman Catholic women use the birth control pill as frequently as non-Catholic women do, leaving us to ponder the point of a rule almost everyone seems to be breaking. The real threat of the pill centers on the sexual freedom it allows young women. Naturally, a confirmed virgin won't need the pill for sexual purposes (she may, however, use it to modulate her period). The rate at which unmarried women use the pill provides the clearest evidence that virginity is increasingly out of fashion these days.

It may be objected that I am describing only one of two cultures in the United States—the liberal, largely well-educated segment of America.[33] That may be, yet I remain skeptical that the other culture will remain different in the twenty-first century—at least not in this regard. What's increasingly aberrant is the young woman who graduates from college a virgin. Given the way that she might be teased by those who know her secret, it would seem virginity has become a sin.

DRAWING LINES

At base, virginity comes down to medical and legal definitions. These definitions reflect the difficulty of formulating an answer to the question of purity, as well as the need our forebears felt for an answer. That answer has been a woman's body, specifically a hymen. If the hymen is broken, the deal is off (even Princess Diana had to undergo an examination of this sort in order to gain the Crown's permission to marry Prince Charles).[34]

Is fidelity like virginity? Yes and no. We may feel the attraction of a technical view (has X occurred or not?), although the complicating factors hide behind brute facts ("well, no, not exactly . . ."). Infidelity doesn't come down to the question of penile-vaginal penetration; plenty of Americans consider other erotic activities capable of constituting infidelity (interestingly enough, Americans may hotly debate this question as well, as in the confirmation hearings of Clarence Thomas and the Monica Lewinsky sex scandal). Former cheaters constitute a curious class, one akin to alcoholics who are "on the wagon." Even after conquering a drinking problem, people will insist they are still alcoholic. Former cheaters must live with anxiety that they might slip again.

But what about former cheaters? Is the popular saying really true—"Once a cheater, always a cheater"? To encourage spouses who have fallen off the wagon, we have to deny that one illicit experience robs a person of self-control. People who say "Once a cheater, always a cheater" really only remind us that some people think about sex a lot. That someone thinks about sex all the time doesn't mean that he or she will always fail at self-control.

In principle, the wayward spouse can return to fidelity, but he'll never be a technically "faithful" husband again. We need words to distinguish between a faithful spouse who has never strayed (a virgin, in the sense of betrayal) and a once-errant spouse who has reformed. Is someone who once voted Democratic always a Democrat? Clearly not. And someone who cheated in his first marriage may never stray in his second. Forgiveness and redemption make conceptual sense. We have to deny that one incident of misbehavior will necessarily lead to others if we intend to motivate cheaters to turn over a new leaf. The Zamboni effect can save a marriage, and one of the principal costs of atonement fatigue is the traditional marriage.

Fidelity does resemble virginity, yes, but it is important to remember that our understanding of virginity seems to have evolved. That doesn't mean we feel completely comfortable about that evolution. Medical advances and sex research have combined to disarm our already jittery confidence about carnal matters. Think of infants born with the sexual organs of both sexes. We feel queasy about such infants. Jeffrey Eugenides' Pulitzer Prize–winning novel, appropriately named *Middlesex*, probes the anxiety such persons cause us.[35] By the same token, we want set categories (e.g., heterosexual/homosexual and male/female) to remain unchanged. As more and more people change their biological sex (from male to female or vice versa), we moderns struggle to accept these bold "corrections" of nature. Joanne Meyerowitz's study *How Sex Changed*[36] similarly details the strategies by which we have resisted the pleas of transsexuals to accommodate genital reassignment.

Infidelity is more like the question of homosexuality. Many young Americans wonder about self-identifying as gay; some feel terror over it. Does a single homosexual encounter, even with a close friend, make you gay? More men than women are apt to answer yes. Both men and women may squirm at the assertion that sexual identity bends and changes over time.[37] We may like to think that a straight person will always be straight and that a gay person will always be gay, but the stories of real people frustrate this pat schema.

A more interesting question to ask might be, Why do we care? or Why are we asking the question? The answer must be that many of us really *do* care about sexual identity. Even more of us care about fidelity. Caring, however, doesn't make for easy answers.

Perhaps this is where the parallel between virginity and fidelity breaks down. And this is where a book on fidelity could begin to help well-meaning spouses. Infidelity as an automatic deal breaker just doesn't seem to resonate with contemporary culture. In fact, infidelity has crept its way through Western cultures and centuries. If we could stop ignoring that, we'd stop fearing infidelity quite so much. We'd see better what we really value (e.g., long-term commitments), what we really fear (that we can't control events like death and deception), and who we really are. Once we learned to relax about the idea we were marrying a nonvirgin (who may have been monogamous in previous relationships), we were on the way to relaxing about the idea that our spouse had fallen off the fidelity wagon—briefly, of course, and apologetically.

Part of the reason we cherish our youth is that we know we can never get it back. Virginity, a symbol of sacred power, is the same: once it's gone, it's gone for good. Parents once found it natural to lie to their adopted children about lineage, thinking that the truth would only hurt them and complicate life unduly. Would-be spouses who genuinely loved someone might find a ready reason to lie about purity if the intended cared deeply about this detail. A culture that shrugged indifferently at virginity would remove that incentive but simultaneously devalue the sacrifice of a person who had been saving him- or herself for the love of a lifetime.

We should notice here that Western countries have excluded gay and lesbian people from the chance to offer the gift of virginity on the night of a wedding to one's true love. If we believe that no other wedding-night gift could surpass virginity in value or beauty, then what a great shame it would be for gay and lesbian people who agree here to find themselves unable to offer up the same gem. Americans (and other Westerners) have conceptually ranked penile invagination above monogamy. The stuffing of an orifice in a very particular way has counted for more than the well-considered movement of a faithful heart.

Those who oppose gay marriage must now explain how and why the sexual intercourse of a monogamous, same-sex couple exceeds in immorality the casual coupling of heterosexual and unmarried pleasure seekers. It is not clear that the heartfelt sexual activity of monogamous gay and lesbian couples vitiates the so-called sanctity of marriage any more than heterosexual premarital sexual escapades do. If we're going to prize virginity, we should allow for the worth of gay and lesbian virginity. If we don't, we'll appear simply cruel when we bless sexual veterans who marry in the heterosexual way and condemn sexual virgins who profess a romantic love for someone of their own genitalia.

AN OPTION, NOT A REQUIREMENT

Once your needs are met, you don't need them anymore. A virgin who marries may see his or her asceticism as a ladder to be discarded once having arrived at the destination. Virginity is not needed anymore; it becomes a gift to the beloved and a badge of honor, proof of moral mettle. Is fidelity always needed? Or is there a point in a monogamous relationship in which partners can say to one another, "OK, OK, I see that you're devoted to me. Now go have your fun, provided that I remain the one you come back to."

If you believe in true love, if you believe that one single person can satisfy all your needs and command your full attention for the rest of your life, then infidelity will be repugnant to you. What seems rare in the West today is the man or woman who sincerely believes another person will hold him or her spellbound for that long.

Defenders of fidelity may say that the struggle against temptation is what elevates fidelity. The harder it is to achieve, the more it means to us. There is something to this logic. The question to be answered, though, is whether we should view this Olympian achievement as a prerequisite for all marriages. Plenty of school kids and college athletes train for and compete in, say, swimming competitions without believing they want or need the Olympic Games to validate what they're doing. Why is marriage any different? Why does marriage have only one speed—all or nothing? Why can't we choose from a menu of speeds?

In effect, this is precisely what Americans are doing: choosing from a menu of speeds, a variety of levels of commitment, a smorgasbord of ways of showing a spouse or spouse equivalent that they're extraspecial. It's not that fidelity loses its value in the contemporary world but rather that fidelity becomes simply one option among several. Americans like choice, and Americans work to create more choices. This work holds intriguing consequences for marriage in particular and morality in general.

Does anyone care anymore if a prospective spouse is no longer a virgin? Probably not. In various memoirs (e.g., Sandra Scofield's *Occasions of Sin*, Lisa Palac's *The Other Side of the Bed: How Dirty Pictures Changed My Life*, and Jane Juska's *A Round-Heeled Woman: My Late Life Adventures in Sex and Romance*), high school– and college-age virgins describe their purity as a millstone around the neck, something onerous to be gotten rid of once and for all.

Does anyone care anymore if a prospective spouse has had a homosexual romp? Does anyone care if a prospective spouse admits to having cheated in his or her former marriage? Does anyone care anymore if a spouse has an affair? The answers to these last two questions, unlike the first two, will tend to be yes. What's the difference between these various scenarios? And what can those emerging shifts tell us about America's moral culture? Sex is unlike anything else, save perhaps God. Sex remains a mystery to us; we may know very well that we don't want the person we love to sleep with anyone else, but most of us struggle to offer reasons more persuasive than "because that would hurt me very much." We have been conditioned by a largely religious culture to resist the idea that a married person might need some time to run wild and prefer instead to think in terms of sinister genital escapades.

As we ponder the worth of sexual virginity (either male or female), it is worthwhile to ask whether we have attributed too much value to virginity. It is possible to do just this. Sexual freedom may ultimately emerge as an even more moving wedding-day gift than virginity is. Even the most experienced of sexual athletes can still offer up his or her sexual freedom on any given day. It is arguably more difficult for a sexual veteran to give up sexual freedom than it is for a virgin.

It is a bad idea to fixate on the wedding day while neglecting the rest of a marriage in which an initial virgin may stray into illicit beds. A one-time sexual tiger who becomes monogamous (through sheer force of will or love) in marriage may deserve quite a bit more applause than the wedding-day virgin who later strays. While virginity may be a very good idea in itself, we must acknowledge that, like getting into an elite university but then simply coasting or perhaps failing out, it is not in itself enough for moral applause.

Sex frustrates us because we have a hard time articulating why we care about it so very much (unlike, say, the characters in Huxley's futuristic nightmare *Brave New World*, who see the pleasure as a simply physical release, lacking an emotional or moral dimension). The different factors that may dictate an individual's response to the questions just posed include

- children;
- privileging today over yesterday (learning that your prospective spouse had a homosexual romp once in the past but now regrets it, learning that your prospective spouse used to cheat but has since reformed;
- homosexual anxiety (could my prospective spouse secretly be gay?);
- disease (what did my prospective spouse perhaps contract in the course of those sexual dalliances, or what could he or she contract after falling off the wagon in our marriage?);
- reputation (what would our friends down at the country club say about this?).

These considerations play some important role in how many contemporary Westerners choose a spouse. Virginity in the traditional sense may count for less today than ever before, but the same kind of purity ("I would be a terrible person if I ever crossed *that* line!") arguably counts for just as much today as it ever did. Although we might call what I'm pointing to "virtue" or "strong character," still it remains that we think about formal sexual relations in terms of past performance, if you will. What a person thinks about virginity, then, tells us a lot about what she will think about fidelity.

Virginity and fidelity resemble one another especially in terms of time. It only takes a moment to undo virginity, which may have been protected over the course of decades. And it only takes a moment to unravel fidelity, which may have characterized a long-standing relationship. The irrevocableness of virginity and fidelity enhance their value and add a certain fascination to the respective states. (Of course, one can be faithful in a second or third marriage, even if one had been unfaithful in the first.)

The difficult and interesting question hovering over this chapter is whether virginity is predictive of fidelity. Is a man or woman who has never had sex before marriage more likely to remain faithful? Can a man or woman who has enjoyed "playing the field" before marriage reasonably be expected to trim his or her sails successfully? I suspect that the answer to the first question here is yes, tout court, and to the second, yes, but only with tremendous effort. Virginity is already on its way to seeming like a quaint childhood hobby. With more and more premarital sex available these days, prostitutes become less and less essential. And with more and more frustrated spouses wrestling with monogamy, the availability of extramarital sex partners who may also be struggling with old-fashioned fidelity blurs the distinction between prostitutes and upstanding people who are trying hard to behave.

MY VIRGIN, MY WIFE

Born inside a prison, the virgin learns to revere the walls of his or her captivity. Let's face it, boys feel less pressure to stay in than girls, although even modern popes such as John Paul II or Benedict XVI will insist that voluntary sexual confinement should span genders.[38] Before your first sexual encounter—an immediately ambiguous experience, as we've seen—you may spot plenty of opportunities to sever your chains, but you should resist. All in the name of keeping the slate clean—of keeping the ice so clean as to make the Zamboni effect redundant.

Traditional, idealized Western marriage resembles virginity. In marriage, we move from having had no sexual partners to having a first. Ideally, and we might emphasize the word *ideally*, you die having had exactly one sexual partner: your spouse. Like virgins, married men and women may spot plenty of opportunities for escape from the realm of low numbers (zero for virgins and one for spouses), although the married are expected to resist these opportunities, just like virgins. In an important way, marriage is just like virginity. Yes, you can have sex while married, but not necessarily with the person you fantasize about. Ambiguity about who qualifies as a virgin dovetails with anxiety about who qualifies as a faithful spouse. Although many of us still care about fidelity, even we may snicker at the idea that a bride and groom should both be virgins. Sin fatigue is the reason for our snickering.

In conclusion, the question is no longer whether a potential partner has had sex but rather whether that sex has been exclusively safe. What has America lost in the passing of virginity reverence? Sex tourism may decline: proper college students may stop taking a semester or year abroad in order to sow their wild oats in a place no one knows them. Perhaps harmful myths about virgins will fade—that you can cure your syphilis or AIDS by having sex with one. Paternity anxiety no longer finds relief in virginity, as a DNA test can determine paternity better than any other alternative. It seems unlikely that many women will ever become nostalgic about the pre–birth control pill era.

Curiously, today we think of two kinds of virginity: heterosexual and homosexual. Losing one's homosexual virginity could be quite useful (you'd know for sure that option's not for you) or quite dangerous (maybe my partner will want to do that again?). This anxiety has nothing to do with purity.

In the late twentieth century, the French public tolerated the infidelity of President Mitterrand and the British public tolerated the infidelity of Prince Charles. One day the American public may move in the same direction. If so, fatigue will be the chief reason for abandoning Puritanical mores.

III

MODERN SINS, DESPITE FATIGUE

5

MODERN SINS

The 2000 film *Bedazzled* opens with an intriguing series of vignettes: We observe busy city streets. Our gaze fixes first on one individual, then another. The frame freezes intermittently, each time isolating a single person. The punching sound of a computer accompanies a tally of the individual's sins, which are then superimposed over the unsuspecting person. We understand that we are seeing straight through people, just as God does.

God has been observing people for a long time. Have the sins he's seen changed much? Yes and no. Certainly, our view of traditional sins has evolved—think of breaking the Sabbath by shopping on Sunday. But the traditional list seems to have expanded to include more sins. Space travel, medical technology, and the Internet, to name just a few, have taken humans to new corners. New sins have emerged from human progress in certain instances; in other instances, we are left with new spins on old sins (e.g., letting personal debt run out of control through student loans, mortgages, and credit cards).

Even a brief examination of modern sins might indicate nothing new under the sun. For the Ten Commandments and seven deadly sins might amount to a kind of periodic chart of wrongdoing; these seventeen proscriptions contain the raw elements of all other kinds of transgression, we might maintain. A more extended analysis of these new sins, though, will show that there *is* something new under the sun. So, in a world habituated to space travel, heart transplants, and the Internet, let's look for new sins. Some candidates will be more egregious than others. Reasonable people may disagree over whether our forebears always considered things like child abuse or schoolyard bullying or sexual harassment sinful. What may have been assumed before is now made explicit, even codified by civil law. Other sins, like being an alcoholic or being gay, have started to disappear as scientific advances have transformed understanding of the human condition.

We should remember that at least since the time of Averröes, Moses Maimonides, and St. Thomas Aquinas, believers have insisted that God's rules make good sense. Far from a whimsical divine fiat, a religious rule should be able to compel anyone who tries hard enough to grasp its intrinsic rationality. "Because God says so" may be a good reason for believers, but this plea in itself will hardly persuade a nonbeliever.

Do we really want to call any of the alleged offenses on the list that follows here a *sin*? What would designating these actions a sin gain us? Getting any of these items on the sin list would enlist God on our side, much in the way that Jews, Christians, and Muslims have tried to do collectively since 9/11. Keep in mind that God cares very much how we treat other people: if we harm them, we offend him. And so we sin.

As I argued in chapter 1, however, it makes little sense to say that atheists sin against God when they misstep. So the stakes of conversion appear quite high: believers may recognize a new urgency in getting nonbelievers (of whom there are relatively few in the United States) to believe, even as the religiously different may exhort each other to do a better job of following the faith they supposedly profess.

Now let's take a look at thirteen modern sins: (1) harming the environment, (2) failing to thrive, (3) obesity, (4) depression, (5) harming children, (6) wife abuse, (7) sexual harassment, (8) denying the Holocaust, (9) homophobia, (10) circumcision, (11) racism, (12) disrespecting other religions, and (13) drunk driving. In these modern "sins" we catch a useful glimpse of the contemporary West, as well as a sense of sin's vast future.

HARMING THE ENVIRONMENT

In the book of Genesis—that is, at the very beginning of the Hebrew Bible or Old Testament—God seems to give the Earth to Adam and Eve. For ages, this passage seemed to grant permission to plunder the environment guiltlessly. Today, many Westerners worry. At risk is our own personal safety, the welfare of future generations, and the viability of the planet itself. Religious believers will add to this list another concern: offending God through a selfish misuse of his marvelous gift, Earth. It wasn't until quite recently that we humans could harm the environment (if in fact we really can), which makes ecological disregard a modern sin. Let's review the anatomy of this new sin.

As numerous commentators have pointed out, Western civilization faces an environmental crisis, facets of which include

- global warming,
- pollution,
- soil erosion,
- deforestation,
- species extinction,
- overpopulation, and
- overconsumption.[1]

Ethicists, theologians, and secular scholars survey the destruction to our planet and its ecosystems since about 1900 (roughly the beginning of widespread industrial activity on the Earth) and worry that the Earth will become too toxic not only for wildlife but also for humans. We humans have not been good stewards of God's gift of Earth, some of us will say.

The 2004 blockbuster film *Day after Tomorrow* dramatized this crisis, specifically global warming. Viewers witnessed the scary destruction of New York City, an area smothered by carbon dioxide emissions from tailpipes and smokestacks. These gases had raised the globe's temperature high enough to halt the thermosaline North Atlantic ocean current, which regulates heat distribution. Suddenly the weather turns against humankind, and major cities such as Tokyo, Los Angeles, and New York suffer catastrophes. Critics pointed to various scientific inaccuracies in the film, all the while affirming that the planet is in fact in trouble. The film is far from science fiction fantasy.

In 2006, former vice president Al Gore published a book and released a related documentary called *An Inconvenient Truth*, both designed to startle Westerners into a deeper realization of the global warming crisis.[2] The harrowing documentary may not have focused on or targeted religious sensibilities, but it appealed to the sense of moral duty underlying many religious actions. The message of both the book and the documentary was clear: we had transgressed, and we need to change our ways. We will suffer the consequences of our actions, unless perhaps God suddenly intervenes to restore our damaged ecology to its erstwhile resplendence (read: a Zamboni effect for the globe).

In affluent economies, factories and refineries consume energy and emit greenhouse gases. Two-thirds of global carbon emissions arise from fossil fuel utilization for power generation, transportation, domestic heating, cement making, gas and coal mining, and industrial manufacturing. It is these emissions that raise the temperature of our planet. At least that's how some scientists see it. Other scientists—perhaps not very reputable ones—continue to contest the global warming theory and question whether humans could ever permanently alter the climate system of the planet.[3] These dissenting scientists view twentieth-century rises in global mean temperatures as the lingering results of the last mini–Ice Age in the sixteenth century. According to that group, contemporary do-gooders are foolish to blame leaders of affluent societies for the modern sin of harming the environment.

As scientists continue to debate man's impact on the environment, it bears asking what exactly pollution might have to do with sin. Ancient Hebrew scriptures link humanity to both the ecological order and the being of God. This linking—in contemporary parlance, this codependency—contrasts sharply with the prevailing ethical individualism of the modern West. The Hebrews believed that moral values issued from the ordering of the natural world. Morality should not be reduced to individual human intuitions and emotions, nor may moral judgment be limited to human experience. The physical reality of created order coalesces with the community of human and nonhuman species in the architectonics of the creation. Although the extension of ethics and law to include animals is often represented as uniquely modern, the Hebrew Torah anticipated the modern animal rights movement by thousands of years. And hundreds of years before the formation of the Society for the Prevention of Cruelty to Animals (SPCA), St. Francis of Assisi was preaching to the animals and birds of Europe.

Church leaders have only recently addressed the sinfulness of environmental harm. In an environmental symposium held at St. Barbara Greek Orthodox Church in Santa Barbara, California, on November 8, 1997, the ecumenical patriarch Bartholomew asserted that deliberate degradation of the environment is sinful—that is, something to which God was opposed and something that requires repentance:

> If human beings treated one another's personal property the way they treat their environment, we would view that behavior as anti-social. We would impose the judicial measures necessary to restore wrongly appropriated personal possessions. It is therefore appropriate for us to seek ethical, legal recourse where possible, in matters of ecological crimes.
>
> It follows that, to commit a crime against the natural world is a sin. For humans to cause species to become extinct and to destroy the biological diversity of God's creation . . . for humans to degrade the integrity of Earth by causing changes in its climate, by stripping the Earth of its natural forests, or destroying its wetlands . . . for humans to injure other humans with disease . . . for humans to contaminate the Earth's waters, its land, its air, and its life, with poisonous substances . . . these are sins.
>
> In prayer, we ask for the forgiveness of sins committed both willingly and unwillingly. And it is certainly God's forgiveness which we must ask, for causing harm to His Own Creation.[4]

Polluting the environment exceeds garden-variety wrongdoing in the eyes of this religious thinker—it qualifies as a sin against God. A theme embedded in the heart of the Christian tradition—respecting the natural world—comes into somewhat urgent focus now, when the natural world appears to be in danger. The breakdown of our natural environment finds a parallel in the general moral breakdown of the West. The same kind of selfishness fuels the different declines.

Moral aversion to pollution takes different forms—from the Green Party in Germany to Greenpeace internationally to the American director John Waters's hilarious send-up of a suburban housewife (*Serial Mom*, 1994) who so objects to neighbors who neglect to recycle newspapers and cars that she kills them with the skill of a professional hit man. It seems difficult to imagine anyone confessing to the sin of environmental disregard (or whatever we want to call it) in the confessional, but that reluctance may itself be a sin. For looking environmental responsibility in the eye and taking it seriously would seem to require a readiness to admit fault when we fail. Part of the problem with this modern sin is its unusually corporate nature: a cluster of individuals cannot save the environment—only nations working in concert can.

FAILING TO THRIVE: NOT REACHING
YOUR FULL POTENTIAL

The Romantic ideal of unlimited human potential has seized the American imagination such that each of us today, children especially, is a diva waiting to hatch. Failing to be a success represents a transgression; obviously, you're not trying hard enough.

Competition and stress: these are the building blocks of American culture. The feelings of inadequacy that gnaw at us may have a practical effect: they may urge us in one direction rather than another. The direction in question can make all the difference to our lives. Dissatisfaction with ourselves may prompt us to refashion how we look, how we speak, and how we hope. Several best-selling American books reflect ambitious and ongoing preoccupations: *How to Win Friends and Influence People, Seven Habits of Highly Effective People, The Magic of Thinking Big, Think and Grow Rich,* and *How to Have Confidence and Power in Dealing with People.* Highly educated people tend to be more ambitious than those who are not, but college graduates have no monopoly on feelings of entitlement in America today.

The plight of Michael Gonzales represents an important new strain of bravado in American culture. In late August 2000, a federal appeals court ruled that a University of Michigan medical student who had been diagnosed with a reading and writing impairment was not in fact entitled to extra time on a medical licensing test he had to pass in order to remain in medical school. Gonzales had invoked the Americans with Disability Act (ADA) of 1990 to argue for 50 percent more time than the standard twelve hours in which students must complete the exam.[5]

The medical examiners board that denied his request three times (before he appealed it to the U.S. Court of Appeals) noted that Gonzales had qualified for Advanced Placement classes in high school, achieved high grades there, and performed well on the SAT and MCAT—all without extra time or help. The appeals court decided that Gonzales was not the sort of person the ADA sought to protect. The lesson from this case is that if you fail to pass a crucial test, the reason couldn't possibly be that you're not smart enough to pass it. There must be something wrong with the system. If there weren't, you'd be guilty of some sort of sin—although it's hard to say whether the sin would be sloth or mediocrity. Christians may puzzle over this question, given that many of them take inspiration from biblical passages such as "All things are possible" (Luke 18:27) and "You can do all things" (Philippians 4:13).

Failing to thrive can of course be the fault of social structures that hold down certain groups, such as blacks, or Jews, or gays. In the early 1970s, the Australian singer Helen Reddy added fuel to the feminist quest for social equality with a song that proclaimed, "I am woman, hear me roar, in numbers too big to ignore / I am woman, I am invincible / If I have to, I can do anything." Her song became an anthem in the burgeoning women's rights movement. This message began to appear more and more frequently in popular music. At the end of the twentieth century, the American star Whitney Houston musically declared, "You can do miracles, if you believe," and, in "One Moment in Time," she took the opportunity to reinforce the notion that anything is possible if we just try.

The social critic David Brooks argued in 2004 that no single elite (e.g., intellectual, artistic, corporate, athletic, or social) rules America; neighboring tribes of elites barely know of each other's existence. Because there is no definable establishment to be oppressed by, there is no obvious target to rebel against. Meanwhile, everyone preens (or so it sometimes seems). "Everybody can be an aristocrat within his own Olympus." In *On Paradise Drive*, Brooks further observes, "Whereas the Greeks advised, 'Know thyself,'" Americans in various self-reinforcing cliques "live by the maxim 'Overrate thyself.'"[6]

Popular culture endorses in an unprecedented way the belief that we can do anything we want, particularly when it comes to academic achievement.[7] This idea leads some to think that those living in poverty or tedious middle management jobs are to blame for not trying harder. Of course, the world is much more complicated that that. Yet unbounded optimism about our human potential does have a downside—that we are to blame for failing to thrive. Americans have even transferred enthusiasm for thriving to the burgeoning field of cosmetic surgery. At the Final Judgment, God will ask you to account for the gifts he's given you. Denying that you received much in the way of gifts seems an imprudent strategy. Better advice is to get to work before it's too late, excelling in whatever way you can. In the final analysis, the failure to thrive may have more to do with time management than anything else. One of the worst sins of all could in fact be wasting our time, our youth. As a popular bumper sticker once put it, "Jesus Is Coming; Look Busy!"

When he was a student at Cambridge University, Isaac Newton, deeply religious, kept a journal in which to record daily sins. Newton regretted violating the Sabbath, failing to pray sufficiently, to give enough time to God (because he was always solving mathematical problems).[8] The West would in fact have been a poorer place, had Newton spent less time developing his potential. Newton shows the difficulty of dismissing too hastily this sin of failing to reach your potential, for some of us really are divas waiting to hatch. Regardless of our abilities, though, we can agree that life is short. Wasting time, whether you believe in God or not, seems awfully wrong.

OBESITY

According to a 2006 Yale University poll, many Americans would give up a year or more of their lives—even a limb—rather than gain weight.[9] Americans could view obesity as a matter of aesthetics (people look better when they're thin), but gaining weight has become a moral issue: a sign that you are lazy and lack self-control. We could instead look at losing weight as a medical issue; indeed, we would have good reason to do so. In 2004, fully two-thirds of U.S. adults were officially overweight, and about half of those had ballooned into full-blown obesity.

Excess poundage takes a terrible toll on the human body, significantly increasing the risk of heart disease, high blood pressure, strokes, diabetes, infertility, gall bladder disease, osteoarthritis, and many forms of cancer. The total medical tab for illnesses related to obesity was at least $117 billion in 2004, according to the U.S. surgeon general. Poor diet and physical inactivity threatened to overtake tobacco as the leading cause of preventable death in the United States. By 2006, many Americans were too fat to fit into X-ray machines; hospital personnel naturally worried about the expanding predicament.[10] Surely weight is a personal responsibility, Americans seem to agree. So, while perhaps not ignoring medical and aesthetic questions, Americans sometimes tie obesity to sin.[11]

Nineteenth-century attitudes toward obesity reflected guilt over the new abundance of food, as well as the rise of a consumer culture and the growth of sedentary work habits. The self-control necessary for dieting helped reconcile moral concerns about consumer affluence. Especially during the two world wars, Americans heard and read arguments that eating too much and gaining weight were unpatriotic, presumably because of concerns about food shortages. However disparately, dieting fads today link us to the experience of ancient ascetics, who struggled to overcome their hunger way out in the deserts of Africa and the Middle East. The difference today may lie in the wardrobe: the thinner you are, the more clothes you are likely to own. Mother Teresa is an obvious exception here. Princess Diana, who died close to the same day as Mother Teresa, never wore the same dress twice; Mother Teresa owned only one dress.

In 1973, Carolyn Soughers brought the first size discrimination lawsuit in the United States. She had been denied employment with a county civil service agency on account of her size, and she eventually lost her case. It was only in 1993 that the federal Equal Employment Opportunity Commission ruled that "severely obese" people could claim protection under federal statutes that barred discrimination against the disabled. Although the question of defining obesity as a disability remains fluid, we have a hard time thinking of a powerful man or a beautiful woman as fat.

In *Eat Fat*, Richard Klein defends obesity, denies it is a sin, and even makes a case for fatness as the ideal.[12] Given the modern American media's enthusiasm for waiflike beauty (which has been tied to increasing rates of anorexia and bulimia), he seems especially provocative, perhaps even perverse. Klein anticipates with pleasure the day when the aesthetic of Rubens becomes normative again.

This thinness imposed on the body is the sign that marks the body of Franz Kafka's protagonist in the classic short story "The Hunger Artist" (1922). This man starves not because he wills himself thin but because he claims he cannot find any food to his taste. He is a Christ figure of sorts, and one can read the story as a metaphor for the saying "Man does not live on bread alone." The hunger artist craves more than just earthly sustenance; he seeks spiritual nourishment. So, Americans seem to think today, do fat people lack spiritual robustness. The tables have been turned in Kafka's marvelous story, and today we resist food not because it displeases us but because we want to please God with our continence (and look better and live longer in the process).

The old sin of gluttony (enjoying yourself too much, taking more than your due) has been transformed into not looking as good as we might. In America, where money could be spread around in such a way

CHAPTER 5

that everyone would be obese, the offense against an aesthetic ideal of thinness would still prevail.

DEPRESSION

Jesus told his disciples that he had come to Earth so that they should have more joy and have it more completely. Most believers—whether Jewish, Christian, or Muslim—will say that their lives are happier for God's presence. If depression afflicts you, what will you do about it? Now that modern science *can* treat depression, it seems you *must* seek treatment. If you don't (assuming you can afford the medical treatment, that is), you would seem to be sinning. And if you think depression spurs your own creative output or helps society produce more and better artists, you may be utterly mistaken.[13]

According to recent research, about 3 percent of Americans—some nineteen million—suffer from chronic depression.[14] More than two million of those are children. Manic-depressive illness, often called bipolar illness because the mood of its victims varies from mania to depression, afflicts about 2.3 million and is the second-leading killer of young women, the third of young men. Depression as described in the American Psychological Association's *Diagnostic and Statistical Manual–IV* is the leading cause of disability in the United States and abroad for persons over the age of five. Worldwide, including the developing world, depression accounts for more of the disease burden, as calculated by premature death plus healthy life-years lost to disability, than anything else but heart disease. Other illnesses, from alcoholism to heart diseases, mask depression when it causes them; if one takes that into consideration, depression may be the biggest killer on Earth.

Depression, like aging and the very inclination to sin, may result from Original Sin. Leaving aside the impossibly difficult question of why God allows depression (which our predecessors referred to as "melancholy") in the world, we can agree that individuals suffering from it might seem to have a duty to fight it. And those who do not suffer from depression might have a moral duty to help lift the depressed out of the dark fog.

Treatments for depression proliferate, but only half of Americans struck by major depression have ever sought help—even from a clergyman or a counselor. About 95 percent of that 50 percent go to primary care physicians, who often don't know much about psychiatric complaints. An American adult with depression stands only about a 40 percent chance of correct diagnosis. Nonetheless, about twenty-eight million Americans—one in every ten—are now on selective serotonin reuptake inhibitors (SSRIs—the class of drugs to which Prozac belongs), and a substantial number take other prescribed medications. Less than half of those whose illness is recognized will receive appropriate treatment. As definitions of depression have broadened to include more and more of the general population, it has become increasingly difficult to calculate an exact mortality figure. The statistic traditionally given is that 15 percent of depressed people will eventually commit suicide; this figure still holds for those with extreme illness.

Public health officials understandably worry about studies documenting an increase of depression.[15] Twenty years ago, about 1.5 percent of the population had depression that required treatment; now it's 5 percent; and as many as 10 percent of all Americans now living can expect to suffer a major depressive episode during their life. About 50 percent will experience some symptoms of depression. Clinical problems have increased; treatments have increased vastly more. Diagnosis is on the up, but that does not explain the scale of this problem. Incidents of depression are increasing across the developed world, particularly in children. Depression now occurs in younger people, with an average onset at about age twenty-six, ten years younger than a generation ago; bipolar disorder, or manic-depressive illness, sets in even earlier. Things are getting worse, it seems.

Despite the great revolutions in psychiatric and psychopharmaceutical treatments, many people continue to suffer abject misery, as Andrew Solomon stressed in The Noonday Demon. More than half of those who do seek help—another 25 percent of the depressed population—receive no treatment. About half of those who do receive treatment—13 percent or so of the depressed population—receive unsuitable treatment, often tranquilizers or unhelpful psychotherapies. Of those who are left, half—some 6 percent of the depressed population—receive inadequate dosage for an inadequate length of time. So that leaves about 6 percent of the total depressed population who are getting adequate treatment. But many of these ultimately choose to go off their medications, usually because of unpleasant side effects. Meanwhile, at the other end of the spectrum, people who suppose that bliss is their birthright pop caval-cades of pills in a futile bid to alleviate those mild discomforts that tex-ture every life.

The moral question here, the link to sin, hovers over noncompli-ance (failure of those who have begun treatment to continue it) and refusal (of those who decline any medical avenues). Various people may decline medical intervention: think of an impotent man who chooses not to avail himself of Viagra or an infertile woman who chooses not to avail herself of (costly and painful) new reproductive technologies. Depression might seem to be more urgent; indeed, our friends and family members might argue that we *owe* them our best efforts to find suitable treatment—and that perhaps we owe ourselves as much as well.

According to Solomon and Kay Redfield Jamison, only about one in four patients who take antidepressants continue the treatment for six months, and a large proportion of those who stop do so because of sex-ual and sleep-related side effects. Once the sexual effects set in, sexual anxiety ensues, so that erotic encounters may become disturbing mo-ments of failure; people afflicted with this burden may develop a psy-chological aversion to sexual interaction, which makes the symptoms worse. Most men with erectile dysfunction are also struggling with de-pression; lifting the impotence may be sufficient to reverse the depres-sion. It seems that about 99 percent of people with acute major depres-sion report sexual dysfunction.

We moderns have good reason to think of depression as a great evil. Like a dogged enemy, it can tackle us suddenly. If we think of sin as something that diminishes us, that distances us from God, that reduces our ability to enjoy the gift of life, then we can begin to see an impera-tive to pull ourselves out of depression. Remaining depressed when we really don't have to—for depression can sometimes be controlled—appears a sin in a world that can now control it. Pride might figure prominently in that sin, although an altogether healthy appreciation for sex may have just as much to do with the sin of noncompliance. The de-pression of people who cannot afford medical care should concern us, for it could be argued that we have a moral duty not only to feed and clothe the poor but also to help lift them out of depression. Compelling indeed is the argument that modern Westerners sin corporately by denying medical aid to those who cannot afford it.

HARMING CHILDREN

Today we worry about harming children physically (we are not to reprimand our own children physically, nor do we allow teachers to do so in public schools) and sexually. As already noted, the rhetoric of our politicians and school board representatives regularly turns to fear of depriving children of opportunities (the "failure to thrive"). We used to think of children as incompetent adults, slowpokes who needed a little prodding in order to carry their own weight. When they stepped out of line, whether at home or at school, we beat them. We worried less about their sexual initiation—whether it was propitious or awkward—and focused more on the social economies of unwanted pregnancy. We seemed to worry more about the harm children could do to adults or possibly themselves than the harm adults could do to children.

The concept of childhood was supposedly only born about 150 years ago. According to the influential French historian Philippe Ariès, European societies before the eighteenth century did not recognize what we now call childhood, defined as a long period of dependency and protection lasting into physical and social maturity. Until the mid-1700s, he argued, children learned to adapt what they said and did to adult expectations, not vice versa.[16] Other scholars have subsequently explained that a child of seven might be sent off to become a scullery maid or a shoemaker's apprentice; by fourteen, he could be a soldier or a king, a spouse, and a parent. Life expectancy was much shorter then, and if you were only going to make it to forty, you'd better start living as soon as possible. At the same time, if your kids stood a good chance of dying before, say, age seven, then you might do well to withhold emotional attachments for a while.[17]

Ariès's theory has undergone furious debate and significant revision since he advanced it in 1960 (the field of childhood history has taken off since then).[18] While many historians accept his basic notion that the young did not in centuries past enjoy the special protections now extended them, an important number of historians nonetheless insist that adults and children in the past did recognize a category of person, the Child.

Scholarly debate aside, it is interesting to note that children were not automatically considered innocent, pure. In Puritan America, in fact, the opposite seems to have been the case. Infants were conceived and born in sin, but they were considered perfectible through religious guidance and the development of good habits. Early colonial toys and children's furniture, writes Karin Calvert in her history of the material culture of childhood in America, propelled the child forward into contact with adults and the adult world. Adults shared beds with children and generally regarded the young as apprentices making an important, if rushed, journey to maturity. There was no point in dawdling along the way.

Romantic philosophers and writers in the mid–eighteenth century celebrated children as unspoiled, unaffected, noble. The complications adults had heaved on Locke's tabula rasa or Rousseau's *beau savage* came in for blame; the child deserved our special sympathy, as his innocence was endangered by the sad fact of entering a rotten world, of the necessity of working (often very hard) for a living. By the late nineteenth century, that innocence could actually inspire politicians and moralists: adults might do well to imitate children—to the extent possible (bringing children up did require circumspection, after all). In any event, the child deserved to inhabit a sphere blissfully free of sexual knowledge and desire. Ironically, just when adults demanded less from children in the workplace, fear of a child's sex life mushroomed.

The angelic child came in for lots of skepticism from Freud. In his *Interpretation of Dreams* he spoke of a sexual "instinct" born in the child. This instinct grew into sublimated sexual desire for a parent and then eventually transformed into adult passion or ambition. Neurotic suffering was the fate of those who failed to vent this sexual instinct properly. Freud deserves credit for raising awareness about the extent of what would now be called sexual abuse of children. Part of the problem with understanding the sexual abuse of children was grasping the difference between prepubescent children, postpubescent children, and full-fledged adults. Around the 1930s, a new class of people further confounded the dividing line between childhood and adulthood: teenagers.

A combination of war, economic scarcity, and television left teenagers more vulnerable to the harshness of life and the fierceness of carnal desire. By the end of the twentieth century, the traditional landmarks of adult enfranchisement had been scattered into disorder. Marriage can now follow the establishment of a household, a career, and a credit history; the birth of a child can predate all of these. Preteens enroll in college; adults return to school at midlife or, increasingly, in old age; young surrogate mothers gestate babies for women who want to start families after their reproductive years are past. Many grown-ups live single and childless all their lives. And many teenagers view their virginity with embarrassment early in the new millennium.

By the end of World War II, Western mores had evolved to the point that it was morally unthinkable to deprive a child of an education, just as it was impermissible to force a youngster into "child labor." Similarly, the idea that a child would simply "get over" any sexual contact an adult had initiated drifted into perversity. Laws forbidding sex with children, as well as child pornography, gathered widespread support.[19] It took a little longer to leave off with physical punishment, but many American and European parents seem to have broken with that long tradition. Increasingly, believers see as a sin the failure to appreciate children as a sacred gift from God (notwithstanding the commandment exhorting children to obey their parents) or at least as creatures deserving of protection from the harshness and perverseness of the adult world.

This question of status plays itself out poignantly in juvenile courts today. How we punish child criminals—some of whom have literally killed for luxury coats and tennis shoes—divides Americans. While some push for stiffer juvenile offender laws, others argue that sending a child to prison for life is itself a crime.[20] Children increasingly take guns to school today and sometimes use them; as schools and communities argue over how to stop the trend and punish wrongdoers, some parents lament the further erosion of that once magical time called childhood.

Society is not to blame when a mother, father, or teacher beats a child. Society will not go to prison, no matter how poor or depressed the abusive parent, no matter how awfully the child behaves. For today, harming children is a sin. Anyone who harms a child can find him- or herself sent off to reeducation camp.

WIFE ABUSE

No doubt for a long time, husbands have beaten their wives. We lack a clear picture of how wives made sense of their plight, for there was no word such as *wife battering* to convey social and moral disapproval. Wives just had to put up with their husbands. Husbands could always remind wives of the traditional wedding vows (now largely abandoned or significantly softened), in which a woman essentially vows subservience to her man.

Today Western communities increasingly provide support services for battered wives, who can hide out in private locations with physical protection and psychological counseling. Today we understand that the violence a woman suffers at the hands of her husband or partner is compounded by the responses of social institutions to mistreatment, discrimination, harassment, and violence that perpetuate and reproduce the violence in women's lives. Violence against wives has sometimes included victim blaming and indifference, even contempt from police, family members, hospital personnel, and juries. Hostility toward battered wives reinforced the idea that women are to blame and perhaps even deserve to be abused. Today we tend to think of denying compassion to battered women as a sin, one as blameful as the batterings themselves.

Violence against women became a major social issue in the United States in the 1970s.[21] Before 1970, most Americans preferred not to talk about rape or wife battering. These were the problems of individual women, to be borne in silence and shame (an important exception here arose when black men were accused of raping white women). The rise of feminism in the late 1960s fueled the impetus to speak publicly about old secrets. Sexual harassment and assault on the street, in the workplace, in educational, medical, and prison institutions became urgent, political concerns. Toleration of personal violence (private) led to toleration of institutional violence (public), Americans came to see. Talk of wife abuse led to renewed concern over prostitution, female sexual slavery, pornography, and the international trafficking of women and girls.

An anthology of scholarly essays entitled *To Have and To Hit* makes a useful distinction between wife beating and wife battering, with *battering* defined as a beating that is sufficiently severe to cause injury or death.[22] Although wife beating is not a cultural universal, it is much more common, at both the individual and societal levels, than wife battering. Cultures that accept, and even advocate, wife beating may be strongly opposed to wife battering. The sanctions against husbands and the sanctuary for wives are much more likely to be available in cases of battering than in instances where beating is not sufficiently severe to maim or kill. Wife beating appears to be quite prevalent across cultures, according to scholars. Although wife beating is now considered morally despicable, this volume reminds us that official positions and enforcement are very different things, especially if policemen and judges beat their own wives or expect that such behavior will be a normal part of the marital relationship.

I mentioned in chapter 2 that under traditional Jewish law, only the husband can grant a religious divorce decree, or get, to his wife. Without a get, a woman cannot remarry within Orthodoxy. These rules present obvious difficulties to battered women locked in Orthodox Jewish marriages. Even in Orthodox Jewish communities, we now see cries for change. Some Orthodox Jewish women have begun to fight domestic abuse through changes to divorce law. A rare religious decree called a Heter Meah Rabonim, the rough equivalent of an annulment, releases husband and wife from a troubled marriage.[23]

Hard to find nowadays is the person who will claim that a man's house is his castle and that his property includes his wife and children, but domestic abuse did not arouse widespread public concern until the 1970s. Few would argue that Judaism or Christianity condoned domestic violence, but it is worth pondering whether these traditions simply counted on men behaving well, as opposed to actively shaming and blaming men who attacked their wives physically. Because so few people talked about domestic beatings in the past, it's hard to say that such an abuse of power qualified as a proper sin. Yet many Jews and Christians will reasonably maintain that revulsion to such a practice runs throughout their traditions. Things are clearer today, and Americans and Europeans are fortunate to live in a society that explicitly condemns this particular abuse of power.

SEX WITH SUBORDINATES: SEXUAL HARASSMENT

Prior to the 1960s (World War II being something of an exception), Western women did not work in numbers comparable to the twenty-first century (of course, there were plenty of schoolteachers, nurses, secretaries, and housekeepers). Thus, sexual harassment in the workplace did not happen so often (men taking sexual advantage of their housekeepers, think of Samuel Pepys's diary here, came to constitute a fairly large class). It can't be said that sexual harassment is just like domestic abuse, then—it had always been going on, we just didn't recognize it. Overlooking what used to be called "hanky-panky," sexual harassment is a new way professional men and women can disappoint God and therefore sin. Interestingly, the very sin of sexual harassment seems to require women to do something to which some religious conservatives continue to object—that is, to work outside the home. That said, American laws against sexual harassment certainly do not emerge from religious tenets.

Sexual harassment in the school, university, or workplace is now firmly established in federal and state law as a form of gender discrimination and a ground for tort liability. The ordinary standards of justice applicable to other aspects of public life, including norms against discrimination in hiring and firing, now govern sex in the workplace (universities are, after all, workplaces). Threatening to penalize a business subordinate for refusing sexual advances is a kind of injury the law already has the tools to remedy.

The move to criminalize sexual harassment initially foundered. Workplace sexual harassment violated the equal employment laws, Catherine MacKinnon and other legal scholars argued in the 1980s. Critics insisted that one cannot know whether another person is interested in a particular sexual interaction unless one asks, that legally imposed silence or restraint would lead to less sex when more sex is a paramount good, and that people could fend off harassers depending on their own, internally constructed sexual preferences. Legal critics said that to regulate sexual harassment is to violate the protections of free speech and privacy and to lead to totalitarianism or, at the least, Senator Joseph McCarthy's witch hunts. Sexual harassers became the real victims, persecuted by zealous and repressive feminists hostile to the natural and normal desires of heterosexual males.

Some thinkers, such as Jeffrey Rosen of *The New Republic*, tried for years to create a groundswell for repeal or narrowed definitions of sexual harassment in law. Thwarted by a unanimous Supreme Court application of the law in sexual harassment cases in the late 1990s, Rosen and *New Yorker* magazine legal analyst Jeffrey Toobin reopened the subject of repeal of sexual harassment laws as part of a perceived social revulsion against punishing a popular president (i.e., Bill Clinton) for sexual misconduct.[24] Toobin was particular exercised over Yale University's prohibition of faculty-student sex, enacted in the aftermath of an incident involving a seventeen-year-old freshman failing mathematics and the thirty-one-year-old math teacher she sought out for help.[25] Although the professor was dismissed, he insisted that the sex had been consensual each time it occurred. In an interesting but unrelated coda, the writer Naomi Wolf petitioned Yale in 2004 to reprimand or fire Professor Harold Bloom, whom she accused of having sexually harassed her when she was a Yale undergraduate in the early 1980s.[26] Wolf's reasoning for making the request some twenty years after she left Yale was, she said, to protect current female undergraduates. Yale declined to dismiss Bloom, who was by then reportedly quite ill and physically feeble.

Sexual harassment may or may not involve the sin of adultery. Whether lust or malice motivates the harassment of an inferior by a business superior, harm is done. Nonbelievers will see that people who believe in God will naturally insist that sexual harassment offends him. Most of us need to earn a living, and it is now illegal of our bosses to impose erotic conditions on our continued employment or eventual promotion. Of course, much more is involved in the legal definition of sexual harassment than asking for sexual relationships. Think of pin-ups affixed to office walls, workplace outings to geisha houses, and sexually explicit conversations without accompanying overtures. Laws against what we now call sexual harassment have no doubt cut down on such situations, even as such laws have fanned the flames of desire for some. Those who find the forbidden sexually stimulating will only welcome the law against sexual harassment as a new aphrodisiac.

DENYING THE HOLOCAUST

Believing in God seemed to get harder in the twentieth century, the most violent and bloody of all. One particular genocide stands out from all the others, the one for which Hitler will be remembered. Even non-Jews struggled to understand how a good and omnipotent Father could have allowed six million Jews to go to their death in Nazi death camps, usually after unspeakable tortures. Today Westerners regularly invoke the Nazi as the prototypical bad guy, the sinner of sinners. Yet a new sinner now rivals the Nazi's heartlessness: the person who insists the Holocaust never happened.

In a preface to the book *Denying History: Who Says the Holocaust Never Happened and Why Do They Say It?* Arthur Hertzberg asserts:

> The attack by the Holocaust deniers is, in a very deep sense, the most hurtful that has ever been leveled against the Jews. We have long been prepared to defend our religion and our corporate character (to the degree to which it might exist), but the immediate reaction by Jews to the

Holocaust deniers is outrage so complete that we cannot think of an appropriate response. How, indeed, can a people answer the charge that it has imagined or invented its greatest tragedy?[27]

Today, neo-Nazis have an obvious interest in making their predecessors look better. The accounts of Auschwitz, they insist, are wildly exaggerated or even invented. One of their arguments is that the gas chambers were simply not large enough, or efficient enough, to have been the place of execution for many hundreds of thousands of people in a very short time. Along similar lines, Holocaust deniers argue that the same Communists who worked to portray Nazis in the worst possible light deliberately exaggerated the number of the Nazis' victims and the number of extermination camps.

Of course, we know of other genocides. To this day, Turks deny the Armenian massacres.[28] Although various other examples (e.g., in Rwanda) suggest themselves, the Holocaust has arguably captured the Western spotlight. One reason why Holocaust deniers act as they do comes down to a fascination with Jews and with things Jewish. Another reason: a classic case of blaming the victim, insisting that Jews have brought any anti-Semitism on themselves and now have only themselves to blame. Others insist that Jews invented the Holocaust in order to gain the moral high ground. Yet another reason is the need for enemies: an external enemy clears away internal strife. An enemy in life, like an opponent in sports, gives focus and meaning—someone to defeat, something to overcome. Anti-Semitism lies at the heart of complex and multifaceted motivations for denying the Holocaust.

Doubting the Holocaust, or denying it altogether, happens in part because of the fluidity of history. Unlike the scientifically sophisticated approach of a chemist or a physicist, a historian's search for truth must make its way through a minefield of human biases and foibles. Facts emerge murkily from the past, as flawed people press them into service of some explanation or political agenda. Facts cannot exactly speak for themselves but instead rely on ventriloquists. The testing of hypotheses in historical scholarship is tricky; it takes some skill to hold them apart from cultures and epochs.

It is one thing to bear false witness (in direct violation of a commandment) and another thing to accuse someone else of bearing false witness (in this case, the Jews). As if the extermination of six million Jews in Nazi death camps were not enough, some today persecute Jews further by insisting that Jews simply fabricated what must be one of the darkest moments of the twentieth century.

Part of the controversy surrounding the release of Mel Gibson's blockbuster film *The Passion of the Christ* (2004) involved his father, a conservative Roman Catholic who stated publicly his doubts about the scope of the Holocaust. Only a couple of years earlier, Emory University professor Deborah Lipstadt had found herself sued by David Irving, a British historian who had referred to the Holocaust as "only a legend" and thus dismissed her scholarship. The author of an acclaimed 1993 book, *Denying the Holocaust: The Assault on Truth and Memory*, she defended herself against libel charges and won in British court (in Britain, unlike the United States, the defendant must prove the truth of what she wrote). The debate underlying that court case, like the publicity over the views of Mel Gibson's father, stings Jews. Questioning whether the Holocaust happened or doubting accounts of its extent has become a sin, one linked murkily to genocide and racism.

HOMOPHOBIA

Throughout most of the twentieth century, homosexuals were essentially forced to lead double lives of deception. Double lives can be exhausting. That kind of secretiveness and closetedness can ravage a person. Shackling one's amorous passion, refusing ever to give in to it, can lead to a crippling coldness, creating a vicious circle. It is not hard to understand why gay men and women entered heterosexual marriages or why so many of these marriages failed. Before domestic partner benefits, before nondiscrimination laws, before Stonewall, before the word *gay* meant anything but homosexual, it was all right to shun gay people. Today, with few exceptions, it is no longer all right. Not exactly.

In the 2004 elections in the United States, gay marriage aroused widespread debate among liberals and conservatives. Conservatives opposed to the legalization of gay marriage won the day, but even most of them were careful to hold apart two separate threads—namely, opposition to gay people and opposition to gay sex. It was considered unseemly to hate gay people but laudable to deny the morality of gay sex. In this distinction, Americans largely followed the Vatican.

The Vatican has certainly condemned gay bashing, but it has also condemned gay sex, and in such terms as to make comprehensible that ordinary people might infer that beating up moral criminals is basically all right. By no means has the Vatican been alone here: until the U.S. Supreme Court decision *Lawrence v. Texas* (2003) reversed *Bowers v. Hardwick* (1986), plenty of ordinary Americans also inferred that gay people deserved whatever bad things happened to them.

In 1994, Jack Hampton, a Texas state district court judge, gave a killer of two gay men a thirty-year sentence instead of life in prison after remarking that the men wouldn't have been killed "if they hadn't been cruising the streets picking up teenage boys."[29] In 1997, forty states in the United States still allowed known homosexuals to be summarily fired from their jobs without cause.[30] In 1998, 54 percent of Americans still believed homosexuality to be a sin, and even more—59 percent—believed it to be morally wrong; 44 percent believed that homosexual relations between consenting adults should be illegal.[31] At the close of the twentieth century, the murder of Matthew Shephard (a gay twenty-one-year-old college student) by two self-proclaimed homophobes spoke volumes of the viciousness of homophobia in America. As the debate over gay marriage steamed up in the first decade of 2000, some liberal activists charged that hatred of homosexuals remains the last acceptable prejudice in America.

In the 1970s, Catholic theologians stepped in to denounce the emerging sin of homophobia—emerging, because it had previously been assumed that avoiding contact with any gay person was what the righteous did. In the 1970s as now, Catholic moral thinking judges homosexual orientation sinless, homosexual acts (gravely) sinful. Two documents in particular have defined contemporary discussions of Catholic homosexuality. The first, the *Declaration Regarding Certain Questions of Sexual Ethics*, was issued by the Congregation for the Doctrine of the Faith (CDF) at the end of 1975. The second, the *Letter to All Catholic Bishops on the Pastoral Care of Homosexual Persons*, was released in the fall of 1986. Both the *Declaration* and the *Letter* are signed by the prefect or head of the CDF—in 1975, by Cardinal Seper; in 1986, by Cardinal Ratzinger. Each was approved for publication by the reigning pope (Paul VI and John Paul II). The 1986 declaration further states that it was written at the pope's command. These documents distinguish between *being gay* (not a sin) and *having gay sex* (a sin); these documents carefully called homophobia a sin, even as they muddied the waters (for it can be difficult to resist understanding a person in terms of what he wants).

The private advice of the CDF in 1992 opposing equal civil rights for homosexuals came in "Some Considerations Concerning the Response to Legislative Proposals on the Non-Discrimination of Homosexual Persons." While deploring acts of violence against homosexuals, the document defended such violence as understandable, essentially because homosexuals did not take enough care to conduct themselves as heterosexuals (i.e., to conform to "gender norms"). The document even went so far as to suggest barring gays and lesbians from certain areas of employment—such as schoolteachers, youth counselors, or athletic coaches—from being temporary parents for foster children, and from military recruitment. In the summer of 2003, the pope himself appealed to Canadians and Americans to oppose gay marriage, which had neared legal passage in both places.

The term *homophobia* is now popularly construed to mean fear and dislike of homosexuality and of those who practice it. One basis for this fear, many argue, is the perception that homosexuality and homosexuals disrupt the sexual and gender order supposedly established by what is often called natural law. Another source of homophobia is the fear that the social conduct of homosexuals—rather than homosexual behavior alone—disrupts the social, legal, political, ethical, and moral order of society. Male homosexuality has been the primary target of homophobia. One modern sin (homophobia) belies another (misogyny), as people who dislike gay men are often the same people who disapprove of women taking on traditionally male roles (e.g., CEO or priest). Meanwhile, many conservatives will insist that they neither fear nor hate homosexuals; conservatives resist the label "homophobes" and, with perhaps good reason, insist that the word *homophobic* only applies to people who hate gays.

With regard to Roman Catholic theologians and priests who inveigh (often hypocritically) against gay people, some scholars have linked homophobia to despair, especially for lesbian and gay youth, and even the spread of AIDS.[32] In the secular culture, then, a modern sin has emerged: to deprive gay and lesbian adolescents of hope, to encourage self-loathing, to deny gay and lesbian people the right to marry. This secular culture clashes with Catholic culture, making the orthodox Catholic position sinful (in the eyes of liberals). Of course, Catholics were not the only ones to take this position on gay marriage: fundamentalists and Evangelicals such as James Dobson (Focus on the Family) and Jerry Falwell (The Moral Majority) thought along similar lines.[33] Such conservatives insist on the intrinsic sinfulness of gay marriage and point out that homophobia does not describe them, because they do not fear homosexuality—they simply condemn it. Meanwhile, moral questions have arisen: If you're a man who sexually desires only other men, is it a sin to marry a woman? Even a woman who adores you and pretends not to notice your sexual lack of interest in her? Reasonable people will disagree here.[34] What seems clear is that the world has become much more finely attuned to sin, picking up on the radar screen such offenses as domestic abuse and gay bashing that would have previously been hushed up and hidden, if not outright excused.

CIRCUMCISION

Circumcision, whether of infant females or males, has sparked heated opposition. Opponents resort to rhetoric that resembles the language of sin to stress the moral wrong of the act. By no means do I want to suggest that circumcision ranks beside anti-Semitism or gay bashing on the spectrum of possible moral failings, only to indicate the range of moral objections in the early twenty-first century. Well known is the fact that many Western women spoke out publicly against female circumcision in the late 1990s. Less known is opposition to male circumcision.

In March 1999, the American Academy of Pediatrics (AAP) released a policy statement on the circumcision of newborn males, stating that the putative health benefits of circumcision do not merit recommendation as a routine procedure.[35] The withdrawal of medical support for routine circumcision raises intriguing implications for sin. If it makes sense to speak of the right to be born, to speak of respect for the rights of a fetus, it might make sense to speak of the right of an infant male to decide the fate of his foreskin.

It is now illegal in the United States to perform genital alteration on female minors, no matter how minimal the surgery or how safe and sanitary the procedure. Newborn male genital alteration, however, is an accepted procedure in the United States. Despite some controversy, circumcision remains a familiar part of life in America. The law takes no cognizance of the male procedure, with no records kept of circumcisions performed outside hospitals and with no oversight or licensing of ritual practitioners. The American culture of circumcision is slowly shifting, raising the question of sin. Humans can harm one another in a panoply of ways, but genital mutilation must be one of the most intimate. After listening to the men who protest their unwitting circumcisions, we'll have to decide whether only a hard-hearted person would exclude infant circumcision from the list of modern sins. In circumcision we reach the outer limit of the sympathy others can reasonably expect to elicit from us.

Medical research confirms the intuition that cutting an infant's penis causes pain, though the implications of this pain for an individual's later development are disputed. Nevertheless, the larger question about circumcision, as with any clinical intervention, is whether it improves patients' health. Medical researchers have yet to confirm whether circumcision increases life span or reduces the incidence of disease. In an era of managed care, insurance companies naturally question whether any health benefits outweigh the costs.

In preventive medicine, the general rule is that the intervention should match the risk. When the risk is large, aggressive interventions make sense. The smaller the risk, the more caution one should exercise. And in moral theology, a sense of proportions governs discussions of sinfulness. Is the very application of sin to circumcision simply frivolous? Should we take seriously the anger of *anyone* who tells us that he has been wronged? What's particularly interesting about circumcision is the fact that God wanted it—indeed, commanded it. After all, he commanded Abraham five thousand years ago to have all Jewish men circumcised.

Some American men have protested the routine circumcision of newborn infants; these men have gone so far as to claim that they had been harmed—indeed, psychologically scarred—by the attempt to "protect" them. These protesters wanted to regain the sensitivity they felt had been stolen from them along with their foreskins. These men referred to circumcision as "the universally shared wound of males in America." Through the 1970s and early 1980s, the rare man who wanted to reverse his circumcision usually met with skepticism or derision from physicians. With the formation of Brothers United for Future Foreskins (BUFF) in 1982, some activists urged public discussion of "the Nonsurgical Foreskin Restoration Method." The budding movement gained steam in June 1987, when a *Donahue* show devoted an hour to circumcision. A guest named Richard Steiner extolled the virtues of foreskin restoration.

In the audience that day sat Jim Bigelow, who founded a new association for men who suffered from foreskin removal, the UNCircumcising Information and Resources Center (UNCIRC). Several other groups coalesced around the same time (e.g., the National Organization of Restoring Men [NORM] and the National Organization to Halt the Abuse and Routine Mutilation of Males [NOHARMM]). Men who embarked on the painstaking course of foreskin restoration often described their decision as a quest for wholeness, not unlike repentant sinners doing contrition. They frequently compared foreskin restoration with the familiar use of plastic surgery to construct women's breasts after cancer surgery.

The example of circumcision as a modern sin tests our sensitivity to people who tell us they are suffering. What can we say about a black professor who occasionally complains of her discomfort every time she visits the university swimming pool or tennis courts? We may insist that she has nothing to feel sorry about—all the white people there are enlightened, and the university community abhors racism, but she still may insist that she feels uncomfortable being the only black person around. Furthermore, the example of circumcision pits two forces against one another: the autonomy of an infant who may later resent having been circumcised, and the will of God, who instructed Abraham to circumcise all male infants. In any event, it seems highly unlikely that a hospital or national health care would reimburse a man for the cost of his foreskin reconstruction procedure. Whereas everyone seems to take transsexualism, or sexual reassignment surgery, quite seriously, some people may struggle to take the uncircumcision movement seriously. Our heightened sense of sensitivity today may have limits, and circumcision might be just the example to illuminate those limits. If we were to dismiss male circumcision from the list of modern sins, we would have to provide a good explanation for why male circumcision differs morally from female circumcision. Religious Jews and Muslims may find it convenient to reach for Hebrew scriptures in the attempt, once again invoking the language of sin.

In a separate vein, circumcising infants has perhaps encapsulated a larger and more difficult question—whether it is perhaps objectionable to baptize an infant without asking him or inculcating a religious tradition in him more generally. Violating the autonomy of others worries us moderns in a variety of ways.

RACISM

Racism is perhaps the most familiar modern sin in contemporary Americans. The struggle for civil rights in America, like the struggle to end apartheid in South Africa, figures into the curriculum of virtually all high school students in these respective countries. Many Americans think of the civil rights movement as a struggle against sin. This movement began in earnest in the early 1960s, when Governor George Wallace refused to desegregate the University of Alabama, when James Meredith attempted to enroll in the University of Mississippi (only to meet with mob violence), and when Birmingham police officers turned high-powered fire hoses on black protesters.

Hating or discriminating against other people has become a cardinal sin today. Less obvious and much more threatening is the legacy of racism, according to which Caucasians reap the fruits of an unearned privilege of being white in a white supremacist society.

Racism will likely endure in the West, notwithstanding an increase in interracial dating and marriage. In the 1960s, black leader Malcolm X decried the tendency of African Americans to prefer the lighter children in their families and the lighter adults in their communities. In his autobiography, Malcolm X maintained that such preferences masked self-loathing. While such a deeply ingrained tendency may prevail for at least several generations to come, it should be noted that scientific advances will make it more difficult for lighter-skinned people to congratulate themselves on distance from darker-skinned neighbors. DNA testing often reveals that white people are racial mongrels, with forebears spanning several different racial groups.[36]

One hierarchy or another will emerge—either that it's better to be white than black or that it's better to be black than white (as Elijah Muhammad, d. 1975, the leader of the Nation of Islam, insisted). Much more will be said on the sin of racism in chapter 6, "The Sins of Our Fathers," when I discuss the American policy of affirmative action in the context of intergenerational justice and Greek tragedy.

DISRESPECTING OTHER RELIGIONS

The ecumenical turn of the late twentieth century came close to ending religious triumphalism, or the belief that one single religion would ultimately prove correct and all others simply wrong. The fanaticism pursuant to September 11, 2001, initially threatened to return many in the West to an earlier, my-way-or-the-highway mentality, but the remarkable gains of the late twentieth century seem to be rather firmly anchored in our reflexes.

In the wake of 9/11, various television commentators and journalists raced to assure Americans that terrorism did not marry well with Islam. As Princeton professor Bernard Lewis wrote in *What Went Wrong?* "There is nothing in Islamic history to compare with the emancipation, acceptance, and integration of other-believers and nonbelievers in the West; but equally, there is nothing in Islamic history to compare with the Spanish expulsion of Jews and Muslims, the Inquisition, the *Auto da fés*, the wars of religion, not to speak of more recent crimes of commission and acquiescence."[37] It would be a great mistake to single out Muslims as an example of believers who disrespect other believers. Many Muslims spoke out against Elijah Muhammad, the American leader of the Nation of Islam in the 1960s and 1970s; they maintained that his Nation of Islam was a separatist organization, as opposed to a community of believers. Elijah Muhammad's successor, the American Louis Farrakhan, has taught that white people in general but Jews in particular bear the blame for the problems of African Americans. It would be a mistake to seize on Farrakhan as an example of Muslim disrespect for Christians and Jews, as Farrakhan does not come close to representing mainstream Muslim sentiments.

Catholics serve as a better example here. We can measure twentieth-century ecumenical gains by the Roman Catholic Church. In the late nineteenth century, Pope Leo XIII came close to affirming the importance of non-Catholic religions. Other, more conservative Catholics pummeled him for this inclination. The reactions to Leo's liberalism surfaced in the condemnation of "Americanism."[38] A substantial group of conservative Catholics, led by Archbishop Corrigan of New York and Bishop McQuaid of Rochester, campaigned for a complete withdrawal of Catholics from the state educational system in America. Others, led by Archbishop John Ireland of St. Paul, wanted a compromise that would allow continuing Catholic participation in the public schools. Archbishop Ireland's attitude reflected a more general openness to the distinctiveness of American social and religious culture, which was demonstrated by the participation of Cardinal Gibbons in the Chicago Parliament of Religions during the exhibition there in 1892. For ten days Christian churches and denominations took part with Buddhists, Hindus, and Muslims in a public affirmation of "basic religious truths." Gibbons closed the proceedings by leading the assembly in the Lord's Prayer and giving the Apostolic Blessing—a sharing in public worship with Protestants and even non-Christians unheard of at the time, for which, remarkably, he had obtained permission directly from Leo XIII.

Such a display of "indifferentism" would have been inconceivable in Europe, and many in America were disturbed by it. Leo himself condemned "inter-Church conferences" in 1895. The continuing eagerness of "progressive" Catholics to participate fully in American life and to integrate Catholic values as fully as possible into the "American way" led many to fear a dilution of Catholic truth. Monsignor Satolli, the apostolic delegate in the United States, having initially supported Ireland and the progressives, came increasingly to feel that there was "nothing of the supernatural" about the American church. The question was whether to adapt Catholic teaching to the modern world. This sort of adaptation required a new respect for Protestants, as well as an articulation of the extent to which one should affirmatively show respect for competing faiths. In 1899, Leo sent *Testem Benevolentiae* to Cardinal Gibbons. This letter condemned the new idea that the church should adapt itself (specifically, its doctrines) to the age in order to win converts. How far the church has come since 1899.

Two of the more influential documents of the Second Vatican Council (1962–1965) stressed the importance of respecting the religious faiths of people who do not worship as Catholics do. *Lumen Gentium* (1964) and *Nostra Aetate* (1965) paid special attention to Jews, emphasizing that anti-Semitism was henceforth to be considered a grave sin. Coming on the heels of the Holocaust, the documents tried to respond to the horrific slaughter of six million Jews. Remarkably, the documents even spoke of the possibility of salvation for Jews, who by definition deny that Jesus is the Messiah.

Pope John Paul II labored strenuously to make the world safe for Judaism. The first pope to visit the synagogue of Rome, he also prayed at the Wailing Wall, recited Kaddish (the Jewish prayer for the dead) in the Vatican, allowed international scholars to begin to investigate the role of the Vatican in the tragedies of World War II, and publicly urged Jews to take pride in their Jewishness. Because of John Paul II, Catholics inhabit a different moral universe, one in which they are taught to respect the faith of their neighbors and are explicitly forbidden from anti-Semitism, a grave sin. Consequently, Catholic respect for the faithful of other religions is now expected, too.

DRUNK DRIVING

At the outset of the twentieth century, only the wealthy could afford cars. Everyone else walked to work or perhaps relied on a horse and carriage. By the end of the twentieth century, cars were much more than a luxury—they were largely essential in most of the developed world.

Long before the invention of cars, we knew what alcohol was. And we liked it. We may never know how many men died on horseback, en route from a party, but today we keep track of how many people drink and drive. We take away their driver's licenses in many instances, and we prosecute them as murderers when they kill people with their vehicles. As astounding as it may be to young Americans today, we used to let drunk drivers walk away from their crimes. We merely thought it a shame—a "tragedy," as adults might have said in the 1970s. And that was that. But today, the deaths wrought by drunk drivers constitute a crime. It makes sense to call drunk driving a sin because carelessness can no longer cloak murder. In 1980, Mothers against Drunk Driving (MADD) started with a loosely assembled group of brokenhearted mothers.

Today, it is the largest crime victims' assistance organization in the world with more than three million members and supporters.[39] MADD helps us see clearly how much social attitudes toward even unintentional wrongdoing can change.

Since MADD's inception, alcohol-related traffic fatalities have declined remarkably. The story of a little girl served as the match that started the fire. Five-and-a-half-month-old Laura Lamb became one of the world's youngest quadriplegics in 1979 when a repeat drunk driving offender traveling at 120 miles per hour hit Laura and her mother, Cindi. After the crash, Cindi and some supporters waged a war against drunk driving in their home state of Maryland. Less than a year later, on the other side of the country in California, thirteen-year-old Cari Lightner was killed at the hands of a drunk driver. Two days earlier, the offender had been released on bail for a hit-and-run drunk driving crash. He already had two drunk driving convictions with a third plea-bargained to "reckless accident." At the time of Cari's death, the drunk driving offender was carrying a valid California driver's license.

Enraged, Cari's mother, Candace Lightner, and friends gathered at a steak house in Sacramento. They discussed forming a group named MADD—Mothers against Drunk Drivers. Lightner and Lamb joined forces, and by the end of 1981, MADD had established eleven chapters in four states. MADD began to receive donations from victims and concerned citizens and was awarded a $65,000 grant for chapter development from the National Highway Traffic Safety Administration (NHTSA).

By the fall of 1982, more than seventy MADD chapters were operating, primarily initiated by aggrieved family members. In March 1983, NBC produced a made-for-television movie about MADD entitled *The Candy Lightner Story*. By the end of the month, 122 more MADD chapters had opened, covering thirty-five states. By its tenth anniversary, MADD had grown to 407 chapters and thirty-two state offices, with affiliates in Canada, England, New Zealand, and Australia. Shortly thereafter, a Gallup survey revealed that Americans cited drunk driving as the number one problem on the nation's highways. Three years later, a second Gallup poll showed that the public had become less tolerant of drunk drivers and more supportive of stiffer penalties. A modern sin was born.

In the 1980s, MADD popularized the concept of "designated drivers." Today, it is a household term, and bars and restaurants nationwide ask patrons to "designate a driver"—one of MADD's ongoing awareness and prevention messages. The organization's most well-known legislative accomplishment came in 1984 when a federal law required all states to increase the legal drinking age to twenty-one or else forfeit highway funding. In the mid-1980s, MADD launched an aggressive anti-impaired driving campaign and also undertook a legislative agenda that focused on administrative license revocation, open container laws, a maximum blood alcohol content of 0.08 percent, Dram Shop laws, Victim Bill of Rights, crime victim compensation, and several other measures.

The proliferation of Starbucks cafés around America in the 1990s might have had something to do with a heightened awareness of the dangers of drinking and driving. Whereas it was once difficult for adult friends who wanted to socialize after work to find a venue other than a bar, it is now relatively easy (if you live in an urban or suburban area) to find a café. Getting home after coffee avoids a set of worries that would beset a friend who parted from someone who entered a car after a few drinks. Starbucks removes drinkers from the occasion of sin, and drunk driving constitutes a sin in the modern West.

SIN TODAY: AN UPDATE

With the exception of harming the environment, there wouldn't appear to be any new sins against God. There wouldn't appear to be any new sins against others (at least not without new categories of persons, such as working woman, child, or public homosexual), just more precise examples (and admittedly new ones) of cruelty, negligence, and unkindness. One important exception here is spiritual smugness. In the twenty-first-century West, criticizing another person's faith is a sin; go ahead and lambaste his political views, but leave his spiritual beliefs alone.

Where we really see new sins is in the area of relations with the self. How we manage or fail to take care of ourselves offers the examples of genuinely new, utterly modern sins.

Some sins apply only to a particular religious group (e.g., in vitro fertilization and Roman Catholics). Other sins may appear to be new, but in fact are not—for example, artificial birth control and abortion did not just show up on the scene in the twentieth century but have been around for centuries as illegal ventures. Downloading pirated music from the Internet (think Napster) represents simple theft, although in a somewhat ambiguous context.

Other sins have died away—marrying outside your faith (Orthodox Jews being an obvious exception here), shopping on Sundays, disrespecting your parents by blaming them for all your problems, and so forth. For many years now, some Americans have been pressing for national health care, particularly for children. America still does not have it, and the blame may rest with individual Americans who, deep down inside, really don't want to pay higher taxes. Is this a sin? If you believe in God, you may well believe he is unhappy about this. At the least, he would wish that Americans treat each other better.

Perhaps the most obvious modern sin, the one requiring no explication, is racism. In addition to the unearned privilege of being white in a white supremacist society, we now recognize that people of color can just as unfairly hate white people. Sin cuts both ways, when it comes to hatred or withholding respect.

As always, sin comes down to boundaries, that is, overstepping boundaries. Because the boundaries keep shifting, life stays interesting. Boundaries will never disappear entirely. Traditional Jews, Christians, and Muslims are likely to populate the West for at least another century or two. This means that sin fatigue will not lead to the end of sin. Sins will be renamed and reconfigured, but they will remain. Sin fatigue may make a name for itself as an important sin in its own right, but sin fatigue will not eradicate sin. Sin will not leave us until we want it to, and we are not ready to let it go.

6

THE SINS OF OUR FATHERS: PAYING FOR AFFIRMATIVE ACTION

In September 2002, the president of Harvard University kicked off the new academic year by condemning what he termed "growing anti-Semitism" at Harvard and elsewhere. Students and professors on campus had demanded that the university remove all Israeli investments from its endowment. "Serious and thoughtful people are advocating and taking actions that are anti-Semitic in their effect if not their intent," said President Lawrence Summers, referring both to the push for divestment and to actions by student organizations at Harvard and other campuses to raise money for groups found to have ties to terrorist groups.[1] Summers was responding to a popular petition that encouraged the United States government to respect the human rights of the Palestinians by divesting from Israel (in May, 283 professors, including a number of Jewish faculty at Harvard, had signed the petition calling for an estimated $600 million divestment).

Leaving aside the sometimes-virulent debate Summers's comments aroused,[2] I want to consider the logic of considering both the effect and intent of social policies, specifically affirmative action.[3] At the end of the same school year initiated by President Summers's comments quoted here, the U.S. Supreme Court voted to uphold the contentious social program. Affirmative action does not intend to punish Caucasian people, but that may well be its effect. In this chapter, I examine the effects of American racism through the lens of college admissions and question how broadly the responsibility for rectifying social imbalances should be distributed.

AFFIRMATIVE ACTION AND THE SIN OF RACISM

Jews and Christians both condemn racism as a sin. Both groups believe that it offends God to penalize human beings—by withholding sympathy, protection, or civil rights—on the basis of their skin color.[4] The sticky question at the heart of affirmative action in the United States is how to justify helping African Americans through a social policy that seems to harm Caucasian Americans in the process. The sin of affirmative action stems from the apparent perpetuation—indeed, institutionalization—of racism. According to a familiar argument, affirmative action discriminates against white people.

Affirmative action really only affects forty or fifty American law schools and two hundred or three hundred American colleges (most of the other law schools and colleges will take just about everyone who shows up).[5] Since Supreme Court Justice Lewis Powell decided the famous case of Alan Bakke (*University of California Regents v. Bakke*) in 1978, Americans have regularly argued over the fairness of affirmative action.[6] In casting the swing vote on *Grutter v. Bollinger* in 2003, Justice Sandra Day O'Connor implicitly affirmed the unfairness of the policy by stipulating that the ruling should probably be discontinued in twenty-five years. Faute de mieux solutions need not be temporary (Freud considers Western civilization itself a faute de mieux solution in *Civilization and Its Discontents*), but Americans on both sides of the political spectrum look forward to the day when affirmative action will no longer be necessary (i.e., look forward to the day when people of color will have made more significant social and material inroads).

Recent scholarship has highlighted the astonishing extent of racial injustice in the United States and pointed out that affirmative action initially favored white people, not people of color.[7] Despite frequent criticism that affirmative action perpetuates racism, Justice Lewis Powell's policy consciously strived for moral fairness over time.[8] The fairness of affirmative action remains a rich source of material for moral philosophers and grist for debate in the public square. This social doctrine combines the bubbling wellsprings of moral psychology: envy, resentment, revenge, justice, fairness, ambition, "sour grapes," and humility. A volatile subject in contemporary America, affirmative action sometimes devolves rapidly from a political debate to an ugly exchange of charges of immorality and racism.

Criticism of affirmative action is sometimes interpreted as a thinly veiled attack on black people. This is unfortunate but understandable. Indeed, some may criticize President Summers's September 2002 remarks as a symptom of the same tendency: on this logic, anyone who criticizes Israel expresses hostility (sometimes sublimated, sometimes quite explicit) toward Jews. Lost is the possibility that someone may be interested in justice. It may be that few still believe in justice.

Philosophers since Nietzsche have debated whether sophisticated, modern talk about justice differs in any meaningful respect from old-fashioned revenge.[9] Nietzsche didn't think justice amounted to anything more than revenge; neither do many other contemporary philosophers. If affirmative action represents social justice, then it might seem to amount to a kind of revenge as well. Writing for the *National Review* some two months after the Supreme Court handed down its decision in *Grutter v. Bollinger*, Barbara Grutter, the lead plaintiff in the case, insisted, "As the polls indicate, the majority of Americans care deeply about fairness and equality, and they are not fooled by terminology. They know that when the odds of a minority applicant being accepted are 234 times that of other applicants with the same college grades and test scores, different admissions criteria are being applied based on race, and that race is not *a* factor, but *the* factor."[10] Grutter decried the unfairness of punishing white people. Although she never used the word *revenge*, it dovetailed with the spirit of her reaction to the court case.

Applying the logic of "justice = revenge" to the affirmative action debate, African Americans once suffered and now it's time for whites to take their turn. I reject this simplistic logic and accept that affirmative action amounts to *restitution* for wrongs suffered. Some African American leaders have even demanded publicly that the U.S. government financially compensate all descendents of black slaves from the antebellum South. Fair restitution of this sort would require impossibly complex algorithms. Perhaps not surprisingly, black demands for monetary restitution have not produced the desired results (although, in a separate vein, Germany does now provide restitution to concentration camp survivors, and various Catholic archdioceses in the United States have compensated victims of priestly sexual abuse).

It's not so very hard to see why someone might initially equate affirmative action with revenge, however inarticulately or subconsciously. The God of Judaism and Christianity tells us in the Hebrew Bible, "For

I, the Lord your God, am a jealous God, punishing children for the iniquity of their parents" (Exodus 20:4). This is presumably the logic that justifies Elie Wiesel's 1968 exhortation, "Every Jew, somewhere in his being, should set apart a zone of hate—healthy, virile hate—for what the German personifies and for what persists in the German. To do otherwise would be a betrayal of the dead."[11] This is not the kind of statement we would expect from someone who would later win the Nobel Peace Prize (in 1986), but it does mesh with God's logic (of course, the Hebrew Bible does present varying portraits of God's logic). Curiously, Wiesel, a concentration camp survivor, later changed his mind. Writing an op-ed piece in 2001 for the *New York Times* entitled "Only the Guilty Are Guilty, Not Their Sons," Wiesel stated, "We Jews do not believe in collective guilt. I have repeated over and over my belief that only the guilty are guilty: the children of killers are not killers, but children. I know from my own experience with German students that their burden is, at times, difficult to carry, heavy as it is with painful memories and questions about their fathers' and grandfathers' roles in the most terrifying genocide in history."[12]

Affirmative action does not aim to punish white people who may or may not have descended from slave owners. (Within two years of Summers's remarks, black students at Harvard would publicly protest that affirmative action should only benefit blacks who descended from American slaves, not black students from Africa or the Caribbean.) No one intends to seek revenge, and if the system of affirmative action happens to look or feel like revenge to white people, we must insist they are wrong. Yet young white people are being punished for the sins of their fathers, much as God told the ancient Israelites that he would punish sons for the sins of their fathers. Discrimination against talented white candidates for competitive universities cries out for recognition, but recognition as what? We must persuade white people such as Alan Bakke or Jennifer Gratz—a twenty-three-year-old white woman who was rejected from the University of Michigan in 1995 and then sued the school for racial discrimination—that *restitution*, not revenge, is at work.

Yet the plaintiffs mentioned here certainly feel as though *someone* has taken revenge on them. Will we disagree with them? I will have more to say about the difficulty of sympathizing with these specific plaintiffs later. For now, it is worth reconsidering another passage from Hebrew scriptures, a particularly zesty one. Abraham, curious about how God makes executive decisions, questions the decision to obliterate a debauched town (Genesis 18:16–33). What if there were fifty virtuous people living in the town, would you destroy them in order to take revenge on the debauched? No, God responds. What about forty-five? Forty? Ten? Abraham keeps pushing God, until God agrees that punishing even one innocent person seems immoral. Getting back at a large group that deserves to suffer doesn't justify making innocent bystanders weep and wail. Did Justice O'Connor bear this in mind while writing her opinion? Or was there some other factor, a more important and perhaps less apparent one, that overrode the suffering of the innocent? Surely Justice O'Connor would answer yes, someone else's suffering took priority here. The O'Connor example does not neatly parallel Abraham's niggling, as the O'Connor example does not exactly involve a choice of whom to "harm" but entails rather an issue of punishment.

If we allow that Bakke and Gratz suffer in the course of such social restitution, we run into another problem: Who will make restitution to Bakke and Gratz for the wrongs they suffered? Is there anything other white people can do for them? Is there anything powerful white people such as Justice O'Connor can be said to owe hopeful but disappointed white students? White students in their twenties may reasonably feel they are paying for the sins of their fathers, but it is not clear that Justice O'Connor has.

New generations of African Americans can be said to benefit from the fact that their forebears were victims. (Some black students oppose affirmative action for the reason that they suffer under it as well: they fear that all other students and faculty automatically assume that black students are inferior and gain admission to elite schools only because of affirmative action.) Do we see any way in which Bakke or Gratz will ever profit from being victims? Gratz had to settle for a less prestigious school, but her life went on. Part of her life included fighting what she took to be injustice in the University of Michigan system. Other white students in Gratz's place might well play "sour grapes"—disavow that the elite institution that rejected their application really mattered to them. No doubt this will sometimes occur, a transparent effort to save face and disguise disappointment.

Gratz applauded the fact that the old admissions program, which was scrapped after the lawsuit was filed, was declared discriminatory in federal court in 2000. "I'm excited that they were wrong and they're being told that they were wrong," said Gratz, who had to attend the university's less prestigious Dearborn campus instead of the flagship at

Ann Arbor.[13] She didn't opt for a sour-grapes strategy but voiced her disappointment and chose to fight back instead. The next generation of white students, with the support of their parents, may do the same. In the meantime, who will affirm the suffering of young white students? Note that Elie Wiesel (in the quotation cited earlier) affirmed the suffering of young Germans and acknowledged that they carry a "heavy burden." It would be a sin to dismiss hastily the suffering of young white Americans.

Most selective colleges and universities now use race as a factor in admissions, a practice that has been under attack in recent years (due in significant part to the efforts of Ward Connerly, a wealthy African American who opposes affirmative action). Michigan's system was seen as vulnerable because it is explicit, whereas other institutions use more subtle and subjective approaches. The judge, Patrick J. Duggan of the Federal District Court in Detroit, ruled in December 2000 that the university had violated the United States Constitution from 1995 to 1998 with a two-tiered admissions system that admitted white and minority applicants under different criteria. But he said Michigan's current policy, in which black and Latino applicants automatically receive a 20-point boost on a 150-point scale, was perfectly legal. The case reached the Supreme Court in the spring of 2003; the Court upheld Judge Duggan's ruling.

If we agree that it is only fair for white people to shoulder some of the burden involved in moving toward racial equality in the United States, then it will become important to spread that burden equitably among white people. As it stands, young white people seem to shoulder more of the burden than older, professionally secure white Americans do. This discrepancy should worry us.

"WHITE PRIVILEGE"

Those who support affirmative action sometimes point to "white privilege" as the moral basis for their support. From this viewpoint, white people, *simply because they are white*, enjoy a variety of social benefits of which they may not even be aware. Jennifer Gratz and other white students may boast superior SAT scores and grade point averages, but that is supposedly because they have profited from an unjust social structure that deeply favors white people. Gratz would never have even become a competitive applicant to elite colleges had she not supposedly received invisible and tangible boosts along the way, it might be objected. Affirmative action is a way of leveling the playing field, of putting a thumb on the scale for black students. This is one way of justifying affirmative action.

It is conceptually impossible to defeat this idea of "white privilege," for the more a white person succeeds, the more he or she fails. The reason for the success will always come down, at least in part, to white privilege. It is this idea that frustrates and sometimes exasperates white people living in the lower classes. One way to improve social justice in American would be to target economic status instead of race (some universities are doing precisely this, partly out of fear of race-based lawsuits). Affirmative action pivots on race, though, perhaps in an effort to atone for the sins of white fathers. It is not clear when, if ever, black people will agree that white people have done enough atoning.

Berkeley professor John McWhorter, himself an African American, argues provocatively in *Losing the Race: Self-Sabotage in Black America* that African Americans shoot themselves in the foot by portraying themselves as victims (and white people as victors).[14] According to McWhorter, African Americans would do better to emphasize and publicize the many African Americans who have succeeded in America despite an abundance of enormous social obstacles in their way. Inspiring African Americans will do more good for them, McWhorter insists, than enraging or infantilizing them.

McWhorter chips away at the idea of white privilege. Such privilege was and is unfair, but it has already diminished in power. Aging, lower-class white Americans will scoff at the idea that they enjoy vast privileges just because of their skin color, and the story of Jennifer Gratz makes it easy to see why. The Gratz story is just one, to be sure, but it may be enough for conservative and lower-class white Americans to start insisting that African Americans enjoy more privilege than they are willing to admit. It is not my point to claim here that African Americans do not deserve special help; rather, I want only to draw attention to the difficulty of ending an argument by appealing to something called "white privilege."

It must be said that Jennifer Gratz, or any white student protesting affirmative action, cannot claim with certainty that she would have been admitted to an elite school absent a policy that "boosted" the applications of racial minorities. She can never know for certain that *she* would have been admitted to Michigan's Ann Arbor campus. Yet we should take her worry seriously. We take seriously the pleas of racial minorities that they suffer from subtle discrimination. Even when an African American cannot prove that he has suffered from unspoken racial discrimination, many sympathetic white Americans will believe their black neighbors. Young white people applying to elite schools may suffer as a result of something like "black privilege," and they also deserve our sympathy.

It may be impossible to pin down and highlight the boundaries of "white privilege" or "black privilege," but that doesn't mean neither exists. Take any virtue or vice—compassion or hatred, integrity or dishonesty—and we will run into the same difficulty in making concrete certain ideas or emotions.

White privilege, such as it is, can only take you so far. We may not know for certain that race kept Gratz off the Ann Arbor campus, but we know that it might have. Everyone will agree that taking an unfair advantage over the competition is wrong, but not everyone will agree on the crucial term *fair*. Invoking "white privilege" to explain away the success of white students may raise skepticism in the same way that invoking "the achievement gap" in defense of underperforming black students sometimes does.

INTERGENERATIONAL JUSTICE:
PULLING THE LADDER UP AFTER ME?

Intergenerational justice is a big term for a certain brand of thoughtfulness. One generation, swimming in natural resources, may live it up, metaphorically speaking. That generation may pollute the environment and never worry about the consequences of harming nature, even though scientists may warn that the environment will give out in a century or so. "Who cares?" people living for the day may wonder. It never occurs to them that their children will be left holding the bill for all the damage they've wrought. *Intergenerational justice* invokes the moral appropriateness of treating other generations as fairly as we expect coeval individuals or societies to treat one another.

At base, this chapter concerns intergenerational justice. There is something suspect about a Caucasian man, or a group of Caucasian men, preaching about affirmative action from a comfortable perch. What does it cost white people in power to root for the racial underdog? What does it cost white people with no apparent power to root for the racial underdog? Big difference.

Original Sin presents an excellent model through which to understand this problem of intergenerational justice. Just as an apparently innocent infant is born with the stain of Original Sin, so apparently are white infants born into American culture with the stain of racial hatred. No matter how well meaning the white child, she is often understood to be a menace to black people.[15] Although she may have never harmed or spoken ill of a black person, she is presumed to be an oppressor. She is morally inferior to black people. Suffering can confer a kind of moral superiority, and black people will as a group suffer because of some white people—white people who may be impossible to pinpoint.

Part of the problem is the implicit assumption that black people are any different from white people. It could be that, had black people settled the United States, they may have employed slavery as well. It could be that, were black people in the majority in America, they would treat white people every bit as badly as white people have treated black people. It could be that black people are more like white people than any of the well-meaning liberals has let on. A thoroughgoing moral analysis of race relations would emphasize that no race is likely to be more moral than any other. Racism appears to be a widespread problem internationally, which would mean that white faults are human faults.

What can we do for young white people who find themselves unwillingly cast in the role of brute? Unlike Christians, who can remove the stain of Original Sin through baptism, white Americans cannot wash off their blemish. That is the tragedy in America. Young white people must blame themselves for the nagging problem of racism, even though young white people may feel it wildly unfair—immoral even—to blame themselves.

Meanwhile, older white Americans who enjoy positions of power earn credit for in effect punishing younger white Americans. There is something dashingly romantic about any person in power rooting for an underdog (think of FDR here, or JFK or RFK). Who will deny that it was evil of southern plantation owners to enslave black people? Who will deny the crippling legacy of the inner-city ghettos? Of course people in power can earn applause through appealing to our compassion, our sense of moral urgency. That is cheap applause (admittedly, it cost FDR rather a lot: he was vilified as "a traitor to his class").

But what about putting your money where your mouth is? Actions speak louder than words. That's why Americans favor political candidates who have served in the military, particularly those who have gone into combat to protect their country. We see in these veterans-turned-candidates proof of their convictions. They don't just *say* they love America; they offer us *evidence* that they have risked their lives for America. And so we believe them. Americans elected Bill Clinton, who had wriggled out of military service in Vietnam, but they never stopped sneering at him for that evasion. If you want to know what a person believes, watch what he does. A white corporate CEO or university president who pleads with his white counterparts to endorse affirmative action asks them to accept very real sacrifices. Jennifer Gratz, the woman in Michigan, is one such sacrifice. She and her parents may have worked very hard indeed to propel her to the level of excellence necessary to enter the University of Michigan. She failed. She bore a painful part of the cost of redressing racial injustice in the United States.

What does a white university president have to lose? What would he be willing to give up in order to promote racial injustice? A part of his salary? His job? Lee Bollinger left a prestigious post as president of the University of Michigan for an even more prestigious post as president of Columbia University. Did he ever suffer? Will his children? Unlikely. But he arguably did benefit from championing a cause that made him look wonderfully sympathetic. Robin Hood stole from the rich to give to the poor, but Robin Hood was not rich. Lee Bollinger is.

It might be thought that an elected white person in power risks his very job when he publicly supports affirmative action. True enough. Given that perhaps a majority of Americans disapproves of affirmative action, it is certainly true that the university president or foundation head might be said to risk something. But there are big risks and small risks; this must be considered a small one. For in the present climate, a university president could win not only the admiration of posterity but also converts to his view by forfeiting his job. No university president yet has lost his job over supporting affirmative action. Were he to do so, he would be canonized a secular saint by liberal fellow-travelers and find his way to another job, perhaps an even better one (e.g., running the Mellon Foundation). No, the university president doesn't risk much. And if he were a politically shrewd, calculating soul, he might well throw himself behind affirmative action even if his heart wasn't in it. He feels the pull of the tide.

Former Princeton University president William G. Bowen assumed leadership of the Mellon Foundation and has since argued publicly in favor of maintaining affirmative action in American universities. In the wake of a widely publicized scandal in 2006 at Duke University involving white male lacrosse players and black female strippers, Richard Brodhead, the president of Duke, invited Bowen and Julius Chambers, a former director of the NAACP Legal Defense and Educational Fund, to analyze the incident, which involved rape allegations.[16] Brodhead also appointed an internal committee to investigate the problem. In their report, Bowen and Chambers concluded, among other things, that Duke had been "handicapped by its own limited diversity." By this, Bowen and Chambers meant to criticize the composition of Duke's internal committee, which was comprised of five white men, an Asian American man, and a white woman. Bowen and Chambers seemed to imply that white people, if left to their own devices, would naturally behave as racists. It is not clear that such a finding will help America move beyond racism. The message some young Americans—both white and black—may have taken from Bowen's comment is that white people are not to be trusted. Such a message increases the burden of young whites who oppose racism but cannot convince blacks of their sincerity. (The white lacrosse players emerged victorious in the suit, after the testimony of one particular stripper proved quite faulty and after allegations that the police chief had acted to undermine the case of the lacrosse players.)

What does the generation of established white professionals born before 1955 owe white Americans born after 1960? Anything at all? If we accept what I take to be the most compelling argument in favor of affirmative action—that it is patently unfair to ask African Americans to accept the whole cost of moving to a racially just society—then we are left with the proposition that white people must help. But *which* white people? Young white people are footing the bill for the magnanimous social rhetoric of older white Americans. Although white Americans today are not guilty of the sin of their fathers, young whites are paying for the sins of their fathers. The distinction between guilt and punishment is key here, as is the matter of agency: young white people are not guilty of their forebears' racism, but they suffer the punishment for it. Young white people did not choose to suffer for their fathers; young white people find themselves almost without choice (there is, of course, the choice to fight against such punishment or to complain about it).

Another argument to which a white university president might resort is that it's easier to change the system from within than from without.[17] This argument, familiar from Marx, appeals to plenty of gay Catholics, for instance, who explain to gay people furious with the church that they stay within it because they stand a better chance of effecting reform from within than from without (the same could be said of gay Baptists, gay Republicans, etc.). Fair enough. But does this argument hold for university presidents?

University presidents, in either public or private institutions, do not elect themselves. They are elected. But they can define their jobs to a significant extent and allocate responsibility for certain tasks to whomever they see fit. Have we ever heard of a white university president keen on affirmative action sharing part of his job with a person of color? Have we ever heard of a white president allocating part of his salary to young Caucasian Ph.D.'s who cannot find an academic post in a market that explicitly courted candidates of color?

No. Part of the problem here is that we can never point to an instance in which people will say, "That person of color got a job because of his race" or "That Caucasian person was passed over for a job because of her race." Yet it is fair to say that Caucasians whisper such allegations.[18] What can a university president dedicated to hiring more faculty of color do to help aspiring faculty members who find themselves at a disadvantage because of their race? Again, young white people are on their own, paying for the sins of their fathers. Older white leaders remain in power, experiencing affirmative action as a policy rather than an obstacle.

Case studies could help enormously as moral philosophers examine the ethics of affirmative action. People in power have always managed to find loopholes to free them from the restrictions of the masses. How many powerful white people will watch silently and passively as their hardworking children are denied admission to the best colleges?

In their book *The Shape of the River*, former Princeton University president William G. Bowen and former Harvard University president Derek Bok leaned on a flawed analogy to persuade us that white students who fail to gain admission to elite colleges lose their places to less qualified students of color.[19] When nondisabled people covet an empty parking spot reserved for wheelchair users, the nondisabled might swear to themselves and say something to the effect of "If only that spot weren't reserved for the disabled, I would get it now." No, the authors assert—that spot could just as easily have gone to some other nondisabled person. But when it comes to university admissions, it is simply not the case that white applicants are wrong when they say, "If only there weren't affirmative action, I would have gotten admitted to Elite U." For as long as statistics indicate that the test scores and grade point averages of people of color lag significantly behind those of white applicants, it is accurate to say something like "If only there weren't affirmative action, some white students—perhaps even I—would have received the spot now occupied by (some) people of color." The analogy assumes that we are selfish, only interested in benefits for ourselves; it could be, however idealistic it may sound, that some people are interested in social justice.

What's at issue is the relative contribution to redressing racial injustices that certain generations make. Just as previous generations of African Americans suffered terribly under Jim Crow laws, today's African Americans enjoy unprecedented opportunities unthinkable to their parents. And today's generation of white Americans is called on to make sacrifices their white parents by and large do not make. Who will care about the white students who slip through the cracks? Or about the lower-middle-class white kids left behind?

Philosophers have spoken of intergenerational justice in terms of the environment (especially pollution, global warming, butchered forests, etc.) and national debt, but no one seems to have noticed that it bears importantly on affirmative action as well. Young people in America pay for the sins of their fathers in a variety of ways, and older Americans ought to think long and hard about the consequences of their actions as well as how to foot the bill equitably. (I will have more to say about university presidents and affirmative action in my discussion of humanism.)

THE SUFFERING OF THE FACELESS

As I've indicated, part of what makes affirmative action interesting is the impossibility of pinpointing personal suffering. Barbara Grutter, Jennifer Gratz, and a countless host of faceless Americans may fume that they have been discriminated against, but they can't *prove* that they would have been admitted to the school of their choice, absent a policy of affirmative action. It is therefore easy for defenders of affirmative action to rest their case, concluding simply that Barbara Grutter would not necessarily have seen her dream come true without affirmative action. It's as if there are no real losers in affirmative action decisions—everyone wins.

But does that mean that Barbara Grutter or Jennifer Gratz never really suffered? Certainly not. They did and perhaps still do. They felt entitled to admission, which doesn't mean that they should have been admitted. Still, they can point to objective measures such as grade point averages and SAT scores, measures universities respect and depend on, and complain that they, or people like them, are being discriminated against (of course, elite universities insist that admissions decisions follow on a complex amalgam of criteria). No one wants to be a victim of racial discrimination, but the sins of American fathers have doomed young Americans today to the role of social oppressor and, in certain cases of employment decisions and university admissions, to premature rejection.

Jennifer Gratz is not Rosa Parks, but that doesn't mean that Gratz should disappear from the list of people Americans care about. Parks, a real person, suffered discrimination. What makes the Rosa Parks bus incident so very compelling is the sense that this African American stood in for, suffered for, so very many other African Americans. Gratz stands in for plenty of other white Americans as well, but these Americans are invisible. University admissions offices will never release names of white students who lost their place to minority applicants (such lists do not exist), but that doesn't mean that some white students don't suffer discrimination. True, many disappointed white applicants may include themselves inaccurately in the group of superior-but-rejected applicants. Nonetheless, we can be certain that some rejected white applicants really would have been better off in a race that prohibited the use of race as a criterion in admissions decisions.

More and more whites will notice the cost of affirmative action and perhaps see in that cost the sin of fathers long dead. I have not yet mentioned the 1998 lawsuit that became known as the Hopwood case for one plaintiff, Cheryl Hopwood. Four rejected applicants to the University of Texas law school charged in 1992 that the law school's admissions policy discriminated against whites. The school had supposedly set low test score standards for black and Latino applicants in an effort to increase enrollment from those groups. Judge Sam Sparks of Federal District Court denied the several plaintiffs' request for admission to the

University of Texas law school and for the more than $5 million in damages they claimed. Instead, he awarded them $1 each plus about $776,000 for attorneys' fees, court costs, and interest, to be paid by the university. In a crucial move, a coup de grace, Judge Sparks added, "The court finds the law school has proved by a preponderance of the evidence that none of the plaintiffs would have been admitted to the law school under a constitutional admissions system."[20] The judge essentially told the plaintiffs, "You wouldn't have made it, anyway," dodging the question of whether other white applicants that year would have made it but didn't.

It would be interesting to audit the admissions process of the law school, or to compel it to produce the names of white applicants who would have been admitted, absent a policy of affirmative action. Of course, admissions offices insist that the process of admitting students never comes down to simple lists or computing numerical averages, but the dean of the University of Virginia's law school told the *New York Times* in 2003 that there would be few black students at his law school if it weren't for affirmative action (Dean John Jeffries used this point to underscore his support for affirmative action because, he said, black students enriched the culture of his law school).[21]

Because a school does not keep a list of white applicants who "would have been admitted . . . under a constitutional admissions system," no individual white student can ever prove discrimination, as I have said. Poof, discrimination disappears, just like that. Meanwhile, Grutter, Hopwood, and others believe they have been discriminated against. They think of affirmative action as a kind of revenge. They see themselves paying for the sins of their fathers. More and more white Americans will see themselves in Barbara Grutter and Cheryl Hopwood; more and more Americans will see themselves paying for the sins of their fathers.

It might be thought that, given how terribly American blacks have suffered in the ugly legacy of slavery and Jim Crow laws, the suffering of an above-average but not exceptional cross section of white America is not enough to dismantle affirmative action. But this justification is not good enough. It amounts to saying to Barbara Grutter and others, "Keep your mouth shut. We don't care about you, we have more important people to worry about." We need a more sensitive understanding of the costs of affirmative action. We should care about the almost successful but disappointed white applicants whose names we'll never know.

Even though we may not be able to say precisely which white students have suffered under affirmative action, we can still maintain that *some* have. And that is enough to merit public sympathy. We may not be able to do any better than affirmative action until 2020 or so, but we can still acknowledge its costs for young whites burdened by the sins of their fathers. At the same time, we can try much harder to improve inner-city elementary and middle schools, so that economically disadvantaged children receive an excellent education before they apply to college.

SIN AND TRAGEDY

Two questions about sin find difficult answers here. Those questions ask (1) what to do as a society about an apparent conflict of duties with regard to helping African Americans overcome a legacy of racism, and (2) whom to blame for the mess twenty-first-century Americans have inherited.

Kant dissolves the problem I point to in this chapter with a simple insistence that one moral rule can never conflict with another. He reasons:

> Because . . . duty and obligation are in general concepts that express the objective practical necessity of certain actions and because two mutually opposing rules cannot be necessary at the same time, then, if it is a duty to act according to one of them, it is not only not a duty but contrary to duty to act according to the other. It follows, therefore, that a conflict of duties and obligations is inconceivable (*obligationes non colliddunter*). It may, however, very well happen that two grounds of obligation (*rationes obligandi*), one or the other of which is inadequate to bind as a duty (*rationes obligandi non obligantes*) are conjoined in a subject and in the rule that he prescribes to himself, and then one of the grounds is not a duty. When two such grounds are in conflict, practical philosophy does not say that the stronger obligation holds the upper hand (*fortior obligatio vincit*), but that the stronger ground binding to a duty holds the field (*fortior obligandi ratio vincit*).[22]

Our intuitive feeling that there is a conflict of moral rules is simply wrong, Kant concludes. Practical reasoning overrides intuitive feeling. (Kant overlooks or simply ignores an important cultural dimension to the working of practical reasoning.) Duty and practical necessity go hand in hand in such a way, I believe, as to support the Supreme Court in its decision of the *Grutter* case. What, then, becomes of Barbara Grutter and all the other Americans who see themselves in the same boat? They must suffer the punishment due our fathers.

The Jewish philosopher Hermann Cohen finessed this conflict a bit more persuasively. Late in the nineteenth century, he tied the sins of our fathers to tragedy in a way consonant with Nietzsche's influential work *The Death of Tragedy* (1872). Cohen wrote:

> It is a peculiar feature of biblical thinking that the object of its reflection and astonishment is not so much the guilt of the ancestors in its connection with their descendants but rather the discrepancy between the guilt of the parents and the punishment of the children. The mythico-tragic thinking about the inheritance of guilt seems not to have any roots here; it is as if one were in no way able to think that God is capable of burdening guiltless man in such a way. On the other hand, the religious consciousness, for the earliest times, in the case of Abraham with regard to Sodom, resists the daily experience which suggests that the guilt of the parents subsequently brings about the misfortune of the children.
>
> This misfortune of the children appears as the aftereffect of the guilt of the parents in the punishment of the innocent children. For the children are never conscious of their own guilt, and the contemporaries, too, pay more attention to the guilt of the parents than to the possible guilt of the children. Perhaps it is already a step forward in religious consciousness if only the punishment is considered hereditary, but not the guilt itself.[23]

Cohen, who admired and took inspiration from Kant, shows us the way out. Grutter takes a hit for our fathers (see "taking one for the team" in chapter 1), which is not to say that the policy allegedly harming Grutter is immoral. Although she is not guilty, Grutter is punished as if she were. This tragedy foregrounds American social life in the new century.

Barbara Grutter and her sympathizers must continue to articulate what it feels like to be harmed in the way they claim. In the process of the struggle, we must listen carefully and show them precisely where they fail to persuade us. Grutter appeals to simple fairness (as understood to be the opposite of racism), yet she would profit enormously from returning America to a more robust sense of sin, so that she can blame someone for the suffering caused by affirmative action. The venialization of sin I have described makes this move seem inadvisable:

America keeps moving farther and farther away from a robust sense of sin, and neither she nor any movement she might ignite would be strong enough to counter that force. The sinners here—our fathers—have died, so there is no one left to blame. All who suffer in Grutter's way find themselves, in effect, new Antigones. Affirmative action isn't about sin fatigue, except perhaps as a death knell. Without sin fatigue, affirmative action would scarcely be possible; the apparent conflict of moral rules to which Kant points would tip the scale in favor of sin fear—that is, against affirmative action as a form of racial discrimination.

Affirmative action points up the tragedy of race relations in the United States: Sin is embedded in the structure of current laws. Disposition counts for little, as well-meaning white people may simply be faking their sympathy for black people. The argument that all white people profit from a social privilege resulting from their skin color makes it harder to take seriously the professed concerns of white people. Given how very much black people have suffered in the United States, it is hardly surprising that they should find themselves suspicious of white people. And given how earnestly many young white Americans want to move beyond racism, it is hardly surprising that they should find frustrating laws or social policies which seem to institutionalize the focus on race that gripped earlier Americans. In a society in which the real criminals—or at least the original ones—are all gone, the innocent suffer the consequences. We find ourselves like characters in a Greek tragedy, locked into a plight from which we cannot escape.

WHAT BECOMES OF THE BROKEN-HEARTED?

Separating the cause from the effect of an action, as Lawrence Summers did in 2002, is nothing new. That logic underlies the famous principle of double effect, by which Roman Catholic physicians justify performing what amounts to an abortion. (Roman Catholicism strictly forbids abortions.) In the event of an ectopic pregnancy (when the embryo lodges in the fallopian tubes) or cancer of the uterus, a Catholic doctor may morally (and legally, according to canon law) perform an abortion on a woman. How? According to the principle of double effect, the death of the child is a *foreseen* but *unintended* consequence of the medical operation to remove a woman's uterus. Various thinkers have derided this mental somersault as patently hypocritical, ridiculous. Yet

I allow it. Just as Summers urged us to focus on the unintended effects of divestment on Israel, so might a considerable number of social conservatives exhort us to focus on the unintended effect of affirmative action on white youth. That effect should concern all of us.

What, then, will we call Jennifer Gratz and Barbara Grutter? Sore losers? Delusional? Insensitive to the more important struggle of racial minorities? Few, if any, supporters of affirmative action meant to discriminate against Gratz or Grutter. Yet the effect of affirmative action might seem to be precisely that. When you get hit by a car, it doesn't matter whether the driver intended to strike you or not. You still suffer.

Praise for diversity on American college campuses discourages consideration of costs (moral and monetary) of affirmative action for young white people. Because we don't know precisely which white students suffer, all white students in a sense suffer (that is, because we don't know which white students fail to land an offer with their first choice of colleges, all students worry they will suffer racial discrimination). Given the increasing number of stories of American students with near-perfect SAT scores and glorious records of school activities and community service being nonetheless denied admission to their Ivy League school of choice, bias becomes increasingly difficult to prove. Yet we know that the *possibility* of racial bias remains protected by law. Even if we don't know *which* white students suffer, we know that *some* do.

As the United States continues to struggle with the reverberations of black slavery and Jim Crow laws, affirmative action has come to represent sin more vividly than past transgressions, such as homosexuality, drug dealing, or shopping on Sundays. Affirmative action raises anew an old question, whether the sins of our fathers should count against our own moral expectations and social hopes. Affirmative action can be at the same time morally objectionable and socially necessary. Both supporters and opponents of affirmative action can argue persuasively for their views. Meanwhile, affirmative action remains legal in the United States. If young people are doing the work (or making the sacrifices) for which older Americans are taking credit, then young whites deserve acknowledgment. It is important to give credit where credit is due. It is a sin to tell Jennifer Gratz and Barbara Grutter we don't care about them—their professional goals, their personal aspirations. It is a shame to run out of sympathy, but sympathy fatigue follows on the heels of sin fatigue. We've run out of sympathy for Gratz and Grutter; we find ourselves in a stance both tragic and all too human.[24]

EPILOGUE

Gratz did not ultimately get what she wanted, but she emerged some-what victorious. Early in 2007, the University of Michigan agreed to pay $10,000 to each of the two white plaintiffs (Gratz and Hamacher) who had sued in 1997 on the grounds that the university's admissions sys-tem had discriminated against them. Under the deal, the plaintiffs agreed to drop their claims against the university. By the time the plain-tiffs received their settlement, it seemed that a majority of Michigan voters had thrown their sympathy to the young white students—in the process illustrating once again that the very notion of sin remains up for grabs.

CONCLUSION

7

THE BEST WE CAN DO

Alas, sinfulness is the best we can do. That useful insight can prevent plenty of hand-wringing down the road. We do well to avoid perfectionism, which the Catholic Church calls the sin of scrupulosity, a sense of failure over not living up to lofty ideals. We do well to turn away from utopian fantasies that don't resemble any possible real world of human behavior.

By predicting regular failures in the game of virtue, we acknowledge our limitations. Where do we go from here? We should take care not to slip into what psychologists refer to as "learned helplessness." We must fight to rise above our limitations and take some solace in knowing that at least some of the battles can be won.

The cliché of a glass that is both half empty and half full anchors the question of what we can realistically hope for. What we can hope for depends on what Westerners have learned about their moral and cultural potential after many centuries of confessing sins. Just when the weariness of sin fatigue and atonement fatigue sets in, the past returns. We want to hold on to sin and evil in some fashion. As Andrew Delbanco has put it, "Americans have always wanted Satan back and . . . they raise a hue and cry when he gets away."[1] An interesting world requires both good and evil, much as Milton argues in *Paradise Lost*. Even when the party is roaring, many revelers will wonder about their moral standing. To take just one example: Fifteenth-century Florence, with its rampant hypocrisy, lechery, and famously dissolute pope (Alexander VI), would score quite low on a moral barometer. Yet, as Lauro Martines has argued, frolicking Florentines still honored traditional conceptions of virtue and even yearned to enact them in everyday life.[2] The vastness of sin's future exceeds even the vastness of its past, for we'll never really let the idea go of, nor will we ever stop failing to live up to, moral ideals.

The three major faith traditions evince varying degrees of vitality at the dawn of this new century, but only a fool would bet against their making it into the twenty-second century. Such believers will continue to "connect the dots" between moral mistakes and the Hebrew Bible (or to the New Testament or the Koran). One thing is for sure: we will keep sinning.

The question of how good we can be assumes new importance as medical science uncovers more information about criminal minds, as neurologists come to understand depression and all mental illness in more sophisticated terms and, perhaps most important, as the media shower us with sexual images and voyeuristic violence. What's just as important as the question of how good we have to be is how good we don't have to be: according to Hebrew scriptures, a girl who has been secretly unchaste must be stoned (Deuteronomy 22:13–29). Virtually no one will chide a religious group for failing to carry through on such instructions, although we might reasonably ask why not, if we really want to abide by scriptures. As sinners, we benefit from increasingly sophisticated redefinitions of sin. As judges, though, we lose ground to the advances of science and broader access to higher education. The better educated a person is, the more nuanced his reaction to another's moral shortcoming is likely to be, and the less likely he is to accept draconian punishment without putting up a protest. How to draw a line in the sand separating serious sin from trivial sin is anyone's guess in this venial age, when there is apparently no such thing as mortal sin anymore, only personal conflicts we haven't fully understood yet.

"LEARNED HELPLESSNESS"

Guilt and shame may result from realizing our limitations; sometimes we don't stop at guilt or shame but proceed to handicap ourselves. We sabotage our own chances for success and happiness, in part because we accept any eventual failures more readily (we can, after all, claim credit for having predicted those failures and therefore seem in control of our lives). We may tell ourselves that we are offering up our failures to God, in the hope that he will have pity on us more readily. Learned helplessness seems defective as an atonement strategy, not even a "second-best" accommodation for our genuine weaknesses.

Earnest reflection on a pattern of sinfulness may lead to cynicism. When cynical, we fail to give credit where it is due. Sometimes a person or a situation really is as wonderful as appearances suggest, but the cynical person refuses to allow for that possibility. Likewise, in what psychologists have termed "learned helplessness," we are sometimes more competent than we allow ourselves to reveal. If the result of being honest with ourselves about moral limitations is simply throwing in the towel, then there would seem to be no point in our moral struggle.

Christians have taken pains to show that pride goeth before the fall, that optimism and overconfidence can be self-defeating. Likewise, though, pessimism and a lack of confidence can also be self-defeating. Meditation on our repeated failures at virtuous living can lead us to adopt a passive, withdrawn attitude. We give up and resign ourselves to defeat. We adapt to low expectations in a sorry way, blaming our sinfulness on an inability to do any better than failure. Even when conditions become more favorable, we may cling to the safe vision of ourselves as humans who can always be counted on to err.

It is faith in reform that encourages people to ignore failure and try again. Victims of poverty or discrimination may abandon this upbeat philosophy in the face of bleakness; if you can't work your way out of a system that condemns you to perpetual failure, your resignation makes sense. Surely God does not want his followers to give up hope completely, even though sin will always pull them down.

Even patients faced with a dire prognosis can sometimes manage to see the bright side of whatever days are left to them. In a way, sinners must do the same. Although humans will always sin, they needn't commit serious sins (Calvinists deem *all* sins serious), and they needn't give up the struggle to cut down on the number of sins they do commit. If we follow Abelard's focus on intentions, we see the enormous premium to be placed on the *desire* to be forgiven. So no matter how low you've sunk, no matter how often you find yourself repeating the same sins, the very desire to stop, to be forgiven, may earn you more points in heaven that you allow yourself to imagine.

Both psychologists and economists have conducted studies to assess how accurately people can predict their emotional reactions to future events. Scholars have studied responses to misfortunes ranging from romantic breakups to financial losses, from personal insults to personal injuries, and the results of these studies have led to the conclusion that people typically overestimate the intensity and duration of their emotional reactions to adversity.[3] We do "get over it," as the popular saying goes (at the risk of providing wrongdoers with a ready defense for having harmed us). Humor bubbles up within us, even in bad times, and letting it spill out can be therapeutic. There's nothing humorous about sin, but there's something wondrous about the idea that we can forgive both ourselves and others.

Any benefit of fearing sin should come down to humility in the face of things we cannot fully control, including ourselves. Although we may not always be able to direct our bodies and our minds, we can oversee our aspirations, our sense of how good we can be. That sense can quickly get out of hand. People blinded by hubris is a favorite theme of Greek and Shakespearean tragedy. And when birds of a feather flock together, religious observance of any sort can quickly become cruel and dangerous (slave owners claimed God was on their side, as have those opposed to interracial marriage and same-sex marriage); religiously motivated violence is familiar to even occasional newspaper readers. Not surprisingly, various thinkers who do not believe in God have concluded that we would do better to anchor morality in humanity instead of a divinity. Let's take a look now at humanism, the intellectual attempt to save and enrich humanity simply for humanity's sake. Humanism stands as the first of several effective strategies for overcoming learned helplessness.

HUMANISM

William James characterizes humanism as "the doctrine that to an unascertainable extent our truths are man-made products" and recommends "the humanist principle" that "you can't weed out the human contribution."[4] The idea that truth emanated from God had long held sway in Europe, keeping firmly in place the concomitant supposition that humans were intrinsically flawed, base, fallen. The French Enlightenment thinkers insisted that humans are not sinful, as Christianity had taught, but basically good. Late in the eighteenth-century West, the best we could do got a lot better (if only by returning to Plato's view that people seek the good, and they seek it always).

But how good are people? Humanists are not quite so naive as to answer blindly, "Really good!" Yet, the buoyancy of humanistic thinking does expose a certain vulnerability here, a certain tendency to run blindly in the direction opposite learned helplessness. The American philosopher Thomas Nagel charges humanism with hubris for rejecting the "objective stance" that is the "proper form of humility."[5] His anti-humanism protests what he sees in humanism as "a lack of *humility* . . . an attempt to cut the universe down to size."[6] The risk is that humanism induces us to focus too much on ourselves, ignoring perhaps everything not human. A believer might argue (as Kant did) that only God can grasp the objective order of things, and that people cannot. Most Christians will quite readily see the difficulty, if not impossibility, of a Christian humanism. Jewish philosophers such as Hermann Cohen, though, laid the foundation for what could be called Jewish humanism (a "religion of rationalism").

The link between enthusiasm for humanity (built into humanism) and the rejection of religious belief stems from aversion to the idea that this life (and this world) is merely a warm-up for another. This aversion certainly existed before the eighteenth-century Enlightenment thinkers, but it was notably championed by them. In the nineteenth century, Karl Marx, an atheist, saw the flowering of humanism in communism. Today, we seem to have inherited two distinct meanings for the word *humanism*: Renaissance humanism, which has inspired a classical education grounded in the "humanities," and a modern, secular humanism. This secular humanism is seen as an alternative to, rival with, perhaps a threat to, traditional religious belief.[7] Religiously motivated violence stands as perhaps the best reason to move away from traditional religious belief. The question of violence aside, self-righteousness is not to be discounted as a social problem.

And so the whole question of what we are capable of, what our human limits might be, is up for grabs. Many Christians simply accept human shortcomings (for example, recurrent theft, violence and hatred, even floods and hurricanes) as God's punishment for our fathers' sins. Humanists do not. Both groups should be able to see the enormous value of humility on both the personal and social levels.

HUMILITY: PART OF THE BEST WE CAN DO

Although you don't need a doctorate in philosophy in order to understand what humankind is capable of, studying what it means to be human and getting a sense of what we can realistically aim for can help us avoid unnecessary disappointment on the personal level and arrogant power struggles between communities or nations on the social level. Humility makes us better individuals; humility makes other people better neighbors. We no longer blame other people for alcoholism, mental illness, birth defects, or sexual orientation; we should move to a world in which we no longer blame others for choosing not to join our religion.

At the start of a new millennium, Americans largely embraced racial diversity as a morally commendable ideal, but they have yet to embrace moral diversity fully. Particularly on television shows featuring political commentators, conservatives and liberals exhibit little tolerance for each other, little appreciation for a plurality of beliefs. Certainly by the 1990s, Americans officially disapproved of any reluctance to associate with people on the basis of their skin color. However, Americans not only approve of but sometimes applaud a reluctance to associate with people whose views of sexual ethics, recreational drug use, religious creed, or even the permissibility of smoking in public do not conform with their own. We never used to think that racial diversity would strengthen our country, but now we do. We have not yet moved to a society that values moral diversity. On the issues just cited, liberals and conservatives all too often tend to think of overthrowing the opposition, waiting for them to feel ashamed and keep their mouths shut.

The recognition that we are wrong, that we have made a bad decision, is humbling. Humility usually follows on the heels of this realization. Being forgiven can feel exhilarating; mercy can be intoxicating. But mercy poses a problem in a religion such as Christianity, one that always guarantees mercy. Mercy encourages sin as nothing else can. If you know that you'll always be forgiven for anything you do, you may recognize an incentive for just going ahead and living as if there weren't any hard-and-fast rules for conduct, only suggestions and guidelines.

If believers place their faith in God's infinite mercy and compassion, they should press on that faith in order to squeeze out compassion for people of other religions. As we realize our personal limitations, we should focus on social limitations that have prevented us from treating with sufficient respect believers of different stripes. Analysis of shortcomings on the microlevel can suggest solutions on a broader level: just as we accept that we will never be perfect, so can we accept that other people will disagree with our religious beliefs. Those people can still qualify as moral. With regard to people of different creeds, we can agree to disagree and yet still be friends, even good friends. Sadly, the Catholic Church's official position on other religions remained unkind until Vatican II, which overthrew the policy "Error has no rights." Better late than never. Now we wait for various fundamentalist groups around the globe to make the same move.

Humility is a healthy alternative to learned helplessness. In its own way, hypocrisy can also be healthy, provided it's used as a stepladder to be discarded once we reach our moral destination.

HYPOCRISY

Hypocrisy is the homage vice pays to virtue.

—La Rochefoucauld

As much as we may hate hypocrisy, we should recognize that it is only slightly worse than learned helplessness and perhaps, ultimately, a step in the right moral direction. In pretending to be better than we are, we deceive others and possibly ourselves as well. Denying our sinfulness (or moral vulnerability, if you prefer) spawns more sinfulness, and so we seem trapped. The frustrating sense of entrapment almost recommends pretending to be better than we are, for, in time, we may come to be as good as we've been pretending.[8] This dubious act of will may ultimately have served as the training wheels on the bike of a child who is learning to ride. After a bit of practice, the child is in a better position to throw away the moral equivalent of her training wheels, more confident that she can do it on her own.

If hypocrisy can help us be all we can be, we would do well to consider whether hypocrisy is as despicable as Jesus, for example, said. The answer, we'll see, brings to light different kinds of hypocrisy. One kind, if not exactly *good*, is at least helpful. And so, at the outset, I want to distinguish between hypocrites and what we might call "moral novices" or, less flatteringly, the weak-willed.

What offends us about hypocrites is cheating: they reap an advantage they have not earned. One particular kind of hypocrite, the self-promoting spiritual leader (think of Jimmy Swaggart or Newt Gingrich), deserves special blame. Self-promoting religious leaders take credit for work they have not done and try to manipulate others into giving them that credit, all in the name of God. The self-promoting religious leader may profit from exploiting popular fears of, say, people of color or liberal politicians, and encourage a social climate inhospitable to moral evolution. The self-promoting religious leader or demagogue deserves more blame than those whose hypocrisy comes down to false modesty: pretending to be worse than you are (for it might be argued that he who is falsely modest is also hypocritical).

Hypocrisy conjures up negative associations. Hypocrites are often regarded as morally corrupt, cynical egoists who consciously and deliberately deceive others in order to further their own interests. Most of us can see ourselves as at least occasional hypocrites. Hypocrisy, an ordinary vice, is difficult to avoid. The mere fact that everyone errs in this way, if that could be proven, would not mean that we should simply shrug off this lack of integrity. Hypocrisy cries out for correction, even as it exposes our own precarious moral standing ("Let those without sin cast the first stone"). Hypocrisy raises a challenging question: is it worse to pretend to be virtuous while leading a seedy double life or to be the person who blows the whistle on the hypocrite?

We have to be careful about condemning hypocrites—not only because we may not be much better than they, but also because sometimes we mistake them for the weak-willed. Beyond that, even genuine hypocrites sometimes do the right thing, albeit for the wrong reasons. Enthusiasm for rooting out hypocrisy may do more harm than good. The hypocrite may condemn racial prejudice or homosexuality despite his own susceptibility to discriminating against people of color or gays: this is more blindness than a cover-up. The hypocrite has not yet overcome his prejudices, yet he may earnestly hope to do so. We should encourage good behavior (e.g., treating everyone with kindness) and leave people to work out their confusing and perhaps contradicting beliefs on their own. If we were always to speak as precisely as we perhaps ought, we could insist on a distinction between hypocrisy and weakness of will. Such a distinction would no doubt be useful, as we could reasonably insist that the weak-willed person genuinely wants to practice what he preaches, whereas a hypocrite does not. The weak-willed person will likely regret the gap between what he says and feels, whereas the hypocrite will not. Jesus drove home the precariousness of this gap when he accused the scribes and Pharisees.

The self-righteous hypocrite feels morally superior to others and uses the pretense of moral superiority to manipulate those around him.

The principal problem with the self-righteous hypocrite is his abuse of others: true, he may be lying to himself and to others in the process, but it is the unkindness that should concern us immediately. Think here of Reverend Dimsdale and Hester Prynne in Hawthorne's *The Scarlet Letter*.

Freud argued for the utter pervasiveness of ambivalence and consequently changed our understanding not just of ourselves but of hypocrisy as well. Through classic case studies such as Little Hans, Freud argued that our feelings rarely exclude doubt. More often than not, we love those we hate and hate those we love. Our hypocrisy exposes our aspirations and our disappointments as much as it does our simple duplicity.

Snobbishness makes for a useful case in point here. Many people want the admiration of others. They will brag about having graduated from State U. They will wear T-shirts and attend school football games and proudly display decals in their car windows. They will silently congratulate themselves on having done better than the neighbors. But as soon as an Ivy League graduate wears her college T-shirt or displays a school decal in her car window, the State U. graduate may disapprove, claiming that the Ivy League grad is a snob. Freud labored to help us see our own ambivalence. With or without psychotherapy, moral education (e.g., reading novels, reflecting on film, or moving through a succession of messy personal relationships) can help us see ourselves as hypocrites. Frequent reminders of our own moral weakness can improve our characters, but even here, it is possible to get carried away.

Sincerity is critical for religious belief, but Freud tirelessly showed us how complicated the human psyche can be. We want to improve ourselves, and we don't. We want to love our enemies, and we don't. But hypocrisy sometimes becomes laudable as a stepping stone: you espouse a new belief with the specific intention of making yourself believe it over time. Think of Pascal's famous wager: you force yourself to believe in God out of fear of what will happen to you if you die an atheist, but over time, you actually come to believe. This strategy of claiming to believe something we don't *really* or don't *yet* in the hope that we soon *will* no doubt inspires some of the defense of the social policy of affirmative action in the United States, a subject deserving further scrutiny.

Hypocrisy offers a useful lens on contemporary mores. Hypocritical people have internalized social norms with which they disagree. The struggle of the hypocrite instructs us where to stand in the world and which bullets to dodge. As La Rochefoucauld put it, "Hypocrisy is the homage vice pays to virtue" (*Maxims* [1665]: 218). The struggle for personal authenticity begins in hypocrisy, as we struggle to make the inauthentic authentic. A racist can change his racism, but a closeted gay woman cannot change her sexual orientation, which means that becoming ourselves isn't as easy as forcing ourselves to embody the traits we value. Some things we can't change, although the hypocrite may not know that yet.

The biggest problem hypocrisy poses the spiritual life is discouragement. Some well-meaning people who believe in God will shy away from a church or a synagogue because they feel sinful. Religious life is only for the sinless, they reason, and it would be simply hypocritical for a sinner to join in. A long-term perspective is in order here. You may be a terrible sinner now, but if you join a religious community, you may in time overcome much of your sinfulness. No man is an island, and the goal gets easier with help from others.

Often after critical self-evaluation an earnest believer can repair (or establish) a relationship with God. This means that the burning sense of sinfulness can be a good thing, something to embrace. Far from preventing us from walking down a path to God, it should goad us on. The question of moral motivation resists easy condemnation, for even bad motives can lead to what believers would consider desirable ends. The novelist Graham Greene, for instance, went through with a conversion to Catholicism only because the woman he wanted to marry had laid it down as a condition. In the course of charging through obligatory study sessions with a priest, Greene, who falsely claimed he genuinely wanted to be a Catholic, discovered that he genuinely wanted to become a Catholic. The self-awareness Green gained likely increased his humility and decreased any inclination to moral hypocrisy he might have had (because he realized how undependable even assumptions about ourselves can be). With a wry wit, Greene could write with humor about his change of heart. Humor amounts to a highly effective defense against learned helplessness.

HUMOR

A rich sense of humor, coupled with and arising out of genuine humility, must be an integral part of the best we can hope for. It is fine for believers to take their religion seriously, so seriously that they will brook no criticism of it. But a sense of humor about both faith and life makes us easier to get along with. Humor and nobility, to which I'll turn next, can go far toward making us admirable people.

In a memoir detailing his boyhood experience as the gatekeeper in a cloistered convent, the British literary critic Terry Eagleton remembers the job with a sense of humor. When, for instance, the bishop would come to the convent for the wedding ceremony in which a nun would marry herself to Christ, altar boys played an important role:

> The boy with the crosier had the ticklish task of handing the bishop this ornate, outsize version of a shepherd's crook while simultaneously going down on one knee and kissing the Episcopal ring. Later in life, describing this piece of acrobatics to some agnostic friends, I realized from the ribald laughter that the phrase "going down to kiss the bishop's ring" had a rather more salacious meaning than had occurred to me at the age of ten.[9]

The bewilderment of a young boy, even though Catholic, nicely reflects the curiosity of non-Catholics about Catholic custom. In a similar vein, Eagleton conjures up the strangeness of a nun's wedding in the pre–Vatican II cloister:

> It was my job on these occasions to conduct the young woman's parents into the parlour to see their daughter for the last time. They would kneel shyly on the profane side of the grille, partly out of piety and partly because there was nowhere to sit, while their newly-wed daughter knelt smiling on the holy side, her veil thrown back, chaperoned by a kneeling reverend mother whose veil would be lowered. Catholicism seemed to be mainly a matter of kneeling. There was a touch of the zoo about the scene, as though the young creature behind the bars was some exotic, well-nigh extinct species, the reverend mother was her proud keeper and her parents a couple of venerating animal enthusiasts.

In Eagleton's reminiscences we find irreverence, to be sure, but also a kind of objectivity, a mature point of view that most parents surely hope will be the fruit of the education their children receive. Looking back on the religious dimension of his childhood, Eagleton muses:

> Just as the convent bore only a tenuous relation to reality, so did Catholicism as a whole. Its esoteric doctrines seemed no more applicable to everyday life than trigonometry was applicable to pressing your trousers. Like

magic, it was a highly determinate system but entirely self-confirming, with all the exceptional clarity of an hallucination. Catholicism was less about good deeds than about how to keep the charcoal in your thurible alight or knock another fifty years off your allotted time in purgatory. It was less about charity than candelabras.

Eagleton lacks the single-minded drive we impute to early Christian martyrs, whose faith was no laughing matter. Particularly after 9/11, though, such single-minded devotion to any faith may make us fear fanaticism. Eagleton may be an unlikely candidate for future canonization, but his sense of humor suggests that he would make a much more enjoyable dinner guest than any saint. In terms of Catholic public relations, that must count for something. Perhaps the faithful of other religions will also see some value in the ability of once proud—indeed, triumphalist—Catholics to laugh at themselves.

NOBILITY: THE BEST WE CAN DO

Humility and humor—and at least the goal-setting agenda that lies at the heart of hypocrisy—offer paths to moral self-improvement. The end to which that path leads might suitably be described as nobility. One of the nice aspects of nobility is its nondenominational core. Nobility captures the best that sinners can hope for.

Nietzsche, hardly a cheerleader for either Jews or Christians, left us an excellent sketch of moral achievement in the brief essay "What Is Noble?" which appears as chapter 8 in *Beyond Good and Evil*.[10] Nietzsche defines nobility in terms having nothing to do with strict adherence to a religious creed.[11] Nietzsche's idea comes down to a correct use of our powers. In this, he surprisingly agrees with what I take to be the most useful definition of sin (coming from St. Basil the Great): misusing the powers God gave us to do good.

Nietzsche weaves his thoughts around the central thread of "having claws but not using them." A noble person is one who could use his powers to harm you in some way but chooses not to. Beyond that, a noble person is one who uses his powers only when he needs to, not just in order to amuse himself. "The noble soul gives as it takes, from that passionate and irritable instinct of repayment that lies in its depth."

Illustrations abound here, in literature and popular music especially. In Dolly Parton's rueful ballad "Jolene," the singer addresses a naturally beautiful woman named Jolene who has entranced the singer's boyfriend.[12] The singer understands that Jolene has no sustained interest in the man; Jolene is just testing her powers. Such a test, however, could lead to unexpected and sad consequences for the singer. In the song's refrain, the singer importunes Jolene, "Please don't take him just because you can." We might object that decency, not nobility, is what comes into play here. Jolene would only qualify as noble if she genuinely loved her friend's boyfriend but passed over him nonetheless (much as Britain's Princess Margaret did in the 1960s, when the royal family exhorted to her to end a passionate romance with a divorced man, a man who could not make a suitable husband). Nobility holds us to a higher standard than decency, although decency stands as a worthwhile moral goal in and of itself.

People from a variety of religious backgrounds can agree that the misuse of power qualifies as morally objectionable. Yet such abuses happen regularly, sometimes among the most powerful players of all. President Bill Clinton brought out a voluminous memoir in 2004.[13] The public quite naturally raced to see how he would account for his infamous dalliance with the intern Monica Lewinsky. The media trumpeted Clinton's final explanation for the infamous risk taking: he did it simply because he could get away with it (or so he had thought). Not all who misuse their power are particularly powerful, though. Some seventy years before Clinton, the notorious case of Leopold and Loeb shocked Americans in 1924. Two teenage boys in Chicago killed a little boy in their neighborhood; on being found out, Leopold and Loeb explained that they had killed the little boy not out of malice or vengeance, but simply because they figured out that they *could*. (Some American Jews breathed a sigh of relief that the murdered boy had been a Jew, just as Leopold and Loeb were; had the murder victim been a Christian, Jews would have feared reprisals from not-so-noble Christians.)

A barrage of television shows and films also revolve around the idea of judiciously guarding one's powers. The 1960s produced both *Bewitched* and *I Dream of Jeannie*, American television series that mainstreamed witches and genies. In *Bewitched*, a handsome young advertising executive meets a beautiful blonde, a woman who turns out to be a witch.[14] Determined to break from her eccentric family, the young witch tries hard to live without using her powers but alas frequently fails. The eventual marriage between the two sometimes falters, at other times flourishes—all depending on the ability of the witch to

"hold in her claws," to borrow Nietzsche's image. (A 2005 movie entitled *Bewitched* and starring Nicole Kidman brought the 1960s television
show to the screen.)[15] In *I Dream of Jeannie*, a handsome young NASA
astronaut hides an ancient refugee from Baghdad, a buxom blonde
woman affectionately nicknamed "Jeannie," who lives in a bottle, never
ages, and will literally work magic on demand.[16] A romance between
the two ensues, and Jeannie understands that her master will only
marry her if she learns to live (and agrees to live) without using her
powers. Like the witch Samantha in *Bewitched*, Jeannie frequently falls
off the wagon. Her lapses humanize her and consequently endear her
to audiences, who understand they'd fare no better than she, were they
possessed with magical powers.

Men sometimes possess magical powers as well. The *Superman* comic
strip stars a young man who lands on Earth as a result of an accident in
his home galaxy. The young man, adopted and raised by ordinary
Americans, struggles to keep his superhuman powers a secret, all the
while honoring his duty to help humanity by deploying those same
powers against the forces of evil. Various films have brought the comic
strip (and television series) to the screen. More recently, *X-Files*
episodes deepened the genre; in these shows, mortals sometimes torture the superhumans and threaten to prevent them from doing their
best to overcome the forces of evil.

A much more convincing, and therefore more effective, portrayal of
the seemingly ordinary character with hidden, extraordinary power
surfaces in Lars von Trier's film from 2004 *Dogville*; Nicole Kidman
plays an ordinary mortal who has fled her gangster father in order to
forge a new life for herself among honest, hardworking, small-town
Americans.[17] At the conclusion of a harrowing series of cruel events, the
long-suffering and saintly Kidman embraces her father's nefarious connections and, claiming the powers she had formerly renounced, wreaks
her revenge on the immoral townspeople whose presumed integrity she
had once revered. In no way supernaturally gifted, Kidman's character
gains power from her brutal father, a gangster. That Kidman's character chooses ultimately to avail herself of this dark power casts a deeply
sad shadow over the film's conclusion. Kidman realized she had powers
she did not want. She embraced a mainstream community on the expectation that its people would prove more moral than her gangster father. What turns out to be a heartless community drives her to punish
them in a way only a person with unusual powers could do (or a person

with access to weaponry: think here of the sad parallel with Michael Moore's *Bowling for Columbine*).

When we think of contemporary sins, we see corresponding sources of power. Newly empowered people or groups have a responsibility to exercise their power honestly; taking revenge through indiscriminate use of that new power deserves moral criticism. A woman may unfairly accuse her male employer of sexual harassment (think perhaps of Clarence Thomas and Anita Hill). A person of color may unfairly accuse a white person of racism; the white person may suffer unjustly.[18] A high school or college student may falsely accuse a teacher of sexual misconduct; the teacher may suffer unjustly.[19] A majority religion may persecute members of a minority religion living in the same country or land.[20] Employers may mistreat their employees—think especially of migrant workers and illegal aliens here. The list goes on.

By the same token, a white leader, intent on capitalizing on contemporary political culture, may cause younger white people undue suffering. A white man presiding over an elite American university may earn praise from a liberal media for endorsing affirmative action; that white man, however, doesn't pay any obvious price for casting his support for affirmative action. It's the faceless white applicants who narrowly miss acceptance at the same school who pay the price for his decision. Yale University law professor Ian Ayres, a Caucasian, confesses to having lied about his race on his college application. Ayres believed it unfair to privilege black applicants over white applicants, so he claimed to be black when he was not.[21] A compelling account of why Ayres committed a moral foul should attend to the arguably unfair expectation of white leaders that a certain number of never-to-be-disclosed white applicants would bear the cost of implementing affirmative action. Ayres might be said to have exercised a novel form of "civil disobedience"; breaking laws with which one disagrees on moral grounds has some important precedent in the United States. Beyond that, Ayres may have understood early on that very few people are either "pure white" or "pure black"—most of us are interracial mongrels.

The white university president has claws and chooses to use them, as it were; instead of somehow offering to share the cost for using his claws, he makes others shoulder the cost. Instead of sharing some part of the faceless suffering he creates, the white leader may choose to step back and congratulate himself instead, much in the way a president or senator may send someone else's son off to war in Vietnam or Iraq—but not his own. Let's circle back and take another, final look at the social policy called affirmative action.

THE DAMAGED SOCIETY IN WHICH WE TRY OUR BEST

I have suggested humor and nobility as two concrete goals to which we might aspire. Now let's take another look at what we're up against in this struggle—not just ourselves, but the complicated messes into which we are born. The example of Ian Ayres, on reflection, illuminates the struggle of some white students in America against a system they are reluctant to dismiss as simply sinful.

Part of assessing how good we can be entails looking at the inherited limitations of our little worlds. Just as we're stuck with the bodies we've been born with (although cosmetic surgery is an increasingly popular option for those who can afford it), so we're stuck with the world our parents left us (although we can make all sorts of technological improvements). One of the most important set of limitations Catholics must confront is the inheritance of a terrible erosion of moral authority, stemming from repeated accusations of anti-Semitism and, more recently, of scandalous sexual behavior. Other religious denominations have something to learn from Catholic mistakes.

I have already discussed at some length the social policy of affirmative action, which captures the heart of what is meant by charity and goodwill. I have framed the question of how good we can be in terms of the world into which we were born. The phrase "sins of the fathers" pops up in various contexts today. In a 2004 *New Yorker* piece on infidelity, the American humorist David Sedaris recounts an awkward moment when, at the improbable age of twelve, his father took the opportunity to let his son know a secret on a private car trip. "We'd been silent for blocks, when out of nowhere he turned to me and said, 'I want you to know that I've never once cheated on your mother.' 'Um. O.K.,' I said. And then he turned on the radio and listened to a football game."[22] As an adult, Sedaris ponders what his father meant by this disclosure. It could be that the father wanted the conscience of his son to be clear, his son's marital future to be propitious. Much as child abuse becomes a psychological cycle, burdening its victims to become eventual perpetrators themselves, the father could have wanted his son to know that infidelity did not blight his particular future. Or, as Sedaris imagines, it could be that the father wanted badly to think of himself as moral and, in grasping at reasons on which to justify this self-perception, landed on this biographical fact. Sedaris muses, "It sounds like something you'd read on a movie poster, but sometimes the sins you haven't committed are all you have to hold onto." The two explanations—a father wants respect from his son, a father wants a bright future for his son—start from a common premise, that history, especially family history, can hinder us (or help us).

Or take another example. Tom Hayden, the former California state senator and populist from the 1960s, reflected on the cocky and bemused detachment of his son in the book *Street Wars*. When his headstrong son started gravitating toward a local gang and then defacing public property with graffiti, Hayden allowed him to keep going. "Maybe I was a blind enabler, but maybe, too, he was right to rage against the hypocrisy of the society we had bequeathed him."[23] Hayden sees his own sins, and those of his generation, as a good enough reason for young people to rebel. The sins of the fathers justify the misdeeds of the young. This kind of thinking does not help the juvenile justice system, but it does highlight our link to the immediate past.

I have argued that young white people are footing the bill for the magnanimous social rhetoric of older white Americans. They are not paying for the sins of their fathers. In a country such as France, where blacks were never bought and sold as slaves, affirmative action has more to do with changing entrenched social patterns than with apologizing for human rights abuses (i.e., slavery).[24] Affirmative action has aroused criticism in France, just as it has in the United States: even French president Jacques Chirac and his prime minister Dominique de Villepin criticized the policy, insisting that admissions to elite universities should be based purely on merit.

High-profile white men such as Derek Bok (former president of Harvard) and William G. Bowen (former president of Princeton) have spoken out in favor of maintaining affirmative action. Apart from some admittedly valuable rhetoric, they have arguably done little to pay for the sins of their fathers, though—it's middle-class white Americans who are paying that bill, at least when it comes to university admissions. True, a middle-class student with excellent SAT scores cannot be certain that she would have been admitted to Princeton if it weren't for affirmative action, but she has reason to believe she may have been a sacrificial lamb. Bok and Bowen *know* that they didn't personally suffer an unfair rejection.

Bowen decries lack of fairness when it comes to preferring athletes in university admissions, but approves of favoring blacks. In *Reclaiming the Game: College Sports and Educational Values*, Bowen and Sarah A. Levin claim that a different and seldom-publicized factor—athletic talent—frequently outweighs all the others, that coaching staffs regularly exercise decisive power, and that selective universities rarely tell the truth about the extent to which the demand for top athletes in varsity sports determines admissions policies.[25]

Who are the talented white applicants turned away? Do they really exist if we can't publicly name them? They do exist. They fall into the same category of students with strong scores who are turned away in order to make room for talented athletes with lower scores. Refusing to care about the suffering of middle-class white students, far from a noble commitment to righting the wrongs of our forebears, amounts to a sin of sorts—withholding compassion from people who may well deserve it. Allowing their suffering is the best we can do, given the world we found in America.

Bowen and Levin are troubled in *Reclaiming the Game* by the "opportunity costs" of these policies—the phrase points to the number of academically strong applicants who are turned away when slots are reserved for athletes who are inferior students. They urge that the universities in their study take concrete steps toward reform.

Both the admission of academically underqualified applicants and their favored treatment result, Bowen and James Shulman claimed in an earlier work, *The Game of Life*, "in a persistent and widening split between academics and athletics at selective colleges and universities that offer no athletic scholarships, do not compete at the Division I-A level [of the National Collegiate Athletic Association], and presumably exemplify [the] 'amateur' ideal."[26] A white leader like Bowen raises the question of why universities shouldn't eliminate the preferential treatment of both athletes *and* racial minorities. (Disclosure: The author gained admission to Yale and Princeton as a promising competitive swimmer.)

THE BEST WE CAN HOPE FOR

In the midst of the sex scandal of 2002–2003, some American Catholics objected that the media made the crisis seem much bigger than it was and Catholics much more immoral than they were. If nothing else, the terribly painful crisis drove home to Catholics the lesson that their community, their culture, was every bit as liable to sin as any other in America.

A parallel example pits young white Americans who have never hated or mistreated African Americans against African Americans who know that generations of white people have looked down on them and oppressed them. Young white Americans today are paying the bills of racist fathers long gone (or gone into hiding). Similarly, future generations of American Catholics will feel the sting of association with a group that harbored and protected child molesters. These young Catholics will to some extent end up paying the bills of errant bishops who secretly transferred pedophiles from one parish to another.

Humanism will not do as a statement of the best Catholics can hope for, as it intrinsically opposes an organized religion such as Roman Catholicism. Humanism contents itself with, indeed prides itself on, a partial truth. Catholicism, although it often points to mystery, insists on a complete truth. The coping strategy adopted by the modern (post–Vatican II) church has been not to recede modestly from historic claims of complete truth (i.e., the "one true church" of Vatican I) but rather to admit apparent rivals into the fold (as *Nostra Aetate*, e.g., did with Jews and Muslims), on the understanding that rivals agree with Catholicism more than they may realize. More conservative Jews and Protestants will also reject the notion that humanism can aptly summarize the faith they practice. Humanism works better as a facilitator for the American dream. Curiously, Americans became nicer to blacks (in the Civil Rights Act of 1964) at the same time that Catholics became nicer to non-Catholics (in, say, the document *Nostra Aetate*). Religion helps and hinders progress, just as sin fatigue rises and falls over the course of decades.

Imperfection is not an argument against virtue. The simple fact that you are bound to fail at some point in some way does not justify hedonism or utter lawlessness, does not justify refusing to try to play well with others. An ambitious student beginning college may understand that only a single person can finish first in her class; her resolve to be that person makes sense at the outset. Her resolve to excel, even after it gradually becomes clear she will not finish first in her class, also makes sense. That subsequent resolve to excel is laudable, especially in the light of her lowered performance expectations. Once spoiled, her perfect academic record may haunt her, but it ought not undermine her. She may rue the loss of that first-semester 4.0 GPA, but she should never allow that lost perfection to become her enemy. While it is theoretically possible for a college student to graduate with a perfect 4.0 GPA, most Jews and Christians agree that it is impossible to make it through adulthood with a perfect moral record.

We mortals can find comfort in our inferior status, a reassuring source of boundaries and limits (very few people want to be king all the time). The pursuit of a forum for showing relative deprivation of pleasurable activities, and also for enjoying a sense of relative self-righteousness, is one reason that people in a particular religious group tend to cluster together. Anxiety and fear may prevent us from performing good deeds, but the anxiety and fear don't make us bad people. Preoccupied with retirement account savings and rising interest rates, we may not donate as much to charity as we'd like. Fear of falling economically may lead to visions of ending up like the homeless people whom we would like to help but supposedly can't. It seems awfully cold-hearted to condemn people because they give in to their fears. By the same token, people may not admit to their fears, which means that we may often fail to understand the motivations for the actions of another.

Judaism shows general optimism about what we can accomplish in this life with God's help (Psalm 8; Zechariah 1:3; Malachi 3:7). Humility and nobility recommend themselves as excellent strategies, as we ponder the best we can do. Judaism shows marvelous humility when, for instance, it offers a psychologically invaluable escape clause to men who struggle with monogamy: provided that the man go to a town in which he is not known and, before consorting with potential sex partners, that he "cover his head," a Jewish man can be excused for the occasional act of infidelity.[27] Instead of feeling morally superior to others, we might better say to ourselves, "Thank goodness I manage to remain faithful to my spouse," or "Thank goodness I don't feel the slightest sexual attraction to children," or "Thank goodness I wasn't born with violent tendencies." In any event, moral bragging should count as a sin: it is simply ignoble to point out to others how superior to them we are. Education can reveal how unhelpful a black-and-white understanding of sin ultimately is. In time, neurology and psychiatry will likely guide us to a richer understanding of our moral luck, and of chance's role in however good we may or may not become. In time, self-righteousness may decline.

Meanwhile, we continue to sin. No doubt we occasionally fail to see altogether that we've hurt others. We should conclude, as La Rochefoucauld did, that scarcely any of us is clever enough to understand all the evil he does (*Maxims*, no. 269). That realization—and the humility it should evoke—must figure into the best we can hope for. Ours is a venial age, one in which there is no such thing as mortal sin anymore, only failures to understand someone or something. This broad cultural shift will perhaps compel us to forgive more readily—*tout comprendre, c'est tout pardonner.*

EPILOGUE

Magic, mystery, sin, and atonement never disappear in the West; we just tire of them from time to time. This, then, is the take-home message of this book: that we find ourselves floating faster away from the past. The lost tyranny of sin distances us from the brow-beating of our moral forebears: "Our transgressions and our sins are upon us, and we waste away because of them; how, then, can we live?" (Ezekiel 33:10). Well, we'll find a way, we reason silently, while rushing on to think about more pressing tasks to finish today.

It shouldn't really come as any surprise that sin evolves, given how much else does—art, society, history, and war, for instance. And just as interpretation of the U.S. Constitution changes, so too does interpretation of the Bible. Artists—with their paintings, their photographs, and their music videos—transform Western culture by pressing us to update our thinking on sin. Sin leads Western culture today, even as sin seems gradually to burn itself out, to put itself out of business. Counterfeiters, credit card hustlers, identity thieves, adulterous politicians, and Internet predators looking for teenagers—all of them lead intelligence efforts. Some of our best minds work to thwart the ingenuity of such transgressors. It would not be an overstatement to say that we get smarter, shrewder because they push us to keep up with them. In a moral sense, cutting-edge artists from Picasso to Madonna do much the same thing. (The popular 2002 film *Catch Me If You Can*, starring Leonardo Di Caprio, showcased the genius of a fraud who was later recruited to work for the CIA, which profited from his uncanny ability to counterfeit.)

According to Abraham Heschel, Christians talk about sin more often than Jews do.[1] It could be that Christians are more preoccupied with sin than Jews are. This would mean that a history of sin would matter less to Jews than to Christians—or to Muslims, say, or Hindus. Judaism on the whole has adapted to the modern world more gracefully than Christianity has done. In emphasizing the ethnic importance of Jewish identity, many nonbelieving or otherwise-indifferent Jews would have already prepared themselves for a West in which no one believed in God anymore. They would still be Jews ("cultural Jews"), but Christian identity would largely have collapsed.

This is not to say that believers are down and out for the count, though. We have only to look at marvelously persuasive examples from drama to see that believers are no pushovers. In Fellini's masterpiece *La Dolce Vita* (1960), for example, we see a band of boozy, aristocratic revelers pass out after a raucous night only to march off to Mass the following morning (prodded along by a willful Italian mamma, granted). And in the Broadway hit turned movie classic, *The Boys in the Band* (1970), we see the boozy, lustful protagonist Michael host a homosexual party in his Manhattan apartment, only to leave in time for midnight Mass.

Science poses a new threat, to the extent that it reduces or removes responsibility for wrongdoing. We now understand suicide, alcoholism, and depression, for example, better than our forebears did. Whereas moralists long held writers such as Aquinas, Dante, and Luther to be our contemporaries (brimming over with relevant moral guidelines and justifications for them), now we see that these once-influential men are less relevant. We live in a century dramatically different from the nineteenth and even more significantly changed from others. If geneticists should ever discover the "gay gene," then those who claimed that homosexuality is purely a function of choice will have to reevaluate how or why God created gay people (Catholics already lumbered over this hurdle in 1975, although perhaps not entirely satisfactorily). We no longer regard deaf-mutes as ugly, damaged creatures; minorities of other sorts may be next in line for social redemption.

People will remain the signal constant in the future of sin. They will spur us to sin sometimes and deter us from it at others. More than natural disasters or terrorist attacks, individuals (and groups of them) will disrupt our rest and drive us to ponder unspeakable acts. At the same time, individuals (and groups of them) will deliver consolation more powerful than we are likely to find in Prozac or technological gadgets. People are more important than sin.

Sin's future is sin's past: the power of community. What we as a group will accept or deny is sin's future. The good news is the bad news: what Westerners as a group increasingly acknowledge is that urges are stronger than churches. As a result, we have tired of the notion of sin: We know that it will often overcome our best efforts to resist it. We will reason to ourselves, much as the damned in Dante's *Inferno* did, that at least we're not parent beaters, exploiters of the poor, or people who refuse to recycle glass bottles. At the same time, we're skeptical of the atonement of politicians, movie stars, and neighbors who atone publicly. We suspect that we've seen their true colors, and they'll be back to their old tricks in no time. We may forgive them more generously than our forebears did if we understand what they're up against. To understand everything, we sense, would enable us to forgive everyone. We're almost there.

NOTES

CHAPTER 1

1. William James, *The Varieties of Religious Experience* (New York: Penguin Classics, 1985; orig. pub. 1902), 91.

2. Ned Martel, *New York Times*, June 24, 2004, E8. Karl Menninger had noticed this trend long before the twenty-first century; see *Whatever Happened to Sin?* (London: Hodder & Stroughton, 1973).

3. See William S. Babcock, "Augustine on Sin and Moral Agency," *Journal of Religious Ethics* 16, no. 1 (1988).

4. See, for example, Mary Potter Engel, "Evil, Sin and Violation of the Vulnerable," in *Lift Every Voice: Constructing Christian Theologies from the Underside*, ed. S. B. Thistlethwaite and M. P. Engel (San Francisco: Harper & Row, 1990), 155.

5. David Novak, *Jewish Social Ethics* (New York: Oxford University Press, 1992), 106. It is important to note that Novak's claim represents a minority view among Jewish theologians. For a contrasting view, see James Kugel, *Traditions of the Bible: A Guide to the Bible as It Was at the Start of the Common Era* (Cambridge, Mass.: Harvard University Press, 1998), 127; and Efraim Urbach, *The Sages, Their Concepts and Beliefs*, trans. Israel Abrahams (Jerusalem: Magnes, Hebrew University, 1979), 421–36. See also Miroslav Volf, "The Lamb of God and the Sin of the World," in *Christianity in Jewish Terms*, ed. David Novak et al. (Boulder, Colo.: Westview, 2000), 314–15; in the same volume, see especially Steven Kepnes, "'Turn Us to You and We Shall Return': Original Sin, Atonement, and Redemption in Jewish Terms," 293–304.

6. Augustine commands unusual authority in Roman Catholic theology generally and thinking on Original Sin specifically. For a history of Original Sin, see N. P. Williams, *The Ideas of the Fall and of Original Sin: A Historical and Critical*

Study (London: Longmans, Green, 1927), or Alistair McFadyen, *Bound to Sin: Abuse, Holocaust, and the Christian Doctrine of Sin* (Cambridge: Cambridge University Press, 2000), chap. 2. See also Edward Yarnold, S.J., *The Theology of Original Sin* (Hales Corner, Wisc.: Clergy Book Service, 1971), and William Graham Cole, *Sex in Christianity and Psychoanalysis* (New York: Oxford University Press, 1955).

7. In 1893, Mark Twain put a clever spin on this sad story; he also portrayed Eve as an intellectually curious and altogether sympathetic person. See Mark Twain, *The Diaries of Adam and Eve* (New York: Oxford University Press, 1996).

8. Ian Fisher, "Limbo, an Afterlife Tradition, May Be Doomed by the Vatican," *New York Times*, December 8, 2005.

9. *Catechism of the Catholic Church* (New York: Doubleday, 1995), 109–10.

10. This section owes much to *The New Catholic Encyclopedia*'s summary of Teilhard de Chardin's contribution to Catholic theology.

11. Here and throughout the book, I rely for translations of biblical passages on the New Revised Standard Version (NRSV) of *The New Oxford Annotated Bible*, ed. Bruce M. Metzger and Roland E. Murphy (New York: Oxford University Press, 1991).

12. See Johann P. Sommerville, "The 'New Art of Lying': Equivocation, Mental Reservation, and Casuistry," in *Conscience and Casuistry*, ed. Edmund Leites (Cambridge: Cambridge University Press, 1988), 175. For a more general overview, see Richard Miller, *Casuistry and Modern Ethics* (Chicago: University of Chicago Press, 1996), 34–36. Legal theorist Richard Posner believes mental reservation has tainted casuistry, a moral measuring system to be discussed in the atonement chapter. In *The Problematics of Moral and Legal Theory* (Cambridge, Mass.: Harvard University Press, 1999), 122, Posner writes, "Casuistry in this bad sense is illustrated by the Catholic doctrine of equivocation, 'guiltlessly getting a falsehood across,' as by swearing 'that one has not done something, though one really has done it, by inwardly understanding that one did not do it on a certain day, or before one was born.'" The second passage is a quotation from Blaise Pascal, *The Provincial Letters*, ed. A. J. Krailshaimer (Baltimore, Md.: Penguin, 1967), 140.

13. In contemporary Roman Catholic moral theology, some have tried to reinterpret mortal sin in terms of Karl Rahner's notion of a "fundamental option." Rahner pinpointed not individual deeds but rather the overall orientation of the sinner—either toward or away from God. See Karl Rahner, *Theological Investigations*, vol. 6, trans. Karl-H. and Boniface Kruger (New York: Seabury, 1974), 178–96. For a good account of the loosening of sin in Protestant thought, see Marsha Witten, *All Is Forgiven: The Secular Message in American Protestantism* (Princeton, N.J.: Princeton University Press, 1993).

14. See Jacob Neusner, "The Idea of Purity in Ancient Judaism," *Journal of the American Academy of Religion* 43 (1975): 15–27; and Jonathan Klawans, *Im-*

purity and Sin in Ancient Judaism (New York: Oxford University Press, 2000). Christians individualized sin to a large extent, moving from an ancient concept of the corporate good of the state to a religion of personal salvation. Ted Peters distinguishes between the "essentially moral" notion of sin and the "pre-moral" idea of defilement in *Sin: Radical Evil in Soul and Society* (Grand Rapids, Mich.: Eerdmans, 1994), 141. On Spanish fears of racial impurity, see Mark D. Meyerson, *The Muslims of Valencia in the Age of Ferdinand and Isabel: Between Coexistence and Crusade* (Berkeley: University of California Press, 1991); see also Mary Elizabeth Perry, *Gender and Disorder in Early Modern Seville* (Princeton, N.J.: Princeton University Press, 1990).

15. See Elaine Pagels, *The Origin of Satan* (New York: Vintage, 1996).

16. Hassan M. Fattah, "Stampede During Annual Pilgrimage to Mecca Kills 345," *New York Times*, January 13, 2006, A3.

17. For a sprite history of this place, see Alice K. Turner, *A History of Hell* (New York: Harvest Books, 1995).

18. And Catholics still disagree amongst themselves over what qualifies as a mortal sin. In 2006, for example, an American bishop decreed that kneeling too much in Mass is a mortal sin. See David Haldane, "A Ban on Kneeling? Some Catholics Won't Stand for It," *Los Angeles Times*, May 28, 2006.

19. This section borrows extensively from John Marenbon, *The Philosophy of Abelard* (Cambridge: Cambridge University Press, 1997).

20. See, for example, Alan Wolfe, *Return to Greatness: How America Lost Its Sense of Purpose and What It Needs to Do to Recover It* (Princeton, N.J.: Princeton University Press, 2005); or John Portmann, *Bad for Us: The Lure of Self-Harm* (Boston: Beacon, 2004).

21. Catholic priests, if properly trained, still perform the rite of exorcism. In 2005, the new pope, Benedict XVI, spoke supportively at a conference of exorcists. See Ian Fisher, "The Importance of Being an Exorcist," *New York Times*, September 15, 2005, A12.

22. See Andrew Delbanco, *The Death of Satan: How Americans Have Lost the Sense of Evil* (New York: Farrar, Straus & Giroux, 1995).

23. It could be argued that the idea of hell did hold significant sway prior to the twentieth century. See Neil Gillman, *The Death of Death: Resurrection and Immortality in Jewish Thought* (Woodstock, Vt.: Jewish Lights, 1997).

24. See Patrick McCormick, *Sin as Addiction* (New York: Paulist, 1989), and Linda A. Mercadante, *Victims and Sinners: Spiritual Roots of Addiction and Recovery* (Louisville, Ky.: Westminster John Knox, 1996).

25. See Alan Petigny, "Illegitimacy, Postwar Psychology, and the Reperiodization of the Sexual Revolution," *Journal of Social History* 38, no. 4 (2004): 63–79.

26. Alasdair MacIntyre, *After Virtue* (South Bend, Ind.: University of Notre Dame Press, 1984), 168.

27. Matt Ridley, *Genome: The Autobiography of a Species in 23 Chapters* (New York: HarperCollins, 1999), 147–60.

CHAPTER 2

1. As a useful foil to atonement fatigue, it may help to think of an earlier century. Boyd Hilton has deemed the decades from the late eighteenth century to the mid–nineteenth century as an age of atonement. References to and exhortations for atonement cascaded through the literature of this period and arguably drove the lion's share of political debates then as well. See Boyd Hilton, *The Age of Atonement: The Influence of Evangelicalism on Social and Economic Thought, 1785–1865* (Oxford: Oxford University Press, 1988).

2. See Ruth Westheimer and Jonathan Mark, *Heavenly Sex: Sexuality in the Jewish Tradition* (New York: New York University Press, 1995), 124.

3. In this section I borrow from the *Oxford Dictionary of the Jewish Religion* (New York: Oxford University Press, 1997). I have also benefited from Solomon Schimmel's treatment of the topic in *The Seven Deadly Sins: Jewish, Christian, and Classical Reflections on Human Nature* (New York: Oxford University Press, 1996); Rabbi David Novak's discussion of sin in *Jewish Social Ethics* (New York: Oxford University Press, 1993), 106–11; and Jacob Neusner, Tamara Sonn, and Jonathan E. Brockopp, eds., *Judaism and Islam in Practice: A Sourcebook* (London: Routledge, 2000). Hermann Cohen offers a penetrating analysis of sin (and usefully contrasts unwitting vs. conscious sin) in *Religion of Reason Out of the Sources of Judaism*, trans. Simon Kaplan (New York: Ungar, 1972), chap. 11, "Atonement."

4. On the question of whether God forgives, see Anne C. Minias, "God and Forgiveness," *Philosophical Quarterly* 25 (1975). See also John Milbank, "The Catastrophe of Memory: Derrida, Milbank and the (Im)possibility of Forgiveness," in *Questioning God*, ed. John D. Caputo (Bloomington: Indiana University Press, 2001).

5. In a discussion of Manasseh's sin in 2 Kings 21, we see the same metaphor inverted, to some rhetorical effect. We read that just as all that may be left in a dish is wiped out with a cloth, so all the good left in Jerusalem would be wiped out. The image of the dish wiped and turned upside down closely resembles the effect of a Zamboni on ice.

6. See Nicholas De Lange, *An Introduction to Judaism* (Cambridge: Cambridge University Press, 2000), 104–5.

7. According to the Talmud's dicta, repentance, prayer, and good deeds (but not suffering) substitute for the sacrificial cult. See Alan F. Segal, *Rebecca's Children: Judaism and Christianity in the Roman World* (Cambridge, Mass.: Harvard University Press, 1986), 131. Good deeds are particularly recommended.

8. For a good overview of the Yom Kippur liturgy, see De Lange, *An Introduction to Judaism*, 143–46.

9. See, for example, Daniel J. Wakin, "Judge Allows a Jury Trial in a Case of Jewish Divorce," *New York Times*, January 25, 2002, B4; or Joseph Berger, "Old Ways Bring Tears in a New World; Immigrants Face Family Violence," *New York Times*, March 7, 2003, B1.

10. See Carol Goodman Kaufman, *Sins of Omission: The Jewish Community's Reaction to Domestic Violence* (Boulder, Colo.: Westview, 2003).

11. For a good overview of salvation in rabbinic Judaism, see Segal, *Rebecca's Children*, 166–68 and 170–72.

12. For an account of how American Jews argue among themselves on what it means to be Jewish, see Samuel G. Freedman, *Jew vs. Jew: The Struggle for the Soul of American Jewry* (New York: Simon & Schuster, 2001); more generally, see Noah F. Efron, *Real Jews: Secular versus Ultra-Orthodox: The Struggle for Jewish Identity in Israel* (New York: Basic Books, 2003).

13. See John F. Baldovin, "The Empire Baptized," in *The Oxford History of Christian Worship*, ed. Geoffrey Wainwright and Karen B. Westerfield (New York: Oxford University Press, 2006), especially 120–21. Baldovin writes, "One cannot overestimate the influence the penitential system would eventually have on the piety and liturgical life of Western Christians."

14. Some medieval rabbis adapted the list: "While all other sins, including even murder, are susceptible to repentance, masturbation is beyond atonement: 'What is the reason? They kill other people, but this one literally kills his own sons.'" David Biale, *Eros and the Jews: From Ancient Israel to Contemporary America* (Berkeley: University of California Press, 1997), 110.

15. For an engaging examination of this terrible sin, see Alain Cabantous, *Blasphemy: Impious Speech in the West from the Seventeenth to the Nineteenth Century*, trans. Eric Rauth (New York: Columbia University Press, 2002). Blasphemy overlaps with, but is not identical to, sins against the Holy Spirit.

16. In this section I have benefited from the *Encyclopedia of Southern Baptists*, vol. 1: 502; various passages in Richard McBrien's *Catholicism: A Study Edition* (Minneapolis: Winston, 1981); and Richard McBrien's entry "Sin" in the *New Catholic Encyclopedia*.

17. For more on this, see the following two essays from the volume *Christianity in Jewish Terms*, ed. Tikva Frymer-Kensky, David Novak, et al. (Boulder, Colo.: Westview, 2000): Leora Batnitzky, "On the Suffering of God's Chosen: Christian Views in Jewish Terms," 203–20; and Menachem Kellner, "How Ought a Jew View Christian Beliefs about Redemption?" 269–74. The *New Catholic Encyclopedia*, from which the preceding two paragraphs come, is also helpful here.

18. Christians hold that Jesus, the lamb of God, died for the sins of mankind. One fascinating interpretation of this belief can be found in the pallium worn

by the pope. The pallium, a vestment, is made of the wool of lambs blessed annually on the day of St. Agnes's festival, January 21. The lambs are ritually sheared in the neighboring Roman churches St. Agnese and St. Costanza. The pope symbolically takes on the role of lamb of God when he dons the pallium on Ash Wednesday and exhorts the world to turn away from sin.

19. The theologian John Milbank has aptly summarized the strand of Christian belief to which I point here. According to him, the sinner unleashes social anger on himself or herself, yet a community's goal must be "to reduce this anger to a calm fury against the sin, and to offer the sinner nothing but goodwill. . . . This instance of real punishment is also the instance of its immediate cancellation." John Milbank, *Theology and Social Theory* (Oxford: Blackwell, 1990), 421.

20. Peter Brown, *The Body and Society: Men, Women, and Sexual Renunciation in Early Christianity* (New York: Columbia University Press, 1988), 216. Much of this section relies on Brown.

21. The romance of achieving purity in the desert, or at least far from civilization, may have continued for some time. This ideal forms the basis of Flaubert's superb short story "The Legend of St. Julien the Hospitalier," much as it long provided the appeal of monasteries and cloistered convents.

22. Gregory the Great, *Homiliae in evangelia*, 1.3.4 and 2.35.7, quoted in Alfred C. Rush, "Spiritual Martyrdom in St. Gregory the Great," *Theological Studies* 23 (1962): 579, 580 (Rush's translation).

23. Thomas Tentler, *Sin and Confession on the Eve of the Reformation* (Princeton, N.J.: Princeton University Press, 1977). This section owes much to Tentler.

24. "The discipline of the confessional was formally established in the western church by canon 21 of Fourth Lateran *Omnis utriusque sexus*, which has been called with pardonable exaggeration 'perhaps the most important legislative act in the history of the church.'" Colin Morris, *The Papal Monarchy: The Western Church from 1050 to 1250* (Oxford: Oxford University Press, 1989), 491. The formula "I absolve you of your sins" first came into use at this time (492).

25. The plight of convicted child molesters released from prison makes the point forcefully. Such sorry souls found themselves with nowhere to turn in Iowa in 2006, where the situation had become so dire that some released prisoners took to spending their free time in the local sheriff's office, because there was simply no other place for them to go. See Monica Davey, "Iowa's Residency Rules Drive Sex Offenders Underground," *New York Times*, March 15, 2006, A1. Child molesters could not be trusted by good people, because good people did not believe that child molesters could be rehabilitated.

26. In the early 1980s, the U.S. Congress, worried about inconsistency in sentences handed down by various judges, passed sentencing guidelines that stipulated minimum and maximum penalties for specific crimes.

27. For more on the penitentials, see John Mahoney, S.J., *The Making of Moral Theology: A Study of the Roman Catholic Tradition* (Oxford: Oxford University Press, 1987), especially 5–17; and Thomas Tentler. See also John T. McNeill and Helena Gamer, *Medieval Handbooks of Penance* (New York: Columbia University Press, 1938).

28. McNeill and Gamer, *Medieval Handbooks of Penance*, 22, 123.

29. See McNeill and Gamer, *Medieval Handbooks of Penance*, 24–26.

30. For an excellent account of the history of casuistry, see Albert R. Jonsen and Stephen Toulmin, *The Abuse of Casuistry: A History of Moral Reasoning* (Berkeley: University of California Press, 1988). This summary borrows from their study.

31. Early in 1520, Luther criticized the Roman Catholic sacrament of penance in "Reason for Confession." Luther's audience was the Christian who, like himself, had been tormented by sin and sought peace with God in confessions. He denied that confession was in any sense magic, an external rite that could force God into some sort of bargain to forgive sins. Luther scoffed at the fears of scrupulous priests that stumbling over the words of the canon of the Mass entailed terrible sin. He also criticized the idea that Christians should dig deep into their hearts to dredge up every sin in detail in order to lay it before God. The exercise was futile, he believed, as were vows to God in general (such as, to make a pilgrimage to the Holy Land or to Rome, or to vow chastity if one had not yet even entered puberty). For Luther, confession revolved around the conviction that God will forgive those who seek forgiveness; following a certain formula in the ritual was unimportant. For a good overview of Luther on confession, see Richard Marius, *Martin Luther: The Christian between God and Death* (Cambridge, Mass.: Harvard University Press, 1999), especially chap. 8, "The Controversy over Indulgences."

32. For more on Luther's view of God's forgiveness versus a priest's, see Marius, *Martin Luther*, 156–57; for Luther's view on purgatory, see 141–47.

33. Bernard Häring, *The Law of Christ: Moral Theology for Priests and Laity*, trans. Edwin G. Kaiser (Westminster, Md.: Newman, 1961), 3 vols., 1:58–59. In this section I have also found helpful Stephen Haliczer, *Sexuality in the Confessional: A Sacrament Profaned* (New York: Oxford University Press, 1996), especially chap. 1 ("Auricular Confession and the Crisis in the Church") and chap. 2 ("Confession and Confessors in Transition").

34. John Bossy, *Christianity in the West, 1400–1700* (Oxford: Oxford University Press, 1985), 49.

35. See, for example, Bernard Williams's essay "Moral Luck," in Bernard Williams, *Moral Luck* (New York: Cambridge University Press, 1981); and Claudia Card, *The Unnatural Lottery: Character and Moral Luck* (Philadelphia: Temple University Press, 1996).

36. See Bernard Cottret, *Calvin: A Biography*, trans. M. Wallace McDonald (Grand Rapids, Mich.: Eerdmans, 2000), 307, 324. For a useful analysis of Calvin's theology and influence, see Paul Helm, *John Calvin's Ideas* (Oxford: Oxford University Press, 2004). Particularly recommended is David Steinmetz's *Calvin in Context* (New York: Oxford University Press, 1995).

37. An anonymous reviewer for Columbia University Press pointed out this parallel.

38. See Dylan Loeb McClain, "Media Talk: From Mostly Wrong to Just about Right," *New York Times*, August 31, 1998, D5.

39. Katharine Q. Seelye, "President Goes Forth, to Mixed Reception," *New York Times*, August 28, 1998, A14.

40. See Laura Manserus, "A Governor Resigns: McGreevey Steps Down after Disclosing a Gay Affair," *New York Times*, August 13, 2004, A1; see also David Kocieniewski, "A Governor's Downfall, in 20 Wrenching Days," *New York Times*, August 14, 2004, A1. According to the second article, the most dramatic line the governor eventually uttered—"I am a gay American"—was developed by the gay caucus Human Rights Campaign and had been poll tested. The awkward phrase intentionally reframed the debate about gay causes from one about sexual liberation to one about civil rights. Confessing to a national audience, it seems, requires careful practice.

41. Roughly a year later, the American film *Brokeback Mountain* (2005) pushed the subject of gay men trapped in conventional marriages into public dialogue. Sympathy for tortured men striving to conform to heterosexual ideals crested but did not lead to widespread forgiveness. See Katy Butler, "Many Couples Must Negotiate Terms of 'Brokeback Marriages,'" *New York Times*, March 7, 2006, F5.

42. See Joan Petersilia, *When Prisoners Come Home: Parole and Prisoner Reentry* (New York: Oxford University Press, 2003), and Jennifer Gonnerman, *Life on the Outside: The Prison Odyssey of Elaine Bartlett* (New York: Farrar, Straus & Giroux, 2004). See also David Garland's excellent work *Punishment in Modern Society: A Study in Social Theory* (Oxford: Clarendon, 1990), to which I am indebted.

43. Michel Foucault, *Discipline and Punish: The Birth of the Prison*, trans. Alan Sheridan (New York: Vintage, 1979), 55.

44. Foucault, *Discipline and Punish*, 52.

45. See Andrew Delbanco, *The Death of Satan*. For a thorough profile of Christian denominations in the United States still in the grip of apocalyptic expectations, see Boyer, *When Time Shall Be No More: Prophecy Belief in Modern American Culture* (Cambridge, Mass.: Harvard University Press, 1994); for a broader overview, see Eugen Weber, *Apocalypses: Prophecies, Cults, and Millennial Beliefs through the Ages* (Cambridge, Mass.: Harvard University Press, 2000).

46. See Jeremy Travis and Michelle Waul, eds., *Prisoners Once Removed: The Impact of Incarceration and Reentry on Children, Families, and Communities* (Washington, D.C.: Urban Institute, 2002).

47. Baron de Montesquieu, *The Spirit of the Laws* [1762 translation] (Berkeley: University of California Press, 1977), 88.

48. Montesquieu, *The Spirit of the Laws*, 88.

49. Emile Durkheim, *The Division of Labor in Society*, trans. G. Simpson (New York: Free Press, 1964), 124.

50. Durkheim, *The Division of Labor in Society*, 125.

51. Durkheim, *The Division of Labor in Society*, 126.

52. Durkheim, *The Division of Labor in Society*, 112.

53. Michael Ignatieff and Douglas Hay have continued in the tradition of Montesquieu, de Tocqueville, and Durkheim, and their work informs this section. For an excellent overview of the philosophy and sociology of punishment, see again Garland, *Punishment and Modern Society*. For a philosophical and religious analysis of the pleasure people have felt in the punishment of alleged criminals, see my book *When Bad Things Happen to Other People* (New York: Routledge, 2000). This section borrows much from Garland.

54. See Timothy Gorringe, *God's Just Vengeance: Crime, Violence, and the Rhetoric of Salvation* (Cambridge: Cambridge University Press, 1996); and Sheldon Watts, *Epidemics and History: Disease, Power and Imperialism* (New Haven, Conn.: Yale University Press, 1997).

55. See Ariel Glucklich, *Sacred Pain: Hurting the Body for the Sake of the Soul* (New York: Oxford University Press, 2001).

56. For an authoritative survey of the desire for martyrdom from the church fathers through the late Middle Ages (including helpful distinctions between different sorts of martyrdom), see Louis Gougaud, *Dévotions et pratiques ascétiques du moyen ages* (Paris: Desclee de Brouwer, 1925), 200–19.

57. Biographical sketches of Lovelace abound. I have borrowed liberally here from an obituary of Lovelace. See Joe Bob Briggs, "Linda's Life: A Sad Story, and Its Impact on Us All," *National Review* online, April 25, 2002.

58. See Frances Finnegan, *Do Penance or Perish: Magdalen Asylums in Ireland* (Oxford: Oxford University Press, 2001). Finnegan writes, "Continuing to operate even when the Women's Movement was at its height, the Magdalen System in Ireland lingered on unnoticed, its victims not, apparently, a matter of concern. Tragically, scores of penitents (or 'ladies,' as they were latterly called) were still in the Homes in the early nineteen-nineties, when these once thriving empires were belatedly sold. These women, who dreaded the prospect of leaving, were casualties not of the Victoria Age but of the much more recent past. Their lives were, if anything, more squandered than those of their predecessors, and to less purpose. *At least earlier magdalens had been rejected by a society believing its own propaganda—that sinners must atone and that sex was a sin.*

Recent inmates continued their penance long past the abandonment of such views. Kept ignorant of changing attitudes, demoralised and controlled, they were excluded from the sexual revolution which, far from freeing them, made mockery of their wasted lives" (4–5; emphasis mine). Magdalen laundries operated on several continents in the nineteenth and twentieth centuries. Peter Mullan made the laundries famous through his 2002 film *The Magdalene Sisters*. See also Kathleen O'Malley, *Childhood Interrupted: Growing Up under the Cruel Regime of the Sisters of Mercy* (London: Virago, 2005).

59. See Richard Savill, "Vicar Who Can't Forgive Steps Down from Pulpit," *The Telegraph* (United Kingdom), March 7, 2006.

60. David Novitz, "Forgiveness and Self-Respect," in *In Defense of Sin*, ed. John Portmann (New York: St. Martin's Palgrave, 2002). For a thoughtful exposition of the opposite view, see Solomon Schimmel, *Wounds Not Healed by Time: The Power of Repentance and Forgiveness* (New York: Oxford University Press, 2002).

61. See, for example, Mark Amstutz, *The Healing of Nations: The Promise and Limits of Political Forgiveness* (Lanham, Md.: Rowman & Littlefield, 2004), as well as Schimmel, *Wounds Not Healed by Time*.

62. Marina Cantacuzino, "Grief Encounters," *The Times* (London), June 19, 2004, 30. For an encouraging account of restorative-justice programs, see Charles Tilly, *Why?* (Princeton: Pinceton University Press, 2006).

63. See, for example, Steve Bloomfield, "Power of Forgiveness Offers Hope for Peace in War-Torn Uganda," *The Independent* (London), September 25, 2006.

64. Bernard Schlink, *The Reader*, trans. Carol Brown Janeway (New York: Pantheon, 1997).

65. Catholic theologians didn't really clarify the notion of purgatory until the second half of the twelfth century. "Though Christians had prayed for the dead throughout the history of the church, and had come to use 'purgatorial' as an adjective with a word like 'pain' or 'trial,' there was no clear definition of its status or place. It was only in the 1170s that purgatory became a noun and theologians defined its nature." Garry Wills, *Why I Am a Catholic* (Boston: Houghton Mifflin, 2002), 135.

66. Of course, not everyone lives with such anxiety. Take, for example, three best-selling English journalists, who individually brought out memoirs in the early twenty-first century detailing their return to the Roman Catholic faith after decades of indifference or outright atheism: John Cornwell (*Breaking Faith: The Pope, the People, and the Fate of Catholicism*, which is only partly a memoir), Karen Armstrong (*The Spiral Staircase: My Climb Out of Darkness*), and Tony Hendra (*Father Joe: The Man Who Saved My Soul*). Cornwell and Hendra had already begun formal religious life before leaving it; Hendra had petitioned to be a Benedictine monk but was directed by the monastery to wait, once he was admitted to Cambridge University, where he lost his faith. Armstrong left the con-

vent (and, inadvertently, her faith) for study at Oxford University, and Corn-well left the seminary (and, inadvertently, his faith) for Cambridge University. None of the three expressed fear of damnation, had he died before returning to the faith.

67. For an excellent account of the demise of confession in the United States, see James M. O'Toole, "In the Court of Conscience: American Catholics and Confession, 1900–1975," in *Habits of Devotion: Catholic Religious Practice in Twentieth-Century America*, ed. James M. O'Toole (Ithaca, N.Y.: Cornell University Press, 2004), 131–86. O'Toole argues persuasively and at length that the culture in which confession thrived (until roughly the early 1970s) is now gone.

68. Susan Cheever offers numerous parallels in *My Name Is Bill: Bill Wilson—His Life and the Creation of Alcoholics Anonymous* (New York: Washington Square Press, 2005).

69. See David Allen Karp, *Speaking of Sadness: Depression, Disconnection, and the Meaning of Illness* (New York: Oxford University Press, 1994); Janet Sayers, *Divine Therapy: Love, Mysticism, and Psychoanalysis* (New York: Oxford University Press, 2003); and Steve Salerno, *Sham: How the Self-Help Movement Made America Helpless* (New York: Crown, 2005).

70. See Christina Hoff Sommers and Sally Satel, *One Nation under Therapy: How the Helping Culture Is Eroding Self-Reliance* (New York: St. Martin's, 2005).

71. Rosabeth Kanter, *Commitment and Community: Communes and Utopias in Sociological Perspective* (Cambridge, Mass.: Harvard University Press, 1972), 64–65. See also Leon Festinger, "The Psychological Effects of Insufficient Reward," *American Psychologist* 16 (1961): 1–11.

72. For an excellent account of this magical mystery, see Keith Thomas, *Religion and the Decline of Magic* (New York: Scribner's, 1971). This remarkable book can be read as a prelude to sin fatigue and atonement fatigue. Thomas writes, "We are, therefore, forced to the conclusion that men emancipated themselves from these magical beliefs without necessarily having devised any effective technology with which to replace them" (663). Shortly thereafter, he concludes that it would be a mistake to attribute undue rationality to the seventeenth-century urban dwellers with which he ends the study. The reasons for the mystery fatigue came down to "the growth of urban living, the rise of science, and the spread of an ideology of self-help" (665). Thomas emphasizes that fascination with magic never disappeared, though: "Indeed the role of magic in modern society may be more extensive than we yet appreciate" (667).

CHAPTER 3

1. Although masturbation may be condemned in Islam, male and even female masturbation were not always considered sinful. See B. F. Musallam and

David Morgan, *Sex and Society in Islam: Birth Control before the Nineteenth Century* (Cambridge: Cambridge University Press, 1983), 33–34.

2. See Caitlyn Flanagan, "Are You There God? It's Me, Monica: How Nice Girls Got So Casual about Oral Sex," *The Atlantic*, January 2006, 167–82.

3. Larry David, *Seinfeld*. The episode, named "The Contest," originally aired on November 18, 1992.

4. See Denise Gellene, "The Fat from These Pigs May End Up Helping Your Heart," *Los Angeles Times*, March 27, 2006.

5. Among the many articles that have reached newspapers, see Nicholas Wade, "Life-Extending Chemical Is Found in Certain Red Wines," *New York Times*, August 24, 2003.

6. Among a variety of such articles, see R. J. Ignelzi, "The Perks of Coffee: Java's Cup Runneth Over with Health Benefits," *San Diego Union-Tribune*, July 18, 2006, E1.

7. See, for example, Rachel Maines's excellent history of the vibrator *The Technology of Orgasm: "Hysteria," the Vibrator, and Women's Sexual Satisfaction* (Baltimore, Md.: Johns Hopkins University Press, 1999); Peter Lewis Allen, *The Wages of Sin: Sex and Disease, Past and Present* (Chicago: University of Chicago Press, 2000); Jean Stengers and Anne Van Neck, *Masturbation: The History of a Great Terror*, trans. Kathryn A. Hoffmann (New York: Palgrave, 2001); and Thomas Laqueur, *Solitary Sex: A Cultural History of Masturbation* (Cambridge, Mass.: Zone, 2003).

8. T. G. Morrow, *Christian Courtship in an Oversexed World: A Guide for Catholics* (Huntingdon, Ind.: Our Sunday Visitor, 2003), 89, 90.

9. Lauren Winner, *Real Sex: The Naked Truth about Chastity* (New York: Brazos, 2005), 114–17. Thomas Laqueur peppers his own study of masturbation with fascinating examples of the more conservative Christian revulsion to this practice. See his *Solitary Sex: A Cultural History of Masturbation*.

10. Garry Wills, *Papal Sin: Structures of Deceit* (New York: Doubleday, 2000), 187.

11. Since Pius XII, official Catholic teaching has objected to all forms of artificial insemination. One of the reasons is that the process encourages or condones masturbation. Creating a child, even for an infertile couple desperate for a biological child, did not count in the Vatican as a good reason for IVF.

12. Bernard Häring, *The Law of Christ*, 3 vols., 3:306–8.

13. Bernard Häring, *Free and Faithful in Christ* (New York: Seabury, 1979), 3 vols., 2:62.

14. Häring, *Free and Faithful in Christ*, 562–63.

15. For this and other papal encyclicals, see www.vatican.va.

16. *New Scientist* reported the findings of this experiment on July 19, 2003 ("Can Masturbating Each Day Keep the Doctor Away?" 15). Newspaper ac-

counts then broadcast the findings, although British papers showed much more interest than American ones. See Mark Oliver, "Helping Hand in Cancer Fight," *The Guardian* (London), July 17, 2003, 12. See also "It's in Your Own Hands to Prevent Prostate Cancer," *Daily Mail* (London), July 17, 2003, 19.

17. "Juice 'Can Slow Prostate Cancer,'" July 2, 2006, www.bbc.co.uk/health. The results of the UCLA study, led by Dr. Allan Pantuck, were published in the *Journal of Clinical Cancer Research*.

18. Georges Simenon, *Intimate Memoirs*, trans. Harold J. Samelson (San Diego, Calif.: Harcourt, Brace, Jovanovich, 1984). Quoted in Uta Ranke-Heinemann, *Eunuchs for the Kingdom of Heaven: Women, Sexuality and the Catholic Church*, trans. Peter Heinegg (New York: Penguin, 1990), 311.

19. Richard Ellmann, *James Joyce* (New York: Oxford University Press, 1982), 175, 50.

20. Already in 2004, testing for fetal defects could detect over 450 complications, many of them debilitating or even fatal. See Amy Harmon, "In New Tests for Fetal Defects, Agonizing Choices for Parents," *New York Times*, June 20, 2004, A1. See also Barbara Ehrenreich's trenchant commentary, "Owning Up to Abortion," *New York Times*, July 22, 2004, A21.

21. See Craig S. Smith, "As a Face Transplant Heals, Flurries of Questions Arise," *New York Times*, December 14, 2005, A1.

22. See, for example, Denise Grady, "The Hard Facts behind a Heartbreaking Case," *New York Times*, June 19, 2005, D5; and Bob Herbert, "Cruel and Unusual," *New York Times*, June 23, 2005, A19.

23. See Hélène Cixous, "Le rire de la Méduse," in *L'Arc*, trans. Keith and Paula Cohen as "The Laugh of the Medusa," *Signs* 1 (Summer 1976): 875–99.

CHAPTER 4

1. See Edward O. Laumann and Robert T. Michael, *Sex, Love, and Health in America* (Chicago: University of Chicago Press, 1994), 50–54. This research focuses not explicitly on virginity but rather on the incidence of sex before the age of eighteen. Curiously enough, this mammoth project to illuminate the sexual culture of the United States did not investigate virginity per se. It did document a clearly higher rate of sexual activity in teenagers, few of whom were likely to be married before the age of eighteen. As I was completing this chapter, I learned of a sociological survey from the Guttmacher Institute in New York City that concluded, "Almost all Americans have sex before marrying." See Lawrence B. Finer, "Trends in Premarital Sex in the United States, 1954–2003," *Public Health Reports* 22 (January–February 2007): 73–78.

2. Tara Bahrampour and Ian Shapira, "Sex at School Increasing, Some Educators Say," *Washington Post*, November 6, 2005, C01.

3. Lucien Legrand, *The Biblical Doctrine of Virginity* (New York: Sheed & Ward, 1963), 20. On the previous page, Legrand asserts, "The Old Testament, on the whole, does not acknowledge any religious value in virginity."

4. Well into the twentieth century, popular American Christians (e.g., President Jimmy Carter and the preacher Jimmy Swaggart) were confessing publicly to having sinned in their hearts (and they weren't talking about secretly rejoicing over a rival's defeat). Lust, fornication, and infidelity loom behind the inability of a man to keep his thoughts clean.

5. Laura Kipnis, *Against Love: A Polemic* (New York: Pantheon, 2003), 11.

6. *Letters of St. Jerome*, trans. C. C. Mierow (London: Longmans, Green, 1963), letter 22, "To Eustochium," sec. 7, 140.

7. Aline Rousselle, *Porneia: On Desire and the Body in Antiquity*, trans. Felicia Pheasant (Oxford: Blackwell, 1988), 156–58. Quoted in Robert Nye, *Sexuality* (New York: Oxford University Press, 1999), 38. In his memoir/tribute to his childhood confessor, British comedy writer Tony Hendra writes that a Benedictine monk instructed him that there was no sin in nocturnal emissions. See *Father Joe: The Man Who Saved My Soul* (New York: Random House, 2005), 124.

8. Rousselle, *Porneia*, 156–58. Although fantasies threaten the essential commitment to God, it may be that erotic feelings are apparently relatively uncommon in dreams after adolescence (as few as 6 percent of adult dreams involve feelings of eroticism or sexual activity). See Owen Flanagan, *Dreaming Souls* (Oxford: Oxford University Press), 149. Age would seem to have its advantages, at least for those who shun erotic dreams.

9. See Gregory Black, *The Catholic Crusade against the Movies, 1940–1975* (Cambridge: Cambridge University Press, 1998).

10. Bernard Häring, *The Law of Christ*, trans. Edwin G. Kaiser (Westminster, Md.: New Press, 1966), 3:375–76.

11. David Sue interviewed college students about their erotic fantasies and found that nearly half of women and over half of the men fantasized about forcing someone or being forced to have sex. Women frequently saw themselves as the aggressor in erotic fantasies. See "Erotic Fantasies of College Students during Coitus," *Journal of Sex Research* 15, no. 4 (November 1979). Catherine MacKinnon makes much of this point in her essay "Sexuality, Pornography, and Method: 'Pleasure under Patriarchy'" *Ethics* 314 (1989).

12. See Jerome Neu, "An Ethics of Fantasy?" *Journal of Theoretical and Philosophical Psychology* 22 (2002): 133–57.

13. James Patterson, *The Day America Told the Truth: What People Really Believe about Everything That Really Matters* (New York: Prentice Hall, 1991).

14. Laura Sessions Stepp, "The Buddy System; Sex in High School and College: What's Love Got to Do with It?" *Washington Post*, January 19, 2003, F1. Social conservatives might see a silver lining in this cloud: "As the incidence of oral sex has increased, the proportion of high school girls engaging in inter-

course has declined from 51 percent in 1991 to 43 percent in 2001, according to the Centers for Disease Control and Prevention." See also Caitlin Flanagan's review article, "Are You There, God? It's Me, Monica." She accused the 1999 documentary *The Lost Children of Rockdale County* of creating the "oral sex hysteria" in America. Flanagan also mentioned the influential television talk show *Oprah*; Oprah Winfrey had fanned the flames by devoting an episode to the alleged epidemic.

15. See Christopher Hitchens, "As American as Apple Pie," *Vanity Fair*, July 2006, 52–54.

16. Shari Thurer, "Gen X's Change of Head," *Salon*, July 21, 1999 (www.salon.com).

17. See Richard Posner, *Sex and Reason* (Cambridge, Mass.: Harvard University Press, 1992).

18. We can take Samuel Pepys as more or less representative here (Pepys details the affair with his housekeeper in his diary). See also Steven Nadler, *Rembrandt's Jews* (Chicago: University of Chicago Press, 2003), 117. This tradition extends back to antiquity. See Peter Brown, *The Body and Society: Men, Women, and Sexual Renunciation in Early Christianity*: "Men owned the bodies of their male and female servants. Within the walls of a great rambling house, filled with young servants, over whom the master ruled supreme, fidelity to one's wife remained a personal option. Despite harsh laws punishing married women for adultery, infidelity by their husbands incurred no legal punishment and very little moral disapprobation" (23).

19. See Kristin Luker, *When Sex Goes to School: Warring Views on Sex–and Sex Education–since the Sixties* (New York: Norton, 2006). Luker does not discuss virginity per se; the stress on abstinence from sex has become a new way (arguably a Protestant way) of talking about virginity.

20. Brown, *The Body and Society*, 8–9.

21. Rebecca Langlands, *Sexual Morality in Ancient Rome* (Cambridge: Cambridge University Press, 2006), 62.

22. Wendy Shalit, *A Return to Modesty: Discovering the Lost Virtue* (New York: Free Press, 2000).

23. Tara McCarthy, *Been There, Haven't Done That: A Virgin's Memoir* (New York: Warner Books, 1997), 3.

24. *New Catholic Encyclopedia* (New York: McGraw-Hill, 1967), 703.

25. John D'Emilio and Estelle B. Freedman, *Intimate Matters: A History of Sexuality in America* (New York: Harper & Row, 1988), 184–85.

26. Sandra Scofield, *Occasions of Sin* (New York: Norton, 2004), 39.

27. Karol Wojtyla (Pope John Paul II), *Love and Responsibility*, trans. H. T. Willets (New York: Farrar Straus & Giroux, 1981), 258. In Pope Paul VI's encyclical letter of 1967 *Sacerdotalis Caelibatus*, we read, "Priestly celibacy has been guarded by the Church for centuries as a brilliant jewel and retains its

value undiminished even in our time when mentality and structures have undergone such profound change."

28. See Xiao Zhou, "Virginity and Marital Sex in Contemporary China," *Feminist Studies* 15 (Summer 1989): 279–88.

29. Caryle Murphy, "Faith Programs Help Teens Sort Out Sex, Morality," *Washington Post*, April 6, 2003, A1.

30. See "Guadalupe the Sex Goddess," in *Resurrecting Grace: Remembering Catholic Childhoods*, ed. Marilyn Sewell (Boston: Beacon, 2001).

31. See N. El Saadawi, *The Hidden Face of Eve: Women in the Arab World* (London: Zed, 1980).

32. On testing for the maidenhead, see Jan Bremmer, ed., *From Sappho to de Sade: Moments in the History of Sexuality* (London: Routledge, 1989); and Richard Zacks, *History Laid Bare: Love, Sex and Perversity from the Etruscans to Warren G. Harding* (New York: HarperCollins, 1994).

33. On this, see Gertrude Himmelfarb, *One Nation, Two Cultures: A Searching Examination of American Society in the Aftermath of Our Cultural Revolution* (New York: Vintage Books, 2001).

34. This practice continues in some parts of the world. See, for example, Serap Thahinouthlu-Pelin, "The Question of Virginity Testing in Turkey," *Bioethics* 13, nos. 3–4 (July 1999): 256–61.

35. Jeffrey Eugenides, *Middlesex* (New York: Picador, 2003).

36. Joanne Meyerowitz, *How Sex Changed: A History of Transsexualism in the United States* (Cambridge, Mass.: Harvard University Press, 2002).

37. For a popular illustration of this point, see Laura Sessions Stepp, "Partway Gay? For Some Teen Girls, Sexual Preference Is a Shifting Concept," *Washington Post*, January 4, 2004, D1, D7.

38. According to the Book of Revelation, the Apocalypse will require 144,000 virgins—all of them male. Pockets of reverence for male virgins remain, many of them having ancient or medieval inspiration. See, for example, Samantha J. E. Riches, "St. George as a Male Virgin," in *Gender and Holiness*, ed. Samantha J. E. Riches and Sarah Salih (London: Routledge, 2002).

CHAPTER 5

1. See Michael S. Northcott, *The Environment and Christian Ethics* (Cambridge: Cambridge University Press, 1996); this list comes from him, as do a few other insights in this section. See also Lewis G. Regenstein, *Replenish the Earth: A History of Organized Religion's Treatment of Animals and Nature— Including the Bible's Message of Conservation and Kindness to Animals* (London: SCM, 1991); and Keith Thomas, *Man and the Natural World* (New York: Pantheon, 1983).

2. Al Gore, *An Inconvenient Truth: The Planetary Emergency of Global Warming and What We Can Do about It* (Emmaus, Pa.: Rodale, 2006). See also Eugene Linden, *The Winds of Change: Climate, Weather, and the Destruction of Civilizations* (New York: Simon & Schuster, 2006); Tim Flannery, *The Weather Makers: How Man Is Changing the Planet and What It Means for Life on Earth* (New York: Atlantic Monthly Press, 2006); and Elizabeth Kolbert, *Field Notes from a Catastrophe: Man, Nature, and Climate Change* (New York: Bloomsbury USA, 2006).

3. The novelist Michael Crichton also contests global warming theory. See *State of Fear* (New York: HarperCollins, 2004). President George W. Bush has been given to quoting Crichton favorably.

4. This excerpt comes from Alister McGrath, *The Reenchantment of Nature: The Denial of Religion and the Ecological Crisis* (New York: Doubleday, 2002), 39–40.

5. Sara Hebel, "Medical Student's Impairment Was Not Covered by Federal Disabilities Act, Court Rules," *Chronicle of Higher Education*, August 24, 2000, online version.

6. David Brooks, *On Paradise Drive: How We Live Now (and Always Have) in the Future Tense* (New York: Simon & Schuster, 2004).

7. On the high hourly rates (about $100 an hour) that tutors can charge the college-bound children of ambitious parents, see Fran Schumer, "Tutoring Is Big Business, Especially among Students Who Don't Need It," *New York Times*, June 20, 2004, NJ1.

8. James Gleick, *Isaac Newton* (New York: Vintage, 2003), 195, n. 5. Gleick in turn references Richard S. Westfall, *Never at Rest* (Cambridge: Cambridge University Press, 1980), 10.

9. See Scott Deveau, "What Would You Give Up to Be Thin?" *Globe and Mail* (Canada), May 17, 2006, online version.

10. Harry Mount, "Americans Are Getting Too Fat for X-rays," *The Telegraph* (London), July 27, 2006.

11. See Susan Bordo, *Unbearable Weight: Feminism, Western Culture, and the Body* (Berkeley: University of California Press, 1993); Leslie Heywood, *Dedication to Hunger: The Anorexic Aesthetic in Modern Culture* (Berkeley: University of California Press, 1996); Katharine A. Phillips, *The Broken Mirror: Understanding and Treating Body Dysmorphic Disorder* (New York: Oxford University Press, 1998); and Sander Gilman, *Fat Boys: A Slim Book* (Lincoln: University of Nebraska Press, 2004).

12. Richard Klein, *Eat Fat* (New York: Vintage, 1998).

13. See Peter Kramer, *Against Depression* (New York: Viking, 2005).

14. This section comes largely from Kay Redfield Jamison, *Night Falls Fast: Understanding Suicide* (New York: Knopf, 1999), and what is now perhaps the definitive study of depression, Andrew Solomon's *The Noonday Demon: An Atlas of Depression* (New York: Scribner, 2001), 25–26.

15. See new statistics, released in June 2005: Benedict Carey, "Most Will be Mentally Ill at Some Point, New Study Says," *New York Times*, June 7, 2005, A1. On the basis of wide-ranging studies conducted once a decade, some scholars projected that over half of all Americans will develop a mental illness at some point in their lives. See Carey's follow-up article: "Who's Mentally Ill? Deciding Is Often All in the Mind," *New York Times*, June 12, 2005, D1.

16. Philippe Ariès, *Centuries of Childhood: A Social History of Family Life* (New York: Vintage, 1962).

17. See J. J. Plumb, "The New World of Children in 18th-Century England," *Past and Present* 67 (1975): 66.

18. Particularly notable here is Judith Levine, *Harmful to Minors: The Perils of Protecting Children from Sex* (New York: Thunders Mouth, 2003), xxx. Levine draws on the following works: Karin Calvert, *Children in the House: The Material Culture of Early Childhood, 1600–1900* (Boston: Northeastern University Press, 1992); Marina Warner, "Little Angels, Little Monsters," in her *Six Myths of Our Time* (New York: Vintage, 1994); and James R. Kincaid, *Child-Loving: The Erotic Child and Victorian Culture* (New York: Routledge, 1992). Because Levine's work summarizes so many others, her background information is as useful as her own argument is provocative. Another central figure in this discipline is Lawrence Stone: see his *The Family, Sex and Marriage in England, 1500–1800* (London: Weidenfeld & Nicolson, 1977), and *Broken Lives: Separation and Divorce in England, 1660–1857* (New York: Oxford University Press, 1993).

19. The reach of American law, at least when it comes to sex with children, now extends across the sea. Aware that some of its citizens sometimes went abroad (e.g., to Thailand, Sri Lanka, and Costa Rica) in order to find children to have sex with, U.S. authorities have begun to notify travelers that they can be prosecuted at home for sex crimes committed in a foreign country. See Eric Lichtblau and James Dao, "U.S. Is Now Pursuing Americans Who Commit Sex Crimes Overseas," *New York Times*, June 8, 2004, A1, A20.

20. Among the many relevant cases, see the story of a twelve-year-old Florida boy who stomped a younger playmate to death: Terry Aguayo and Maria Newman, "Tate Is Sentenced to 30 Years and Faces Life," *New York Times*, May 18, 2006, online version.

21. See Linda Gordon, *Heroes of Their Own Lives: The Politics and History of Family Violence* (New York: Viking, 1988); Martha Fineman and Roxanne Mykitiuk, eds., *The Public Nature of Private Violence* (New York: Routledge, 1994); and Beth Richie, *Compelled to Crime: The Gender Entrapment of Battered Black Women* (New York: Routledge, 1996).

22. Dorothy Ayers Counts, Judith K. Brown, and Jacquelyn C. Campbell, *To Have and To Hit: Cultural Perspectives on Wife Beating*, 2d ed. (Urbana: University of Illinois Press, 1999).

23. See Daniel J. Wakin, "Judge Allows Jury Trial in a Case of Jewish Divorce," *New York Times*, January 25, 2002, B5.

24. On renewed arguments to repeal or restrict the sexual harassment cause of action, see Jeffrey Rosen, "When Reckless Laws Team Up," *New York Times*, January 25, 1998; or Jeffrey Toobin, "The Trouble with Sex," *New Yorker*, February 9, 1998, 48–55. Cited in Linda R. Hirshman and Jane E. Larson, *Hard Bargains: The Politics of Sex* (New York: Oxford University Press, 1998).

25. See "Yale Bans Sex between Students and Faculty," *New York Times*, November 15, 1997, B5. See also Emily Bazelon, "Lux, Veritas, and Sexual Trespass," *Yale Alumni Magazine*, July–August 2004, 35–43. Bazelon writes, "It was the Jorgenson case that led Yale to ban all sexual relationships between teachers and their students." Bazelon also analyzes the Wolf case.

26. *New York Magazine* published Wolf's accusation-bearing article in February 2004.

27. Michael Shermer and Alex Grobman, *Denying History: Who Says the Holocaust Never Happened and Why Do They Say It?* (Berkeley: University of California Press, 2000), xiii.

28. See Pater Balakian, *Black Dog of Fate: An American Son Uncovers His Armenian Past* (New York: Broadway, 1998).

29. Gary Boulard, "The Anti-Twinkie Defense," *The Advocate*, June 14, 1994.

30. *The Advocate*, April 1, 1997, 25.

31. *The Advocate*, February 4, 1997, 14.

32. See Mark Jordan, *The Silence of Sodom: Homosexuality in Modern Catholicism* (Chicago: University of Chicago Press, 2000), 225.

33. Of course, numerous other religious groups do. In May 2003, the heads of twenty-six conservative groups formed the Arlington Group, the point of which was to pool resources in order to fight the forces of secularism. The Arlington Group found concrete focus only a few months later, when the Supreme Court struck down a ruling that had declared sodomy illegal. The Arlington Group sees sympathy for gay marriage as a kind of disease. Gary Bauer, president of a similar group called American Values, said that gay marriage is "the new abortion."

34. In *Heavenly Sex*, Ruth Westheimer ("Dr. Ruth" to the radio and television public) argues that gay men should enter traditional heterosexual marriages. Westheimer writes as an Orthodox Jew. See Ruth K. Westheimer and Jonathan Mark, *Heavenly Sex: Sexuality in the Jewish Tradition* (New York: Continuum, 2000), 61–62.

35. Task Force on Circumcision, American Academy of Pediatrics, *Circumcision Policy Statement*, 103 *Pediatrics* 686 (1999). See David Gollaher, *Circumcision: A History of the World's Most Controversial Surgery* (New York: Basic Books, 2000). See also Dena S. Davis, "Male and Female Genital Alteration: A Collision Course with the Law?" *Health Matrix* 11 (2001): 487.

36. See "Debunking the Concept of 'Race,'" *New York Times*, July 30, 2005, A14; and Emma Daly, "DNA Testing Tells Students They Aren't Who They Thought," *New York Times*, April 13, 2005, B8.

37. Bernard Lewis, *What Went Wrong? Western Impact and Middle Eastern Response* (New York: Oxford University Press, 2002), 114.

38. See Eamon Duffy, *Saints and Sinners: A History of the Popes* (New Haven, Conn.: Yale University Press, 1997), 241–42.

39. This history, credited to Janice Lord, comes from the official Web site of Mothers against Drunk Driving (www.madd.org/home).

CHAPTER 6

1. Karen W. Arenson, "Harvard President Sees Rise in Anti-Semitism on Campus," *New York Times*, September 21, 2002, A13. The speech became available on Summers's Web site: www. president.harvard.edu/speeches. Less than four years later, Summers would step down suddenly from the presidency of Harvard, amid complaints that he could not appreciate the intellectual gifts of women.

2. See on the NPR Web site (www.npr.org) both the *Tavis Smiley* show from September 25, 2002, and, much more important, *Morning Edition* from October 22, 2002.

3. This policy originally targeted the workplace, not the university. Then and now, it extends to all racial minorities, not just to African Americans. Few will deny that affirmative action has led to the comparatively recent diversification of police and fire departments, unions, factories, offices, and schools.

4. Charles Marsh has written extensively on mainline Protestant racism and the difficult struggle to overcome it. See *God's Long Summer: Stories of Faith and Civil Rights* (Princeton. N.J.: Princeton University Press, 1999), and *The Last Days: A Son's Story of Sin and Segregation at the Dawn of a New South* (New York: Basic Books, 2001). For an indication of Jewish opposition to racial segregation in the United States, see *The Quiet Voices: Southern Rabbis and Black Civil Rights, 1880s to 1990s*, ed. Mark K. Bauman and Berkley Kalin (Tuscaloosa: University of Alabama Press, 1997). Roman Catholics are to oppose every form of discrimination based on creed as well as on sex and race (*Declaration on the Relationship of the Church to Non-Christian Religions*, n. 5). In February 2007, the Public Broadcasting Company (PBS) broadcast the documentary "Sisters of Selma: Bearing Witness for Change." This production recounts the story of Catholic nuns who answered the Rev. Martin Luther King Jr.'s plea to join the Alabama protests on March 10, 1965.

5. For a solid overview of the issues I pursue in this chapter, see Lani Guinier and Gerald Torres, *The Miner's Canary: Enlisting Race, Resisting Power, Transforming Democracy* (Cambridge, Mass.: Harvard University Press, 2002).

6. According to a CBS News/*New York Times* poll on January 23, 2003, more Americans than ever favored affirmative action in university admissions. Some 53 percent favored programs that make special efforts to help minorities get ahead in order to make up for past discrimination, and 39 percent opposed such efforts. Support for affirmative action had increased from five years previous. Back in 1997, 41 percent thought affirmative action programs should be continued, but more—47 percent—thought such programs should be abolished. See www.cbsnews.com.

7. See Ira Katznelson, *When Affirmative Action Was White: An Untold History of Racial Inequality in Twentieth Century America* (New York: Norton, 2005); Ange-Marie Hancock, *The Politics of Disgust: The Public Identity of the Welfare Queen* (New York: New York University Press, 2004); and James W. Loewen, *Sundown Towns: A Hidden Dimension of American Racism* (New York: Free Press, 2005).

8. See John C. Jeffries Jr., *Justice Lewis F. Powell, Jr.* (New York: Scribner, 1994).

9. Among the many articles in this vein, see Andrew Oldenquist, "An Explanation of Retribution," *Journal of Philosophy* 85 (1988): 464–78. For a longer treatment, see Mark Tunick, *Punishment: Theory and Practice* (Berkeley: University of California Press, 1992); and Nigel Walker, *Why Punish?* (Oxford: Oxford University Press, 1991).

10. Barbara Grutter, "Making Progress: A Response to Michigan GOP Chair Betsy DeVos," *National Review*, August 19, 2003, www.nationalreview.com. Grutter earned a B.S. with high honors from Michigan State University, where she maintained a 3.81 GPA. She graduated in 1978 and scored 161 on her LSAT, but she postponed law school for a career as a health care consultant and manager. In 1986, she founded a successful health care information firm, and in 1996, at age forty-three, she applied to the University of Michigan Law School. Grutter was wait-listed and eventually rejected. She then went back to her business and raising her two children.

11. Elie Wiesel, *Legends of Our Time* (New York: Holt, Rinehart & Winston, 1968), 142. In the same chapter and just after this excerpt, Wiesel stated that he would avoid any travel to Germany.

12. Elie Wiesel, "Only the Guilty Are Guilty, Not Their Sons," *New York Times*, May 5, 2001, A23.

13. Jodi Wilgoren, "Affirmative Action Plan Is Upheld in Michigan," *New York Times*, December 14, 2000, A16. Gratz applied to the University of Michigan at Ann Arbor in the fall of 1994, when she was a high school senior in the Detroit suburb of Southgate. Despite her combined score of 25 on the ACT (83rd percentile), a 3.765 GPA, and experience as a math tutor, athlete, cheerleader, and Class Congress representative, she was wait-listed and eventually rejected from UM–Ann Arbor, the flagship school of the University of Michigan system. After

enrolling in UM–Dearborn to study math, Gratz sued the University of Michigan on the grounds that its affirmative action system had discriminated against her. Patrick Hamacher joined Gratz and Grutter as the third plaintiff in *Grutter v. Bollinger*. A Lansing, Michigan, native, Hamacher applied to the University of Michigan at Ann Arbor in 1996. He scored 28 on the ACT (89th percentile) and maintained a 3.373 GPA while training as a varsity athlete and working several part-time jobs. After he was wait-listed by UM–Ann Arbor, he applied to and was accepted at Michigan State University, where he earned a B.A. in public administration in 2001.

14. John H. McWhorter, *Losing the Race: Self-Sabotage in Black America* (New York: Free Press, 2000).

15. In Sigrid Nunez's novel *The Last of Her Kind: A Novel* (New York: Farrar Straus & Giroux, 2005), for example, we find a character who, as a white teenager entering Barnard in 1968, loathed herself because of her race and felt immediate guilt every time she encountered a black person. She wished she were herself black.

16. See Karen W. Arenson, "Duke Failed to See Gravity of Rape Case, Report Says," *New York Times*, May 9, 2006, A5.

17. Frank Hereford, president of the University of Virginia in the 1970s, lost a lot by virtue of that very decision. His example argues against my point here; surely there are other such examples.

18. John McWhorter, an African American scholar of linguistics, joins in the whispering. See *Losing the Race*, 243–47.

19. William G. Bowen, Derek Bok, and Glenn C. Loury, *The Shape of the River* (Princeton, N.J.: Princeton University Press, 2000), 36–37. The authors borrow this analogy from Thomas Kane.

20. "No Damages for Students over Affirmative Action," *New York Times*, March 22, 1998, A27. In the Hopwood case, a three-judge panel said that affirmative action as approved by the Supreme Court in the landmark 1978 *Bakke* decision was no longer permissible.

21. Steven A. Holmes and Greg Winter, "Test of Time: Fixing the Race Gap in 25 Years or Less," *New York Times*, June 29, 2003, D4.

22. Immanuel Kant, *Introduction to the Metaphysics of Morals* (1797), as quoted in Martha C. Nussbaum, *The Fragility of Goodness: Luck and Tragedy in Greek Tragedy and Philosophy* (Cambridge: Cambridge University Press, 2001), 31. Nussbaum follows the translation proposed by A. Donagan in "Consistency in Rationalist Moral Systems," *Journal of Philosophy* 81 (1984): 284.

23. Hermann Cohen, *Religion of Reason Out of the Sources of Judaism*, trans. Simon Kaplan (New York: Ungar, 1972), 189.

24. I am grateful to Pamela Karlan of the Stanford Law School for discussion about this chapter.

CHAPTER 7

1. Andrew Delbanco, *The Death of Satan: How Americans Have Lost the Sense of Evil* (New York: Farrar, Straus & Giroux, 1995), 229.

2. Lauro Martines, *Fire in the City: Savonarola and the Struggle for the Soul of Renaissance Florence* (New York: Oxford University Press, 2006).

3. See Daniel Gilbert, "Four More Years of Happiness," *New York Times*, January 20, 2005, A23. These insights were taken from his book *Stumbling on Happiness* (New York: Knopf, 2006).

4. William James, "Pragmatism and Humanism," in *The Writings of William James* (Chicago: University of Chicago Press, 1977), 451, 455. Quoted in David E. Cooper, *The Measure of Things: Humanism, Humility, and Mercy* (Oxford: Clarendon, 2002), 7. On humanism, see also "Letter on Humanism," in *Basic Writings: Martin Heidegger*, ed. D. F. Krell (London: Routledge, 1993). Jean-Paul Sartre touched on humanism in his essay "L'existentialisme est un humanisme," as did George Santayana (*The Life of Reason, or The Phases of Human Progress*, 1905–1906) and John Dewey before him (Dewey professed his humanist faith in various books, especially his Terry Lectures, *A Common Faith*, from 1934).

5. Thomas Nagel, *The Last Word* (New York: Oxford University Press, 1997); see Cooper, *The Measure of Things*, 155–56.

6. Thomas Nagel, *The View from Nowhere* (New York: Oxford University Press, 1989), 109.

7. Richard Norman, for example, identifies himself as both a secular humanist and an atheist, the first being a solution to the second. If religion cannot explain what life is all about, he says, "then we had better look for some alternative set of beliefs to live by, and that is the project of secular humanism." See his *On Humanism* (London: Routledge, 2004), 17. He also seems to want to exclude believers from the ranks of humanists: "Humanism as I understand it involves not just the rejection of religious belief but, at the very least, the positive affirmation that human beings can find from within themselves the resources to live a good life without religion" (18).

8. I am not the first to pursue this line of reasoning. See Eva Feder Kittay's skillful defense of hypocrisy "On Hypocrisy," in *Metaphilosophy* 13 (1982), 277–89. She concludes that hypocrisy "is not so much blameworthy as it is a case of making one's way—given the way of the world." Before her useful essay on hypocrisy, William James had noticed much the same thing. Writing of saintliness in *The Varieties of Religious Experience*, he asserted, "Treating those whom [the saints] met, in spite of the past, in spite of all appearances, as worthy, they have stimulated them to BE worthy, miraculously transformed them by their radiant example and by the challenge of their expectation. . . . It is not

possible to be quite as mean as we naturally are, when [the saints] have passed before us. One fire kindles another; and without that over-trust in human worth which they show, the rest of us would lie in spiritual stagnancy" (357, 358). In hypocrisy, then, we inspire ourselves.

9. Terry Eagleton, *The Gatekeeper: A Memoir* (New York: St. Martin's, 2001), 2, 3, 30.

10. Nietzsche, *Beyond Good and Evil: Prelude to a Philosophy of the Future*, trans. Walter Kaufmann (New York: Vintage, 1966), 201–37.

11. For a similar effort, see Eugene Borowitz's essay on being a mensch in *Exploring Jewish Ethics: Papers on Covenant Responsibility* (Detroit, Mich.: Wayne State Press, 1990). Other examples of interdenominational goals present themselves. During the Vietnam War, for instance, Christians and Jews worked together to protest American involvement. See Patrick Allitt, *Religion in America since 1945: A History* (New York: Columbia University Press, 2003), 101–7.

12. Dolly Parton, *Super Hits* (Sony, 1999).

13. Bill Clinton, *My Life* (New York: Knopf, 2004).

14. Bruce Bilson and Jerry Davis, directors, *Bewitched: The Complete First Season* (1964). The show went through eight seasons and 256 episodes. This and subsequent seasons are available for purchase on www.amazon.com.

15. Nora Ephron, director, *Bewitched* (Sony, 2005).

16. Jon Anderson and Michael Ansara, directors, *I Dream of Jeannie–The Complete First Season* (1965). This and subsequent seasons are available for purchase on www.amazon.com.

17. Lars von Trier, director, *Dogville* (Lions Gate, 2004).

18. In March 2006, for example, a black congresswoman accused a white security guard of racism in Washington, D.C. On the face of it, the white guard was only doing his duty. Members of Congress wear identifying lapel pins and routinely are waved into buildings without undergoing security checks. McKinney was not wearing her pin at the time, and the officer apparently did not recognize her, she has said. Her supporters claimed that Congresswoman Cynthia McKinney, in a hurry, was essentially chased and grabbed by the officer. They maintained that she reacted instinctively in an effort to defend herself. Several Capitol Police officials subsequently told the media that the officer involved asked McKinney three times to stop. When she did not, he placed a hand on her and she hit him, they said. See "McKinney Blames Altercation on Capitol Police," *New York Times*, March 31, 2006. Eight days after the incident, she apologized to her colleagues from the House floor. Ultimately, a D.C. grand jury decided against indicting her on charges that she had assaulted Paul McKenna, the white officer. Think also of Vernon Jones, the manager of De Kalb County, Georgia (the Atlanta suburbs), who allegedly started replacing whites with blacks to get "a darker administration." See *Bryant v. Jones*, No. 1:04CV2462 (N.D. Ga., Aug. 24, 2004). The case was decided on January 10,

2007. The court ordered a stay pending appeal on the issue of qualified immunity.

19. See, for example, the documentary *Capturing the Friedmans*. See also Judith Levine, *Harmful to Minors: The Perils of Protecting Children from Sex* (New York: Thunder's Mouth, 2002), 60, 64. Levine offers examples of unhappy children who accused a parent of sexual misconduct and then later recanted the charge. See also Dorothy Rabinowitz, *No Crueller Tyranny*, about the breathless hunt for child molesters in 1980s and 1990s America. And during the masturbation panic of the eighteenth and nineteenth centuries, children sometimes had parents imprisoned by reporting instances of masturbation (children had been encouraged at school to turn in such problem parents); see Peter Lewis Allen, *The Wages of Sin* (Chicago: University of Chicago Press, 2000).

20. For a variety of ways in which religious groups abuse their power, see Roger Kimball, *When Religion Becomes Evil* (San Francisco: HarperSanFrancisco, 2002).

21. See Richard Coniff, "Flipping It," *Yale Alumni Monthly*, May–June 2004, 30–37.

22. David Sedaris, "Old Faithful," *New Yorker*, November 29, 2004, 107.

23. Tom Hayden, *Street Wars: Gangs and the Future of Violence* (New York: New Press, 2004).

24. See Tami Abdollah, "French Explore Affirmative Action: An Elite University Uses Parallel Admissions Process for Minority Recruitment," *Wall Street Journal Europe*, July 27, 2005, A1. The university in question was Sciences Po, "an elite French university known for its wealthy students and high-profile government alumni."

25. William G. Bowen and Sarah A. Levin, *Reclaiming the Game: College Sports and Educational Values* (Princeton, N.J.: Princeton University Press, 2005).

26. James L. Shulman and William G. Bowen, *The Game of Life: College Sports and Educational Values* (Princeton: Princeton University Press, 2002). The authors argue that recruited athletes have a greater advantage in university admissions than both racial minorities and the children of alumni. Of course, many recruited athletes are themselves racial minorities.

27. Ruth K. Westheimer and Jonathan Mark, *Heavenly Sex: Sexuality in the Jewish Tradition* (New York: New York University Press, 1995), 29. Westheimer invokes the counsel of Rabbi Illai the Elder.

EPILOGUE

1. Abraham Heschel, *God in Search of Man: A Philosophy of Judaism* (New York: Farrar, Straus & Giroux, 1955), 363.

SELECT
BIBLIOGRAPHY

Arenson, Karen W. "Harvard President Sees Rise in Anti-Semitism on Campus." *New York Times*, September 21, 2002.

Ariès, Philippe. *Centuries of Childhood: A Social History of Family Life*. New York: Vintage, 1962.

Babcock, William S. "Augustine on Sin and Moral Agency." *Journal of Religious Ethics* 16, no. 1 (1988).

Biale, David. *Eros and the Jews: From Ancient Israel to Contemporary America*. Berkeley: University of California Press, 1997.

Biggs, Joe Bob. "Linda's Life: A Sad Story, and Its Impact on Us All." *National Review*, April 25, 2002.

Bloomfield, Steve. "Power of Forgiveness Offers Hope for Peace in War-Torn Uganda." *The Independent* (London), September 25, 2006.

Bordo, Susan. *Unbearable Weight: Feminism, Western Culture, and the Body*. Berkeley: University of California Press, 1993.

Bossy, John. *Christianity in the West, 1400–1700*. Oxford: Oxford University Press, 1985.

Bowen, William G., Derek Bok, and Glenn C. Loury. *The Shape of the River: Long-Term Consequences of Considering Race in College and University Admissions*. Princeton, N.J.: Princeton University Press, 2000.

Boyer, Paul. *When Time Shall Be No More: Prophecy Belief in Modern Culture*. Cambridge, Mass.: Harvard University Press, 1994.

Brooks, David. *On Paradise Drive: How We Live Now (and Always Have) in the Future Tense*. New York: Simon & Schuster, 2004.

Brown, Peter. *The Body and Society: Men, Women, and Sexual Renunciation in Early Christianity*. New York: Columbia University Press, 1988.

Cabantous, Alain. *Blasphemy: Impious Speech in the West from the Seventeenth to the Nineteenth Century*. Trans. Eric Rauth. New York: Columbia University Press, 2002.

Carey, Benedict. "Most Will be Mentally Ill at Some Point, New Study Says." *New York Times*, June 7, 2005.

——. "Who's Mentally Ill? Deciding Is Often All in the Mind." New York Times, June 12, 2005.

Cohen, Hermann. *Religion of Reason Out of the Sources of Judaism*. Trans. Simon Kaplan. New York: Ungar, 1972.

Cole, William Graham. *Sex in Christianity and Psychoanalysis*. New York: Oxford University Press, 1955.

Dawkins, Richard. *The God Delusion*. Boston: Houghton Mifflin, 2006.

De Lange, Nicholas. *An Introduction to Judaism*. Cambridge: Cambridge University Press, 2000.

Delbanco, Andrew. *The Death of Satan: How Americans Have Lost the Sense of Evil*. New York: Farrar, Straus & Giroux, 1995.

Durkheim, Emile. *The Division of Labor in Society*. Trans. G. Simpson. New York: Free Press, 1964.

Efron, Noah F. *Real Jews: Secular versus Ultra-Orthodox: The Struggle for Jewish Identity in Israel*. New York: Basic Books, 2003.

Ellmann, Richard. *James Joyce*. New York: Oxford University Press, 1982.

Engel, Mary Potter. "Evil, Sin and Violation of the Vulnerable." In *Lift Every Voice: Constructing Christian Theologies from the Underside*, ed. S. B. Thistlethwaite and M. P. Engel. San Francisco: Harper & Row, 1990.

Finnegan, Frances. *Do Penance or Perish: Magdalen Asylums in Ireland*. Oxford: Oxford University Press, 2001.

Fisher, Ian. "Limbo, An Afterlife Tradition, May Be Doomed by the Vatican." *New York Times*, December 8, 2005.

Flanagan, Caitlyn. "Are You There, God? It's Me, Monica: How Nice Girls Got So Casual about Oral Sex." *The Atlantic*, January 2006, 167–82.

Flanagan, Owen. *Dreaming Souls: Sleep, Dreams, and the Evolution of the Conscious Mind*. Oxford: Oxford University Press, 2000.

Fone, Byrne. *Homophobia: A History*. New York: Metropolitan, 2000.

Foucault, Michel. *Discipline and Punish: The Birth of the Prison*. Trans. Alan Sheridan. New York: Vintage, 1979.

Freedman, Samuel G. *Jew vs. Jew: The Struggle for the Soul of American Jewry*. New York: Simon & Schuster, 2001.

Garland, David. *Punishment and Modern Society: A Study in Social Theory*. Oxford: Oxford University Press, 2000.

Gilbert, Daniel. *Stumbling on Happiness*. New York: Knopf, 2006.

Gillman, Neil. *The Death of Death: Resurrection and Immortality in Jewish Thought*. Woodstock, Vt.: Jewish Lights, 1997.

Glucklich, Ariel. *Sacred Pain: Hurting the Body for the Sake of the Soul.* New York: Oxford University Press, 2001.

Gollaher, David. *Circumcision: A History of the World's Most Controversial Surgery.* New York: Basic Books, 2000.

Gonnerman, Jennifer. *Life on the Outside: The Prison Odyssey of Elaine Bartlett.* New York: Farrar, Straus & Giroux, 2004.

Goodman Kaufman, Carol. *Sins of Omission: The Jewish Community's Reaction to Domestic Violence.* Boulder, Colo.: Westview, 2003.

Gordon, Linda. *Heroes of Their Own Lives: The Politics and History of Family Violence.* New York: Viking, 1988.

Gore, Al. *An Inconvenient Truth: The Planetary Emergence of Global Warming and What We Can Do about It.* Emmaus, Pa.: Rodale, 2006.

Guinier, Lani, and Gerald Torres. *The Miner's Canary: Enlisting Race, Resisting Power, Transforming Democracy.* Cambridge, Mass.: Harvard University Press, 2002.

Haliczer, Stephen. *Sexuality in the Confessional: A Sacrament Profaned.* New York: Oxford University Press, 1996.

Häring, Bernard. *Free and Faithful in Christ: Moral Theology for Clergy and Laity.* New York: Seabury, 1978.

——. *The Law of Christ: Moral Theology for Priests and Laity.* Trans. Edwin G. Kaiser. 3 vols. Westminster, Md.: Newman, 1961.

Helm, Paul. *John Calvin's Ideas.* Oxford: Oxford University Press, 2004.

Himmelfarb, Gertrude. *One Nation, Two Cultures: A Searching Examination of American Society in the Aftermath of Our Cultural Revolution.* New York: Vintage Books, 2001.

Hoff Sommers, Christina, and Sally Satel. *One Nation under Therapy: How the Helping Culture Is Eroding Self-Reliance.* New York: St. Martin's, 2005.

James, William. *The Varieties of Religious Experience.* New York: Penguin Classics, 1985. (Orig. pub. 1902.)

Jamison, Kay Redfield. *Night Falls Fast: Understanding Suicide.* New York: Knopf, 1999.

Jonsen, Albert R., and Stephen Toulmin. *The Abuse of Casuistry: A History of Moral Reasoning.* Berkeley: University of California Press, 1988.

Jordan, Mark. *The Silence of Sodom: Homosexuality in Modern Catholicism.* Chicago: University of Chicago Press, 2000.

Kanter, Rosabeth. *Commitment and Community: Communes and Utopias in Sociological Perspective.* Cambridge, Mass.: Harvard University Press, 1972.

Katznelson, Ira. *When Affirmative Action Was White: An Untold History of Racial Inequality in Twentieth-Century America.* New York: Norton, 2005.

Kepnes, Steven. "'Turn Us to You and We Shall Return': Original Sin, Atonement, and Redemption in Jewish Terms." In *Christianity in Jewish Terms,* ed. David Novak et al. Boulder, Colo.: Westview, 2000.

Kipnis, Laura. *Against Love: A Polemic*. New York: Pantheon, 2003.

Kittay, Eva Feder. "On Hypocrisy." *Metaphilosophy* 13 (1982): 277–89.

Klawans, Jonathan. *Impurity and Sin in Ancient Judaism*. New York: Oxford University Press, 2000.

Klein, Richard. *Eat Fat*. New York: Vintage, 1998.

Kugel, James. *Traditions of the Bible: A Guide to the Bible as It Was at the Start of the Common Era*. Cambridge, Mass.: Harvard University Press, 1998.

Langlands, Rebecca. *Sexual Morality in Ancient Rome*. Cambridge: Cambridge University Press, 2006.

Legrand, Lucien. *The Biblical Doctrine of Virginity*. New York: Sheehan & Ward, 1963.

Levine, Judith. *Harmful to Minors: The Perils of Protecting Children from Sex*. New York: Thunders Mouth, 2003.

Loewen, James W. *Sundown Towns: A Hidden Dimension of American Racism*. New York: Free Press, 2005.

MacIntyre, Alasdair. *After Virtue*. South Bend, Ind.: University of Notre Dame Press, 1984.

Mahoney, John, S.J. *The Making of Moral Theology: A Study of the Roman Catholic Tradition*. Oxford: Oxford University Press, 1987.

Marenbon, John. *The Philosophy of Abelard*. Cambridge: Cambridge University Press, 1997.

Marius, Richard. *Martin Luther: The Christian between God and Death*. Cambridge, Mass.: Harvard University Press, 1999.

Martel, Ned. "In a Show about Sexual Exploits, Blushing Is a Sin." *New York Times*, June 2004, 24, E8.

McBrien, Richard. *Catholicism: A Study Edition*. Minneapolis: Winston, 1981.

McCormick, Patrick. *Sin as Addiction*. New York: Paulist, 1989.

McFadyen, Alistair. *Bound to Sin: Abuse, Holocaust, and the Christian Doctrine of Sin*. Cambridge: Cambridge University Press, 2000.

McGrath, Alister. *The Reenchantment of Nature: The Denial of Religion and the Ecological Crisis*. New York: Doubleday, 2002.

McNeill, John T., and Helena Gamer. *Medieval Handbooks of Penance*. New York: Columbia University Press, 1938.

McWhorter, John H. *Losing the Race: Self-Sabotage in Black America*. New York: Free Press, 2000.

Menninger, Karl. *Whatever Happened to Sin?* London: Hodder & Stroughton, 1973.

Mercadante, Linda A. *Victims and Sinners: Spiritual Roots of Addiction and Recovery*. Louisville, Ky.: Westminster John Knox, 1996.

Meyerson, Mark D. *The Muslims of Valencia in the Age of Ferdinand and Isabel: Between Coexistence and Crusade*. Berkeley: University of California Press, 1991.

Milbank, John. *Theology and Social Theory*. Oxford: Blackwell, 1990.

Morris, Colin. *The Papal Monarchy: The Western Church from 1050 to 1250.* Oxford: Oxford University Press, 1989.

Nagel, Thomas. *The Last Word.* New York: Oxford University Press, 1997.

Neusner, Jacob. "The Idea of Purity in Ancient Judaism." *Journal of the American Academy of Religion* 43 (1975): 15–27.

Neusner, Jacob, et al., eds. *Judaism and Islam in Practice: A Sourcebook.* London: Routledge, 2000.

Norman, Richard. *On Humanism.* London: Routledge, 2004.

Northcott, Michael S. *The Environment and Christian Ethics.* Cambridge: Cambridge University Press, 1996.

Novak, David. *Jewish Social Ethics.* New York: Oxford University Press, 1992.

O'Toole, James M. "In the Court of Conscience: American Catholics and Confession, 1900–1975." In *Habits of Devotion: Catholic Religious Practice in Twentieth-Century America,* ed. James M. O'Toole. Ithaca, N.Y.: Cornell University Press, 2004.

Pagels, Elaine. *The Origin of Satan.* New York: Vintage, 1996.

Perry, Mary Elizabeth. *Gender and Disorder in Early Modern Seville.* Princeton, N.J.: Princeton University Press, 1990.

Peters, Ted. *Sin: Radical Evil in Soul and Society.* Grand Rapids, Mich.: Eerdmans, 1994.

Petersilia, Joan. *When Prisoners Come Home: Parole and Prisoner Reentry.* New York: Oxford University Press, 2003.

Petigny, Alan. "Illegitimacy, Postwar Psychology, and the Reperiodization of the Sexual Revolution." *Journal of Social History* 38, no. 4 (2004): 63–79.

Posner, Richard. *The Problematics of Moral and Legal Theory.* Cambridge, Mass.: Harvard University Press, 1999.

Rahner, Karl. *Theological Investigations.* Trans. Karl-H. and Boniface Kruger. New York: Seabury, 1974.

Ridley, Matt. *Genome: The Autobiography of a Species in 23 Chapters.* New York: HarperCollins, 1999.

Rosen, Jeffrey. "When Reckless Laws Team Up." *New York Times,* January 25, 1998.

Roussell, Aline. *Porneia: On Desire and the Body in Antiquity.* Trans. Felicia Pheasant. Oxford: Blackwell, 1988.

Rush, Alfred C. "Spiritual Martyrdom in St. Gregory the Great." *Theological Studies* 23 (1962): 569–89.

Schimmel, Solomon. *The Seven Deadly Sins: Jewish, Christian, and Classical Reflections on Human Nature.* New York: Oxford University Press, 1996.

——. *Wounds Not Healed by Time: The Power of Repentance and Forgiveness.* New York: Oxford University Press, 2002.

Scofield, Sandra. *Occasions of Sin.* New York: Norton, 2004.

Segal, Alan F. *Rebecca's Children: Judaism and Christianity in the Roman World.* Cambridge, Mass.: Harvard University Press, 1986.

Shalit, Wendy. *A Return to Modesty: Discovering the Lost Virtue*. New York: Free Press, 1999.

Shermer, Michael, and Alex Grobman. *Denying History: Who Says the Holocaust Never Happened and Why Do They Say It?* Berkeley: University of California Press, 2000.

Solomon, Andrew. *The Noonday Demon: An Atlas of Depression*. New York: Scribner, 2001.

Sommerville, Johann P. "The 'New Art of Lying': Equivocation, Mental Reservation, and Casuistry." In *Conscience and Casuistry*, ed. Edmund Leites. Cambridge: Cambridge University Press, 1988.

Steinmetz, David. *Calvin in Context*. New York: Oxford University Press, 1995.

Tentler, Thomas. *Sin and Confession on the Eve of the Reformation*. Princeton, N.J.: Princeton University Press, 1977.

Thomas, Keith. *Religion and the Decline of Magic*. New York: Scribner's, 1971.

Toobin, Jeffrey. "The Trouble with Sex." *New Yorker*, February 9, 1998, 45–55.

Turner, Alice K. *A History of Hell*. New York: Harvest Books, 1995.

Twain, Mark. *The Diaries of Adam and Eve*. New York: Oxford University Press, 1996.

Urbach, Efraim. *The Sages, Their Concepts and Beliefs*. Trans. Israel Abrahams. Jerusalem: Magnes Press, Hebrew University, 1979.

Volf, Miroslav. "The Lamb of God and the Sin of the World." In *Christianity in Jewish Terms*, ed. David Novak et al. Boulder, Colo.: Westview, 2000.

Watts, Sheldon. *Epidemics and History: Disease, Power and Imperialism*. New Haven, Conn.: Yale University Press.

Weber, Eugen. *Apocalypses: Prophecies, Cults, and Millennial Beliefs through the Ages*. Cambridge, Mass.: Harvard University Press, 2000.

Westheimer, Ruth K., and Jonathan Mark. *Heavenly Sex: Sexuality in the Jewish Tradition*. New York: New York University Press, 1995.

Wiesel, Elie. "Only the Guilty Are Guilty, Not Their Sons." *New York Times*, May 5, 2001.

Williams, N. P. *The Ideas of the Fall and of Original Sin: A Historical and Critical Study*. London: Longmans, Green, 1927.

——. *Legends of Our Time*. New York: Holt, Rinehart & Winston, 1968.

Wills, Garry. *Papal Sin: Structures of Deceit*. New York: Doubleday, 2000.

——. *Why I Am a Catholic*. Boston: Houghton Mifflin, 2002.

Witten, Marsha. *All Is Forgiven: The Secular Message in American Protestantism*. Princeton, N.J.: Princeton University Press, 1993.

Wolfe, Alan. *Return to Greatness: How America Lost Its Sense of Purpose and What It Needs to Do to Recover It*. Princeton. N.J.: Princeton University Press, 2005.

Yarnold, Edward, S.J. *The Theology of Original Sin*. Hales Corner, Wisc.: Clergy Book Service, 1971.

INDEX

ABOUT THE AUTHOR

John Portmann is assistant professor of religious studies at the University of Virginia in Charlottesville. He is the author of *When Bad Things Happen to Other People*, *Sex and Heaven*, and *Bad for Us*.